FATHERLOSS

FATHERLOSS

How Sons of All Ages

Come to Terms

with the Deaths

of Their Dads

NEIL CHETHIK

HYPERION   *New York*

Grateful acknowledgment is made to the following for permission to reprint previously published material: Navajivan Trust, for use of material from Gandhi: An Autobiography (copyright 1957 by Beacon Press); New Directions Publishing Corp., for use of "Do Not Go Gentle Into That Good Night," from The Poems of Dylan Thomas, by Dylan Thomas (copyright 1952 by Dylan Thomas); Penguin Putnam, for use of excerpts from Rebound: The Odyssey of Michael Jordan, by Bob Greene (copyright 1995 by John Deadline Enterprises); Scribner, a Division of Simon & Schuster, for use of material from One Life by Christiaan Barnard and Curtis Pepper (copyright 1969 by Christiaan Barnard), and from My Early Life: A Roving Commission, by Winston Churchill (copyright 1930 by Scribner; copyright renewed 1958 by Winston Churchill); Simon & Schuster, for use of quotation from Damned to Fame: The Life of Samuel Beckett, by James Knowlson (copyright 1996 by James Knowlson).

Library of Congress Cataloging-in-Publication Data

Chethik, Neil.
Fatherloss : how sons of all ages come to terms with the deaths of their dads
/ Neil Chethik.—1st ed.
p.   cm.
Includes bibliographical references.
ISBN: 0-7868-6532-6
1. Deprivation (Psychology)   2. Loss (Psychology)   3. Paternal deprivation.
4. Fathers and sons.   5. Bereavement—Psychological aspects.   I. Title.
BF575.D35   C48   2001
155.9'37'0854—dc21   00-044965

Design by Abby Kagan

FIRST EDITION

10   9   8   7   6   5   4   3

For my son, Evan

You have to dig deep to bury your father.

—GYPSY PROVERB

CONTENTS

FOREWORD   *xi*

INTRODUCTION   *1*

PART 1 / THE IMPACT OF FATHERLOSS

John F. Kennedy, Jr.   *13*

Chapter 1: Torn Asunder – Birth to Age 17   17

Michael Jordan   *42*

Chapter 2: Too Soon – Ages 18 to 32   46

Dylan Thomas   *66*

Chapter 3: The Body Blow – Ages 33 to 55   69

John Quincy Adams   *89*

Chapter 4: Closing the Circle – Ages 56 and Up   93

PART 2 / REBOUNDING FROM FATHERLOSS

Mahatma Gandhi   *109*

Chapter 5: Preparing for FatherLoss   *112*

Dwight D. Eisenhower   129

Chapter 6: The First Days After   132

Ted Turner   149

Chapter 7: Men's Styles of Mourning   153

Christiaan Barnard   174

Chapter 8: How Spouses Help   177

H. L. Mencken   192

Chapter 9: Life Changes   195

Ernest Hemingway   212

Chapter 10: Does Therapy Help?   214

David Halberstam   228

Chapter 11: Lingerings   232

Part 3 / The Lessons of FatherLoss

Chapter 12: Affectionate Fathering   249

Appendices

Appendix I: The FatherLoss Survey   273

Appendix II: Resources for Men Facing Loss   279

Appendix III: Father Films   284

Sources   286

Acknowledgments   302

FOREWORD

I T HAS BEEN more than four decades since pioneering thana-
tologist Herman Feifel called attention to the widespread "death
taboo" in our society. Since then, we've seen an explosion of
interest and activity in the field of death and dying. Today, there are
more than three thousand hospice and palliative-care organizations
in the United States, and many more throughout the world. Most
colleges and universities, and even some high schools, offer courses
in death education. Even such once-taboo issues as physician–assisted
suicide are today openly debated. Death–related anxiety is still with
us, of course, but more of us than ever before are learning how to
make end-of-life decisions, to support our loved ones in their dying,
to understand our own reactions to those deaths.

Nevertheless, there are still places where shadow and silence have
continued to reign. Should we be surprised that the most neglected
of these outposts is the male psyche?

For a variety of reasons, this is what has happened: Women have
made themselves more available than men to participate in grief

studies, to join grief support groups, to call on grief counselors for help. As a result, most of what we have learned about the grief process and recovery has come from the experiences of women. Society is much the richer for this knowledge, but our understanding has remained incomplete. What's more, because men have been less willing to openly share their experiences of grief, men at times have been portrayed as ineffective in grieving, inferior to women in this respect.

The stereotype of inadequate male grieving should soon be on the way out, and thanks to *FatherLoss*. With his in-depth interviews and authoritative survey, Neil Chethik has given us a rock-solid database on which to ground our understanding of male grieving. Chethik's conclusions are based both on his original findings and on the clinical and research literatures. We are never hung out to dry with airy speculations nor burdened with statistical overload. There is always the author's levelheaded and engaging voice, and very often the voices of men, young and old, who have experienced the death of their father. And the chapter on how spouses can help bereaved men may well save a few marriages!

FatherLoss is clearly in the first tier of well-informed and responsible trade books on the human condition. It demonstrates that men *do* feel, *do* grieve, and *do* find ways to recover from bereavement. Welcome back to the human race, gentlemen! With the publication of this book, our society has become more whole, and that much more of human nature has been reclaimed.

Robert Kastenbaum, Ph.D.
Professor Emeritus
Arizona State University

FATHERLOSS

INTRODUCTION

THE DEATH of a man's father. It happens 1.5 million times a year in the United States alone. Yet few people are aware of its profound impact. When a father dies, we often see the sons performing their "manly" duties: arranging the funeral, delivering the eulogy, comforting fellow family members. Then we imagine these sons going back to their homes, back to their jobs, back, unchanged, to the lives they'd lived before.

It's rarely so. Sigmund Freud called the death of his father "the most poignant loss" of his life. Actor Sean Connery termed it "a shattering blow." Writer Norman Mailer likened it to "having a hole in your tooth. It's a pain that can never be filled." And General Douglas MacArthur, more than fifty years after the loss of his father, still carried his dad's photo wherever he went. "My whole world changed that night," MacArthur said of the death. "Never have I been able to heal the wound in my heart."

Michael Jordan quit his basketball career after the death of his dad. H. L. Mencken launched his legendary newspaper career. And the poet Dylan Thomas, witnessing his father's losing bout with cancer, composed one of the most oft-quoted couplets of the past century: "Do not go gentle into that good night./ Rage, rage against the dying of the light."

Like all rites of passage, the experience of losing a father—no matter when or how it occurs—tests the strength and suppleness of a son. And the son's reaction may surprise both himself and others. In the worst of circumstances, the loss can propel a son toward despondency and even self-destruction. In the best, as we will see ahead, it can inspire in the son a new appreciation for his life and move him with urgency to make the most of his remaining years.

My own interest in father-death began sixteen years ago with the most memorable words my father ever said to me. I was twenty-seven years old at the time, between journalism jobs, living just a few blocks from the small Miami Beach apartment my paternal grandfather had set up after his retirement. It was the first time in my life that Grandpa was close-by, and along with meals of pot roast and potatoes, I soaked up the stories of his harrowing childhood in Eastern Europe, desperate emigration, and eclectic life experiences spanning the century.

Then one day I got a phone call from a doctor. "I'm sorry to tell you this," came the voice, "but your grandfather has had a heart attack, and he has expired." I was stunned.

The next day, my father flew to south Florida from his home in Michigan. I picked him up at the airport, and we drove in silence to the hospital to identify Grandpa's body, collect his watch and wallet, and make arrangements to ship the body north for burial at my grandmother's side.

Then my father turned the key to my grandfather's home, and we began sorting the material remnants of the old man's life. We discovered curled black-and-white photos from the early years, as well as key chains, checkbooks, matchbooks, coins, coupons, and a pack of stale generic cigarettes. Working in different rooms, we'd occasionally exclaim to each other about a special find. Mostly we sorted in silence.

We kept at it until the glow of the afternoon sun had waned. Then my father and I collapsed in my grandfather's heavily pillowed living-room chairs, glasses of the old man's scotch in hand. We shared memories for a while, then grew quiet. Finally, as the room faded into near-total darkness, I heard a guttural groan. At first, I was startled. Then I realized what was happening. I had never before heard my father cry.

I rose and went to kneel by his side. After a couple of minutes, he spoke. "I am crying not only for my father, but for me," he said. "His death means I'll never hear the words I've always wanted to hear from him: that he was proud of me, proud of the family I'd raised and the life I've lived."

My father then directed his voice toward me, and he uttered the words that continue to resound: "So that you never have to feel this way too," he said, "I want to tell you now how proud I am of you, of the choices you've made, of the life you've created."

Much of the pain that is inherent in father-son relationships dissolved for me in the calm resonance of that blessing. And in the months that followed, I felt stronger and more confident, especially as I restarted my career. At the same time, I had to marvel at the potency of the event that had brought my father, then a successful, fifty-two-year-old university professor and psychotherapist, to such depth of grief, and spurred him to a proclamation of a kind he'd never made before.

I soon learned that my father's reaction was not unusual. As I reached my early thirties, my male friends began losing their fathers in increasing numbers. For many, it was a watershed event. Some cried for the first time in years. Others feared for their own lives. One man decided to become a father for the first time. Another decided to quit his job.

Each man, it seemed to me, experienced a significant reordering of his inner landscape. As a forty-eight-year-old minister friend told me: "When my father died, it was as if I had lived in a house my whole life, a house with a picture window looking out on a mountain range. Then one day, I looked out the window, and one of the mountains was gone."

That image stuck with me. And in 1995, after launching a syndicated men's column, I started writing on the subject of father-death. The reaction to these columns was intense among men, most of whose previous letters and e-mails to me had focused on the intellectual. Now, many wrote with emotion, telling of the "void," the "hole," the "emptiness" that they'd felt after the death of their fathers. Some seemed startled that a man they had once viewed as invincible could be boxed, buried, or reduced to a feathery ash.

Some of these men expressed a hunger for more information on the subject, so I went looking. I found rich treatments on the theme of father-death, dating back to the fifth century B.C. That's when the Greek dramatist Sophocles penned his Oedipus cycle, built around the tale of a man who murders his father and marries his mother. Some two thousand years later, William Shakespeare, as his own father was nearing his end, wrote his treatise on the subject of father-death—*Hamlet*. In the play, a tempestuous young prince reacts with anger, despair, delirium, and, ultimately, resolve to the murder of his father, the king.

The theme of father-death also showed up in more contemporary venues, including at the movie theater. In the Oscar-nominated *Field of Dreams*, Kevin Costner's character so yearns for reconciliation with his dead father that he carves a baseball diamond out of an Iowa cornfield to lure the old man's ghost. In *The Lion King*, the youthful Simba struggles with enormous guilt as he's called upon to take over the realm his departed father left to him. And in the *Star Wars* trilogy, George Lucas sends his young male protagonist on a mission to locate and redeem Darth Vader, the masked father, before death overtakes him.

In searching for resources, I also found books on all manner of other losses: mother-loss, child-loss, spouse-loss, job-loss, pet-loss, even hair-loss. I found no similar writings, however, addressing the specific concerns of modern men facing or mourning the deaths of their fathers. Despite the huge numbers of men affected and the growing interest in the father-son relationship, no psychologist, anthropologist, journalist, or other researcher had written a book focusing exclusively on how men react to the loss of this most influential man in their lives.

This book aims to fill the gap. In the following pages, you will be led on a dramatic and ultimately hopeful journey that begins in the echo of the words, "Your father is dead." Your primary guides will be 376 ordinary American men, men who lost their fathers sometime between earliest childhood and their own seventy-fifth birthday.

Between 1997 and 2000, I conducted personal, in-depth interviews with seventy of these men. In these conversations, we focused on each man's relationship with his father before the death and on his struggles and strategies in the aftermath. While this group of sons did not represent a scientific sample, I took care to include men of different ages, races, religions, economic classes, educational levels, geographic regions, and sexual orientations.

In early 1999, to bring greater definition to the early findings, I commissioned the FatherLoss Survey, a scientific telephone survey of 306 American men, randomly selected from across the nation. My chief consultants on this part of the research were Dr. Robert

Kastenbaum, a bereavement specialist at Arizona State University, and Dr. Ronald Langley, the director of the University of Kentucky Survey Research Center. (For a more detailed description of my research, see Appendix I: The FatherLoss Survey.)

I chose to offer anonymity to all 376 men in the research in the belief that they would be more candid if their identities were protected. In the in-depth interviews, I was often amazed by the level of honesty and openness of the men, most of whom I'd never met before we sat to talk. Our culture seems to draw back from male emotion, especially grief, so I half-expected the men I spoke with to be guarded about any personal turmoil that followed the deaths of their fathers.

It did not happen. Rather, sitting with these men in their kitchens, living rooms, and backyards, I found them eager to talk. They *wanted* to recall the good times with their fathers; they *wanted* to revisit the death, even when it drove them back to tears.

Listening to the men, I was struck by the distinctive rhythm of male grief. In recent decades, psychologists and grief counselors have tended to consider crying and talking—the traditionally female style of mourning—as the gold standard for grieving. (The preponderance of widows as subjects in grief studies may have influenced this.) As a result, well-meaning therapists, spouses, partners, and friends have sometimes tried to steer a bereaved man toward his tears. And for some men, it's been effective. Their mourning process is eruptive, not unlike a volcano, tears flowing like hot lava, releasing the pressure beneath.

However, most men in my research seemed to mourn in more subtle ways. Their emotions moved more like tectonic plates, shifting far below the surface, sending out tremors and shudders, perhaps the occasional tear. And the aftershocks often went on for years. These men tended to release any energy around the loss only gradually, in small rushes, often thinking it through and expressing it by moving their bodies and changing their worlds. They could frequently be found honoring their fathers: building with his tools, tending his garden, setting up a foundation to fight the disease that took his life. It was in the *doing* that these sons seemed best able to come to terms with the loss, and let their fathers go.

In the chapters ahead, I have allowed men to speak for themselves, to tell their own stories. (I have also encouraged them to define "father" as they wished; some chose to speak of their adoptive or stepfathers.) While names and some identifying characteristics have been altered to protect specific identities, the stories related here are real. I did not use composite characters. The quotes came directly from audiotapes or from notes made during our conversations. It is in the rich details of these actual events, I believe, that a man going through the loss of his father can best find answers to his questions.

For those of us who still have a living father, the stories hold lessons too. We'll learn in Chapter 5, for example, about the different ways that men effectively prepare themselves for a father's death. In Chapter 6, we'll see the myriad ways that sons react to a death when they're first informed of it.

Women will see themselves in these pages as well; the "masculine style" of grieving is not unique to men. Women also will find ideas (most directly in Chapter 8) for assisting their husbands, boyfriends, sons, or other men through the loss of a father.

As the father of a son, I've also learned much from the stories in this book. Peering behind the rough veil of so many father-son relationships, I have a far better sense of what my own seven-year-old son needs from me, now and later. (I write about these lessons in Chapter 12.) And I've learned that my relationship with my own father, who is healthy at age sixty-nine, can continue to deepen even in these later years together.

I learned this last point by experiencing it. While some fathers might have felt threatened by a son writing a book on father-death, mine embraced the project from the start. He helped finance the early research, gave me permission to tell part of his story, and offered suggestions on the chapters as I wrote them. His is a powerful presence on these pages, as much for his sustained, supportive spirit as for the substance he supplied.

The men who offered their stories would be pleased by this development. Again and again, they told me that helping men examine and resolve their relationships with their fathers—whether the older man was living or not—was a major reason for their speaking out. For many, telling their stories was their way of reaching across the sands of silence that still separate American men.

Each son's reaction to the loss of his father is unique. It is influenced by a network of factors: the quality of the father-son relationship, the personality and temperament of both father and son, and the suddenness of the father's death, to name just a few. There is one factor, however, that seems to stand out in shaping a son's reaction: the age of the son at the time of the death.

Thus, the first part of this book, The Impact of FatherLoss, focuses on the variations in men's reactions to the death of their fathers, based on the time of the son's life at which the loss occurred. The section contains four chapters, each corresponding to the age of the son at the death: childhood (birth to age 17), young adulthood (18 to 32), middle adulthood (33 to 55), and the "young-old" years (56 to 75).

The emphasis in each of these chapters is on *stories*, detailed portraits of boys and men going through the loss of their fathers. I have supplemented these portraits with my own and others' research, which sheds light on how and why sons in each group tend to react the way they do.

One caution here: Necessarily, I have been arbitrary about when each stage begins and ends; I have featured in the same chapter men who are as much as twenty-two years apart. Thus, you may find that the chapter chronologically pertaining to you carries only a part of your story; look for other aspects of your experience in neighboring chapters.

The second part of the book, Rebounding from FatherLoss, moves beyond age to focus on the ways in which sons, as a group, adapt to the loss of a father. As I've mentioned, the traditionally feminine style of grieving—focused on crying and talking with others—is often viewed as "the right way" to mourn. And yet, on the cutting edge of grief research, scholars are finding that a so-called masculine style—emphasizing thinking, acting, and emotional control—is no less effective. Drawing heavily from the FatherLoss Survey and the voices of men I interviewed, this section describes specific strategies men use as they prepare for, experience, and adapt to a father's death.

In the third part of the book, Lessons of FatherLoss, I'll share what I've learned about being a father based on my experience researching and writing this book. I'll address the questions: What makes a good father to a son? How does the role of father change through the life span? And what can a father do to help prepare his son for his death?

Finally, before each chapter throughout the book, I have included short profiles of notable men, both historical and contemporary, focusing on how they handled the deaths of their fathers. The stories of these men suggest that virtually no son can escape the confrontation with father-death, and that the event has the potential to shape not only a man's life, but the world in which he lives.

Woody Allen once said, "I don't want to achieve immortality through my work; I want to achieve it through not dying." Alas, this is not yet the way of the universe. Until it is, we humans will continue to grapple with how best to cope with the loss of our loved ones. Along with the men whose stories appear in the pages to come, I offer this book as a helpful, hopeful companion in that struggle.

N.J.C.

Part 1

———

THE IMPACT OF FATHERLOSS

John F. Kennedy, Jr.

—※—

For much of America, it was an unforgettable moment.

The funeral mass had just been completed. Pallbearers had shouldered the flag-draped coffin outside, through the cathedral doors, then fastened it to the carriage that would bear it away. Near the coffin, amid a throng of darkly dressed adults, a three-year-old boy in shorts and a buttoned-up coat fidgeted in the dazzling late-November glare. Suddenly, a military band began playing "Hail to the Chief." The boy—who, like his famous father, would one day perish in his prime—squared himself to his father's coffin, stiffened his right hand, and offered a final, sad salute.

An unforgettable moment, for everyone except the boy himself. Years later, the only son of President John F. Kennedy would acknowledge that, as an adult, he recalled nothing of his father's death or funeral. His knowledge of the man in that coffin, he would tell an interviewer, came mostly through "the color of others and the perception of others, and through photographs, and through what [I] have read."

Of course, his father's death would change everything about the life of John Kennedy, Jr. Its legacy—not to mention the paparazzi—would follow him, and define him at times, for most of the rest of his days.

Yet, by all credible accounts, John Jr. emerged from his father's death intact. Like many adolescents, he experimented with drugs and alcohol, and rebelled against his mother's tight rein. In his early career, he bounced around. But by his mid-twenties, his life seemed to stabilize. And in the decade before he died piloting his own plane, John Jr. exhibited none of the dullness or anxiety that haunts so many who lose a parent in childhood. While he generally declined to talk about the personal impact of his father's death, John Jr. seemed good-natured, strongly connected to his family, and satisfied in his career as a magazine executive.

For whatever level of balance he attained, John Jr. owed much to his mother. Jackie Kennedy not only helped the nation grieve her husband's death in 1963, she helped her son mourn his father over the years that followed.

After the assassination, Jackie recognized immediately the importance of maintaining in her son's life a familiar, caring, masculine presence. In the months after the death, she invited Robert Kennedy to fill that role. He would often stop by his nephew's home and take the boy to work with him at the Justice Department.

In addition to Robert Kennedy, other men were invited by Jackie to visit with her son. She called on Dave Powers, one of her husband's close aides, to spend time one-on-one with the boy in the year after the death. She asked Secret Service agents, who would protect John until he was sixteen, to teach him self-defense.

And some historians believe one of the reasons Jackie married Aristotle Onassis in 1968 was to provide her then seven-year-old son with a father figure in the aftermath of Robert Kennedy's assassination.

Besides maintaining father figures in her son's life, Jackie also tried to ensure that John Jr. would stay connected to the memory of his real father. In 1963, many young widows and widowers were being counseled to rid their homes of mementos related to the lost parent and to refrain from talking about the death. The belief at the time was that ongoing attention to the loss might produce a depressed child.

Jackie sensed that this was wrong. In the early days after the assassination, she allowed John Jr. to place phone calls to his father's office and to speak to a familiar secretary. Over the years that followed, Jackie encouraged both of her children to collect photos and other keepsakes of their dad; she even provided them with recordings of her late husband's speeches.

In adulthood, John Jr. continued to honor his father's memory. He provided the voice for an audio version of his father's Pulitzer Prize–winning book, *Profiles in Courage*. And until his own death in 1999, John Jr. actively supported the President John F. Kennedy Library.

After John Jr.'s fatal plane crash, some observers wondered aloud whether there was some kind of connection, on a psychological level, between John Jr.'s early death and that of his father. It's impossible to know for sure; as we'll see in the upcoming chapter, the ramifications of an early father-death can be subtle and long lasting. But John Jr.'s own words indicate that he was less consumed by his father's death than were many journalists, filmmakers, and conspiracy theorists.

As he told an ABC-TV interviewer in 1992: "I think [Caroline and I] have a strong sense of my father's legacy and how important it is, and we both respect it enormously. But at the same time, there is a sense of, a realization, that things are different, and that he would have wanted us to go on with our own lives and not reenact his."

*After [my father's death] I never cried again with any real
conviction, nor expected much of anyone's God except indifference,
nor loved deeply without fear that it would cost me dearly in pain.
At the age of five, I had become a skeptic.*
—COLUMNIST RUSSELL BAKER

Chapter 1

———

TORN ASUNDER

———

Birth to Age 17

TOM PLASKY was eight years old, asleep in his bed, short
dark hair pressed against the pillowcase, when a sound
awakened him. He listened at first without moving, heard
the muffled voices of his mother and father, then slid himself off
the bed.

Reaching the threshold of his bedroom doorway, Tom stopped
short. He could see his parents in the early morning glow through
the open door of their room down the hall. His father sat rigidly in
a chair near the doorway, eyes closed, lips in a slight smile, bald head
turned strangely upward. Tom's mother knelt facing her husband.
When she noticed Tom standing in the doorway, she ordered him
back to his room.

Tom did not obey. Suddenly, his father extended his right arm
as if trying to shake someone's hand. The father's hand grasped,
reached, hung in the air, and then dropped like a stone to his side.
The breath rushed out of his mouth, his head and shoulders fell
forward, and he slumped against his wife.

For a moment, everyone was motionless. Then Tom's mother cried out to him: "Go next door and call an ambulance!" The startled child spun toward the narrow staircase, bounded down the flight of stairs, and sprung out into the dewy Wisconsin spring morning.

Dashing for help, barefoot, Tom already knew his father was dead. The old man's impossibly broad shoulders had stooped and weakened during a two-year illness, and Tom sensed correctly that the end had finally come. Nevertheless, in the days and weeks that followed the death, Tom would often feel stunned into silence. It would take more than a decade for the silence to give way to an emotional collapse. And even long after recovering from that, the fallout from his father's death would continue to invade, and haunt, his daily life.

In their brief time together, Tom had felt extraordinarily close to his father, a mechanic and lumberjack on whose fiftieth birthday Tom was born. They had hunted together in the Wisconsin woods, fished in nearby streams, huddled under the hoods of a series of broken-down cars and trucks. The older man had mused about someday building a garage on a piece of land he owned and opening a father-son auto-repair shop.

That dream had died with the father. And so did the family's way of life. Tom's mother descended into a long depression. She was unable to speak with her children about the loss. The family's minister later told Tom he'd never seen anyone grieve so deeply. Eventually beset by money problems, Tom's mother was forced to join the workforce, removing her, at least in Tom's eyes, as a dependable presence in the home.

Left on his own, Tom struggled to cope with his confusion and emptiness. He chose not to attend his father's funeral after his mother told him and his older sister, "It's an adult ceremony, but you can come if you want to." And he held back his tears, at least when others could see. His father had spoken to him about the importance of "guts," so he cried only late at night, as he ached with loneliness in his bed in the dark. According to the FatherLoss Survey, Tom's struggle with tears was not unusual. Forty-two percent of sons who were younger than eighteen when their father died reported that they didn't cry in the month following it; only 21 percent said they cried "a lot."

During adolescence, Tom became disengaged from the people around him. He felt different; he was, in his own eyes, "the boy with the dead father." Throughout his teens, he had few friends and fewer dates. While his sister came through her grief with the support of her friends, Tom recalled that he had a thirteenth birthday party, and no one showed up. Smart but uninspired in school, he dropped out at seventeen, earned his GED, and joined the Air Force.

At first, dressed identically to his fellow recruits, hair in the same buzz cut, he felt that he belonged. But belonging among these men also meant drinking with them, and on a warm May day in North Carolina, two years into his military career, Tom drank too much. With his brain awash in alcohol, he descended into a dark storm of paranoia: His Air Force buddies were whispering about him; his superiors were plotting against him; his mind was betraying him. At the height of his madness, he pulled the fire alarm at a barracks and was arrested and taken to a nearby hospital. There, safely in his own room, Tom's senses shut down, and this reeling nineteen-year-old fell into a catatonic trance.

It was the eleventh anniversary of the day of his father's death.

For seventy hours (Tom would later find out), he sat upright in a chair, unable to eat, swallow, or blink. An attendant put drops in his eyes to prevent them from drying out. Later, Tom remembered nothing about the blackout except waking up from it in a beige, classroomlike space, staring at a loaded food tray. "There is only one answer that I accept for what pushed me over the edge," he told me more than two decades later. "Grief."

Disoriented, Tom hailed a hospital orderly. "What day is it?" he asked. When the man told him, Tom borrowed a dime and called his sister from a pay phone. "I need help," he told her. Together, the family was able to arrange an honorable discharge. As Tom recalled: "I got a one-hundred-percent temporary disability. There were people from 'Nam who got less disability than I did, and they were missing a limb."

About 4 percent of American males lose their fathers before the age of eighteen, and sons who remember the experience almost always describe it in catastrophic terms: hit by a truck, blown away, torn apart. Psychologist Maxine Harris, author of *The Loss That Is Forever*, a book on parent-loss in childhood, believes that even when a boy and his father are at odds, the death of such a monumental figure "registers as a 10 on the [child's] emotional Richter scale."

And the tremors may continue for a lifetime. According to my survey, 25 percent of sons who lost a father in childhood acknowledged that they'd never fully recovered from the event. They attributed struggles, often decades later, with alcohol, drugs, relationships, even impulses toward suicide, to the legacy of their father's early death.

Recent research suggests there may be a biological component to this ongoing turmoil. After a parent-loss, up to half of children experience permanent physiological changes: Heart rates rise, body chemistry is altered. Like war veterans who react anxiously to a passing helicopter, sons who lose fathers in childhood often have heart-pounding, stomach-churning responses to all manner of subsequent losses. Having been through an early trauma of such magnitude, they display the classic symptoms of post-traumatic stress disorder.

Despite the powerful blow, however, three out of four sons I surveyed who had experienced an early father-death said they'd managed to find their balance at some point in their lives. Most acknowledged some period of foundering. And even after regaining stability, they continued to feel the loss keenly, noting the anniversary of the father's death, and their own wistfulness at weddings, graduations, and other family times. Ultimately, however, they were not defeated by the loss. In inventive and sometimes surprising ways, most managed to mourn, freeing them to live fully again.

When I talked with Tom Plasky twenty-two years after his breakdown, he still was far from reconciled to his loss. After his military discharge, he had tried to cope with the absence of his dad by honoring his father's values of hard, honest work. Although Tom could have lived on military disability for years, he chose instead to give it up and get a job. He became a star machinist's apprentice and within a few years was earning $70,000 annually in manufacturing.

While working with his hands, Tom felt connected to his father; sometimes it seemed that the older man was there working right beside him. And Tom was driven toward further success by his continued desire to make his father proud—to prove, in effect, that had his father lived, their dream of operating a business together could have been realized.

But Tom wasn't satisfied with just a good job; he wanted a meaningful personal life too. At first, it seemed that this would be possible. In his early twenties, while attending a Baptist church, he met a woman and entered into his first serious relationship. Soon, they were married. As it turned out, however, it would be in this relationship, and subsequent ones, that Tom would stumble upon the primary legacy of his father's death: the repeated pattern of love, then loss.

The marriage lasted six years. Along with his alcohol abuse, the major issue between Tom and his wife was, not incidentally, fatherhood. She wanted children immediately; he wanted to wait. "I didn't know how to make a family solid, I'd never seen it before," Tom told me. "I thought I might have to leave sometime. Knowing what it would be like to have no father, I didn't want to put someone else through it."

To keep his wife in the marriage, Tom kept suggesting that if they could go six months without a major blowup in their relationship, he would agree to have kids. Not surprisingly, the decisive fight often occurred just before the six-month deadline.

That first divorce, while a relief in some ways, was also a painful blow to Tom. As he had when his father had died, Tom felt abandoned, and he reacted by drinking more than ever. During one ill-fated binge, he tried unsuccessfully to outrace a police car. In the middle of the high-speed chase, he realized that he cared little whether he survived it. This horrified him, and after his legal troubles were over, he joined Alcoholics Anonymous and quit drinking.

But soon, he recalled, he was blunting his emotions with sex. One of his sexual relationships, with a woman whom he described as "a head-turner, gorgeous," actually turned into a marriage. But it was over after just three months.

It wasn't long before Tom was dating again, this time a fellow machinist, a woman he'd met years earlier. Only eighteen months after his second divorce, he married again, and for nine years the relationship seemed solid, if not passionate. But on the eve of his fortieth birthday, Tom's wife revealed that she'd been having an affair with another man for the previous eight years. She wanted a divorce.

The betrayal was another hard blow to Tom. It so echoed his father's death, he told me, that he ended more than a decade of sobriety and seriously considered ending his life. "I had it all figured out," he recalled of the day he nearly killed himself. "I was going to park my car in the garage. . . . I was going to get drunk and take a long trip in the garage." The more he drank that afternoon, however, the less suicide seemed like a suitable option. Eventually, he checked himself into a hospital detox unit, dried out, and sought professional counseling.

When I talked with Tom, he was forty-one. He had finished a year of therapy, during which he'd focused on understanding how much his life has been affected by his early loss. His spirits were rising; when he talked of his counseling, flashes of excitement interrupted his previously monotone voice.

For years, he told me, he'd felt "strange, different, weird," without knowing exactly why. Counseling was helping him see that he was normal—normal for a man who'd suffered a devastating early loss. He said: "I understand now that it's okay to feel sad about losing my father. It's a crappy thing to have happened. I've missed out on a lot. . . . If other people want to say I'm feeling sorry for myself, that's fine. They ought to try walking around in my shoes."

Three decades after the loss of his dad, Tom was still trying to reestablish a sense of order in his life, to calm the emotional turmoil that had commenced in the aftermath of his father's death.

This struggle with powerful emotional swings was a common one among the men I interviewed who'd lost their fathers early. It was as if the father's death had short-circuited the son's emotional regulators; it was typical for these men, even in adulthood, to frequently become emotionally overwhelmed by events in their lives.

Interestingly, however, about equal numbers of those I interviewed about a father-death in their childhood reported a very different, though still debilitating, legacy of the loss. Rather than overwhelming emotional turmoil, this second group of sons, throughout their lives, felt very little emotion at all. Traumatized by the early experience of enormous pain, they literally went numb.

Mitchell Forbes was a blond, curly haired seven-year-old, and an only child, when his father, then thirty-two, succumbed to leukemia. Before the death, no one talked to the boy about the seriousness of his father's illness. A half-century later, Mitchell could remember only the yellow of his father's face the last time they saw each other in the hospital.

Like eight out of ten sons in my survey who'd lost fathers in childhood, Mitchell attended his dad's funeral. But the experience didn't help much. Mitchell's reaction to seeing his father in the casket was abject denial. "That's not him," Mitchell recalled thinking to himself. The most vivid memory of the funeral day, he said, was being scolded by an uncle, after the service, for playing a game of tag with other kids.

Within weeks of the death, Mitchell's everyday life had changed radically. He and his mother moved from their house in suburban Chicago to a small apartment within the city limits, where his mother began working the three-to-midnight shift as a telephone operator. From then on, Mitchell and his mom corresponded mostly by notes left on the kitchen table. They almost never mentioned his dad.

Lonely and confused, Mitchell didn't know at first what to do with his pain. Then he had an idea: A few months before the death, Mitchell had seen a movie in which a mother tells a son that his father is dead; the father, however, actually has been sent to prison. Although Mitchell had seen his father's corpse and had been to his father's grave site, he managed to convince himself that his dad was really alive and in prison.

A good student to that point, Mitchell stopped paying attention to his teachers. Instead, from second to sixth grade, he sat in the back of the classroom, watching out the window for his father's black 1938 Ford to pull up at the curb and take him home.

By the time a teacher noticed Mitchell's preoccupation, he was twelve years old, and his emotional life had flat-lined. Mitchell rarely smiled and never cried. He'd become, by his own later assessment, "emotionally dead." In a sad testament to that fact, Mitchell told me, he'd had no discernible sex drive until he was twenty-two. Employing a curious analogy, he explained, "I understood sex, but it would be like your understanding of murder, assuming you haven't murdered. It was an intellectual understanding."

Mitchell's sex drive finally did emerge, and he married at age twenty-seven. But his emotional life remained frozen. His connection with his wife, children, and pretty much everyone else in his life, he told me, was superficial. When I spoke with Mitchell fifty-one years after his father's death, he was the director of a school library system in suburban Atlanta, overseeing a multimillion-dollar budget and scores of employees. He was clearly excited by his work and apparently quite good at it. He had just been named the region's librarian of the year.

Personally, however, he described himself as still being "on the fringes of human relationships. . . . As far as personal relationships go, I never really matured. I've always avoided closeness, probably in order to never again experience loss. Externally, I am pleasant and well-liked. But those who have tried to get close to me know that I am distant and completely untrusting."

Mitchell did say he'd made strides over the previous ten years. Like Tom Plasky, he had come to see his "differentness" as one of the legacies of his father's death, and not a self-generated flaw in his personality. He had slowly warmed up to his family. Yet his ability to be openly expressive or to feel things deeply had not emerged. Not long before I interviewed him, his eldest daughter, who was then twenty-eight, told Mitchell that growing up with him as a father was like growing up with no father at all. When I suggested that the comment must hurt him, Mitchell responded: "No, it doesn't. . . . It's a description of what happened. No, it doesn't hurt me. Perhaps it should."

Besides the early loss of their fathers, Mitchell Forbes and Tom Plasky had something else in common: a perceived dearth of maternal attention after the loss. Both men told me that in retrospect, they felt tremendous compassion for their mothers, each of whom not only struggled with her own grief, but was suddenly forced to provide financially for her family. At the same time, both sons said they wished their mothers had been able to help them more to make sense of the deaths.

This wish for the mother's attention and assurance was evident in virtually all the sons I interviewed who had lost their fathers in childhood. In the weeks after the loss, sons wanted their mothers to show them, or tell them, how to respond. When the mother was silent or dismissive, sons often reacted by fantasizing that the father would return, isolating themselves, or becoming unduly angry. It became clear to me that a key factor in a boy's recovery from an early father-death was the ability of the boy's mother to relate to, and attend to, his enormous immediate needs.

John Fetzner's mother offers an example of someone who was able to attend to her son, even while she was grieving intensely herself. John was sixteen years old, living in a midsized town in the Southeast, and working at a fried-chicken restaurant one afternoon in 1993 when he received a frantic call from his mother. His father was in trouble, she told him. John left work and sped home, where he learned that his dad, after an angry argument with John's mom, had screeched off in his pickup truck with these cryptic words: "I have to do something I should have done a long time ago."

John guessed that his father had gone to a favorite fishing hole some twenty miles from home, so he and a family friend took off in that direction. By the time they pulled up to the secluded hole, however, it was too late. Emergency vehicles were on the scene. John's father, it turned out, had rolled up the windows of his truck, doused himself with gasoline, and struck a match. He had died instantly.

Though John's father had been increasingly unhappy after a family bankruptcy, it had not occurred to John that his dad was suicidal. John was devastated by the act, as were his two older brothers and especially his mother, Connie. She had met her husband more than twenty-five years earlier, when both were teenagers, and had fallen in love with his gentleness and wit. They'd had some marital problems, but she too had been shocked by her husband's decision to end his life.

Yet instead of retreating into her grief and guilt, Connie joined a support group for widows, attended conferences for those left behind by suicide, and educated herself about the signs and symptoms of self-destructive mental illness. In doing so, she modeled for John an ethic of self-care. And it seemed to have a positive effect on her son. Once, when she came home from work to find John crying, she hugged him and asked if he was okay. His response: "Mom, I'm okay because you're okay."

Still, Connie feared for John. She had learned that the children of those who take their lives often feel angry and rejected, and are many times more likely than others to commit suicide themselves.

Soon after the death, Connie noticed ominous signs. John hurriedly spent his cut of his dad's life insurance money on friends, a car, and fancy electronics. He also started skipping school. "I stopped trying hard," John acknowledged. "My attitude was basically, 'What does it matter?' I figured that bettering myself wasn't the way to go. *Carpe diem*. Seize the day. Make sure I have fun. That was the way to live."

Connie witnessed this self-delusion, but did not criticize John.

Instead, she regularly invited him to talk about his father, the suicide, and its impact on his life. Usually, John resisted. However, just knowing she was available, he told me later, eased his pain.

Finally, three years after the death, when John was nineteen, the force of his grief began to wane. His everyday mood improved. He began apprenticing as an electrician. He moved into an apartment with his best friend. Connie told me that her son's turn for the better was primarily the legacy of her late husband's early love and caring for him.

But when I visited John in his apartment, five years after the death, he disagreed. His mother, he told me, had been the key. Not only had she been willing to hang in there while he acted out, she'd inspired him by taking care of herself and others. He explained: "Here's someone who lost a person she'd been with for so many years, yet she's trying to make a better life for herself. She's getting involved with survivors of suicide, helping other people. She's been selfless."

Among the sons I spoke with who'd lost fathers early, few of their mothers had been able to offer the kind of consistent, unconditional support exhibited by Connie Fetzner. But my survey indicated that the majority of mothers were at least somewhat helpful to sons who lost fathers in childhood. Sons told me they were helped most when they could simply talk with their mothers directly about the loss. A few men said it helped also when their mother cried, at least occasionally, in their presence; seeing her tears made their own seem normal.

Even involved, compassionate mothering, however, is not always enough to usher a boy safely through an early father-death. Several sons told me that in the wake of the death, they needed more than their mothers—more than *any* woman, in fact—could provide.

Phil Bernstein was eleven years old, and the middle child among three, when his dad, a lean and seemingly fit physical-education teacher in San Diego, died of a heart attack while exercising. Before the death, Phil generally had felt close to his father. They had played lots of sports together, and decades later, Phil still remembered fondly how he'd sit behind his father in the car and run his hand along the bristles of hair on the back of the older man's neck.

Although the family stayed in its home after the death, and maintained many of its same routines, the early months were difficult for Phil. One of the worst blows came around the time of the funeral, when an uncle told Phil that he must now take over as "man of the family." The words haunted the boy. Suddenly, he felt, he was being asked, in one awful phrase, to end his childhood. Phil said: "I knew I wasn't a man. I knew I couldn't do what my father had done. . . . There was this pressure to do something I couldn't. It made me feel totally inadequate."

But during his adolescence, Phil rebounded. He attributed it in large part to the extraordinary mentoring of a twenty-one-year-old college student named Sam. At the time Phil's father died, Sam worked as a recreation leader at a local park. In the months after the death, Sam invited Phil to football and baseball games, to movies, even to restaurants for dinner. "He didn't have to ask about my father," Phil told me more than two decades later. "We were dealing with [the loss] just by going to a game together. All those needs were being fulfilled, the holes were being filled. . . . With [Sam], there was always a male figure around to say, 'You're doing okay.' I tell him even today how fortunate I was that by fate, this person was there."

Later, Phil benefited from his relationship with another male mentor, a basketball coach. The two older men's direct influence on Phil lasted into high school, at which point Phil began a small-scale rebellion, hiding his experimentation with marijuana and alcohol, acting in ways he knew his mentors wouldn't like. Yet their words and attitudes continued to echo inside him, helping him maintain a sense of balance. Phil told me: "What I would have missed, but didn't because of these men, was someone imparting me with limits. I don't know how they did it. Looking back, it's extraordinary."

Phil's brother, Brad, who was ten years old at the time of the death, did not receive this kind of male attention. And when I talked with him twenty-five years later, Brad said he felt this was one reason he'd struggled more than his brother ever since the death of their father.

Throughout adolescence, as Phil's spirits gradually lifted, Brad maintained a deep sense of fear and anger. Early on, Brad said, he worried whether his mother would follow his father into death; he would sometimes enter her bedroom late at night to make sure she was still breathing. And even late in his teens, years after the death, Brad found it disturbing when his mother laughed. "I couldn't understand how she could be happy," he said.

When I talked with Brad, he was thirty-five, and a successful entrepreneur in Portland, Oregon. He was passionate about music, science, law, and other subjects. But he expressed some dissatisfaction with his life. He wondered if he was doing anything good for humankind. And, in his personal affairs, he said, he lacked confidence. He hadn't had a significant relationship with a woman for nearly a decade. "I don't get into [relationships] deeper because I'm afraid, fearing the loss of someone," Brad told me, adding that he believed that "some elements of the [early] loss are still holding me back."

Meanwhile, his brother Phil, now a thirty-six-year-old photographer living in suburban San Diego, exuded a sense of confidence and optimism. He said he'd had some struggles in developing closeness with his wife, but chalked them up less to his father's death than to the cultural climate that makes it difficult for men to show any sign of dependency.

The much larger impact of the loss of his father, Phil said, could be seen in his attitude toward his two sons and daughter. He explained: "I never leave my house without kissing my kids good-bye. The same thing at night—a kiss or a hug. When I got laid off . . . , I loved it. I could be Mr. Mom. I could be with the kids. My philosophy is to enjoy them as much as I can. I do this for me. Maybe it's good for the kids as well. But I do it for me. I feel sorry for my dad, and others today, who don't get to see their kids grow up."

In Phil's situation, the son was glad to have the attention of older males. But some sons I spoke with had father-figures thrust upon them—often when their mothers remarried—and tried at first to repel the older man. To these sons, a stepfather often seemed like a rival, an antagonist, a poor substitute for the real thing. Nonetheless, in a good portion of these cases, even this seemingly inadequate fill-in eventually provided something essential to the son.

William Campbell is a good example. He was thirteen and living in west Texas when his father died of a sudden stroke. Like more than 80 percent of sons in my survey who were under eighteen at the time of their father's death, William did not have a chance to say good-bye to his dad. In the first days afterward, William had ambivalent feelings about the death. He was horrified on one level, but also felt relief because his father had been a strict disciplinarian who had used a belt to punish him and forced him into Boy Scouts and other activities William didn't necessarily want to pursue. On the very night of the death, the two had clashed angrily over William's attendance at a Scout meeting; the father, a Scout leader, had ended up going alone to the meeting, where he suffered a heart attack and died.

That night, William's mother huddled with her three children, and broke the news: "God wanted Daddy." Afterward, she was able to help her son deal with his grief. William recalled, for example, that he was ashamed of himself for not crying at his father's funeral, and then weeping copiously a few months later when a pet rabbit died. His mother comforted him, assuring him that his reactions were normal.

I spoke with William more than thirty-five years after the death, at his home in a rural housing development in Texas. His eyes became wet when he recalled the months immediately after his father's death. He called it "my dark period," during which he spent most of his time alone, playing war games and reading maps. Then his mother married again, this time to a man very different from her first husband. For one thing, the stepfather was politically conservative—in William's words, "an Archie Bunker type"—which was a sharp contrast to his biological father, who had been a liberal civil-rights activist.

But the fact that the stepfather was so different from his biological father turned out to be beneficial to William. In his late teens, as William began to rebel against his stepfather, he found himself standing in the shoes of his biological father, using the words the deceased man had used, espousing the same political perspectives. Soon, William was picking up his accordion, an instrument his father had foisted upon him years earlier. "My stepfather helped me to define myself," William told me. "He was the one there when I rebelled. He was the ideal person [for me] to rebel against."

William got married in his early twenties, and started a family soon after. Having adopted his biological father's tenacity and dedication (though not his aggressive disciplinary practices), William was able to forge a fulfilling family life and social-service career. "I have my father's stubbornness, which is very helpful in a marriage. It's an I-don't-quit attitude. My commitment to my wife, kids, and vows is strong. It's very much a legacy to my father."

About his stepfather, William told me: "We never became close confidants; we were too different." But William added that he came to love and appreciate his stepdad, who died when William was in his mid-twenties. "As the years have gone by, I have missed how [my stepfather] would have enjoyed my children," William said. It seemed odd to say, William told me, but "I regret that my kids did not know both my dad *and* my stepdad."

As William's experience indicates, the caring attention of a male adult can serve to mitigate the damage to a boy after the death of his father. I found this to be true among sons who lost fathers at every stage of childhood. Infants, grade-schoolers, and adolescents all seemed to accommodate their loss more readily when a man took a special interest in them in the months and years that followed the death.

Among these different age groups, however, there did seem to be some noteworthy differences in the impact of the death.

The sons I spoke with who were under the age of three when a father died tended not to remember the actual death. One son who'd lost his father at age two told me it was only when he reached school age that he started noticing what he called "a void, a lack." He said he was teased by other kids for being fatherless, and throughout childhood, wished for someone to show him "the man's world." This son also said he felt awkward when adults mentioned that he looked like his dad. For him, and others who lost fathers very early, the primary legacy seemed to be a sense of being different from other children and of being deprived of a potential guide.

Sons who were between the ages of three and eleven when their fathers died also experienced a sense of differentness and the loss of a guide. But unlike the younger boys, these "second-stage sons" usually remembered, and sometimes reexperienced, the acute pain of the loss itself. In the early period after the loss, most also struggled to accept the finality of the death. I found that sons in this age range were the most likely to fantasize about the possibility of the father returning someday.

Adolescents, those who were between twelve and seventeen, generally seemed to recognize that the death was permanent; there were fewer fantasies. From sons in this age group, I often heard about the ambivalence that they felt at the death. Many missed their dads desperately, but also felt relief that their fathers were no longer looming over them. Of course, those who experienced relief usually felt guilty about it.

Despite such struggles, sons I interviewed who were fifteen and older when their fathers died generally seemed more capable than their younger counterparts of managing the loss, especially when they received support from friends and family. Several of these sons told me they actually were able to turn the tragedy into an opportunity.

One example is Bill McConnell, who was fifteen when his father entered a New York City hospital for what was supposed to be routine surgery. The father, aged forty-two, died during recovery. Bill's first reaction was shock: "Your whole life changes instantaneously. I was blown away by the whole thing. It was just not something that had ever entered my realm of possibility."

During visitation at the funeral home a couple of days later, Bill experienced a poignant moment when his mother's father, his oldest living male relative, walked into the room where the casket stood. Bill, who was in the room too, recalled: "I just started crying as much as I ever cried in my life. I don't know why. He's not a huggy, warm, kissy person. He's kind of a loner himself. But when he got there that night, I just needed to see him for some reason. I knew that somehow, if he was there, everything wasn't quite as crazy as it

seemed. . . . This was the first signal in days that my life wasn't over."
When Bill related this memory twelve years later as we sat together
at his kitchen table, he wept again.

In the three or four months immediately after the death, Bill
became depressed. But then he experienced a remarkable turn-
around. It culminated one day during the summer as he visited the
home of a family friend. While there, he started leafing through the
yearbooks of the children in the family, all of whom attended a
private high school. Suddenly, Bill knew that's where he needed to
be. "Up to that point, I had just kind of gone to school without
thinking about it," Bill explained. "But in that house, in the space
of an hour . . . , something snapped inside of me, and I said, 'I'm
going to this school.' I felt like I woke up."

The transfer from public school inspired him: "I was all of a
sudden surrounded by really smart people. Instead of coming home
and watching several hours of TV, doing homework, and watching
several more hours of TV, I came home and did my homework. . . .
I was coming alive and being alive. I was aware of myself more than
ever before."

Bill eventually became a computer programmer and was running
a small consulting business when I interviewed him. He told me that
the pain of his father's death rarely overwhelmed him anymore. But
he added that it continued to shape him in one obvious way: "I want
a son. I want a son desperately. I need a son. I really believe I need
a son to feel complete. It may never happen, so I might be setting
myself up. But I feel I missed out on that friendship that can only
happen between an adult father and an adult son. Since I can't have
a father, it's got to be a son."

This kind of ongoing struggle with the memory of the father was
almost universal among the sons I spoke with who'd lost fathers early

in life. And, as in Bill's case, the grappling usually lasted well into adulthood. According to my survey, 26 percent of sons who were under eighteen when their fathers died said they still prayed to their dead fathers or tried to communicate with them in some other way; 33 percent had taken up hobbies or sports their fathers had favored; 72 percent spent time with mementos, such as photographs, tools, books, and other items related to their dads.

In these and other ways, the sons revisited their relationship with their fathers, replayed the events of the older man's life and death, and in many cases, assured themselves that the spirit of their father was still present in their lives. It seemed to me that the result of these acts was generally positive, bringing the son closer to an accommodation with, if not a full acceptance of, his loss.

Sometimes this accommodation could not be accomplished by a son on his own. Thirteen percent of sons who lost fathers in childhood ended up seeking professional help—usually when they were adults—to deal with the loss. While that may not seem high, the percentage of help-seekers among boys who lost fathers was twice that of sons who were eighteen or older at the time of the father's death. (For more details about the value of grief therapy, see Chapter 10.)

Along with therapy, religion played an important role in the recovery of some sons who'd lost fathers in childhood. David O'Leary, originally from Trenton, New Jersey, was eight years old when his father died of pancreatic cancer. The older man was "the anchor of my life," David recalled; the death was "a tremendous blow. . . . Something essential got ripped away." On the night he learned his father would die, David said, he cried himself to sleep, and then dreamed that he was reaching toward his father, who was gradually floating away. When David awoke, he recalled, his arms were still stretching into the air.

David was given little information about his father's condition in the year before the death, and little extra attention from his mother in the years after. His mother had to go to work full-time; in a sense, David told me, "I suffered a double loss." David managed to survive in part by participating in Boy Scouts and falling in with a group of athletes.

Nonetheless, he said, he never lost the desire to reexperience the feeling of security he had possessed before his father died. At first, he tried to find it at a Congregationalist church he attended with friends shortly after the death. The church, he told me, provided a social anchor, as well as adult male attention. But he soon found that it could not fill "the huge vacuum in the middle of my life." Over the next five or six years, he ventured to other religions, including Judaism and Mormonism.

At age fifteen, still unsatisfied, he switched to a fundamentalist Christian church after hearing a sermon in which he was promised unification with God—or, in David's words, with "the Big Father." He stayed there until he was twenty-two, even attending a Christian seminary for a year. But finally, after failing to experience the rapturous moment when his feeling of emptiness would disappear, he gave up on religion. For the next fifteen years, he stayed away from church, focusing on his work as a schoolteacher, postal worker, and nurse. He married twice during this time, but chose not to have children.

Then, in his late thirties, during a period of self-examination, David recognized how important his spiritual searching had been to him. He started again to read about world religions and to attend a variety of churches and religious groups. Ultimately, he found a path that seemed to hold promise for him.

At age forty, David began studying Buddhist philosophy and meditating in the Zen style: sitting quietly, concentrating on his breath, and attempting to set aside all extraneous thoughts that entered his mind. Through many months of meditation practice,

David told me, he was able to experience occasional flashes of what he called "numinescence"—a feeling of "awe, wonder, holiness, of being united with the universe. The individual consciousness doesn't disappear," he said, "but I feel that I am part and parcel of everything around me."

It was a warm feeling—not unlike the feeling of security he remembered when he was with his dad. After more than three decades of searching, he'd finally come upon something that served, in his words, as "the salve, the antidote" for his loss.

There's a sad postscript to David's story. When I spoke with David, it had been forty-two years since his father's death. David was fifty, but appeared older. His blue eyes were still lively, but he walked slowly, with a cane. His red hair—thick in a photo he showed me from a few years earlier—was mostly gone.

Two years before we met, at nearly the exact age his father had died, David had been diagnosed with an aggressive form of prostate cancer. It was, in a way, "a confirmation" for him, he told me. "I always had this sense of foreboding. It was not something I brooded on. It was always around the corner of my consciousness. By virtue of my dad dying young, I always had an idea I'd die young too."

Six months after we spoke, David died at age fifty-one.

At the end of my last conversation with him, I asked David whether he thought anything could have been done differently when he was a kid to help him through the loss of his dad. He responded that he wished he had been kept better informed about his father's illness and treatment. He didn't get to see his father much toward the end of his life, he recalled, and was never sure what was going on. This was typical among those in my survey who'd lost fathers in childhood; only 17 percent of sons under eighteen were involved in the late-life care of their fathers (compared to about 60 percent of adults), while just one in twenty-five boys talked with their fathers about the death before it occurred (compared to four in ten adults).

Recent studies have found that children tend to benefit by participating in family activities that precede the death of a parent. Dr. Dennis Klass, a psychologist at Webster University in St. Louis, who has worked with bereaved children for many years, explains it this way: "How do you help kids? You include them in the community. Communities can be families, neighborhoods, villages, schools. When we isolate [children] and say, 'Deal with your feelings,' we have taken away the models that they need." Klass added: "You can't protect kids from death. We do a disservice when we try."

I asked Dr. Klass how he'd recommend breaking the news to a boy whose father was dying. He responded: "Probably Dad ought to be the one to talk to him. Then we give the dad a chance to dump as much fathering as he can into those moments. If I were working with the dad, I would at least give him the opportunity to make a tape or write a letter. 'Here's what I would have said to you when you turned twelve. Here's what I would have said to you when you turned sixteen.' "

Dr. Klass and other professionals said it's always important for parents to be sensitive in the way they handle interactions between dying parents and their young children. University of Michigan psychologist Albert Cain, a child bereavement specialist, told me he'd seen dying fathers become paranoid, and even dangerous or violent, in their last weeks or months of life, sometimes because of physiological changes due to their illnesses. In these instances, he said, the well parent may need to create "a firewall" between father and son.

But in most cases, Cain said, contact between father and son is beneficial to the son. And he urged the child's involvement in funeral or memorial services as well. According to my survey, only 14 percent of sons who were children when their fathers died participated in the funeral. Even viewing the father's body, as long as it hasn't been mutilated, usually helps a child begin to accept the loss, Cain suggested (though he added that kids who resist shouldn't be forced into it).

How should a parent tell a child of the actual death? Cain warned against using euphemisms such as the father is "sleeping" or he's gone on "a long trip." Rather, "Your father has died" is usually appropriate, followed immediately with reassuring words: "This is something we can talk about. It's not too overwhelming for me. I'm not going to dissolve into a sea of tears. I'm not going to shut you up or turn you off. We can talk about this again and again."

The goal, Cain said, is to promote periodic conversation about the loss, to let the children know they can speak of the dead parent and of their reactions to the death. A 1999 Columbia University–New York University study supports this keep-them-talking strategy of helping children after a loss. Researchers asked school-aged boys and girls from fifty-eight families in which a parent had died how open to communicating the surviving parent had been before and after the death. The findings were not surprising: Children who felt the surviving parent listened to them, and was otherwise open to their concerns, were less likely to be depressed or overly anxious after the death.

Even in the most nurturing of circumstances, some sons who lose a father in childhood will founder. Studies dating back fifty years have linked early parent-loss to a variety of life problems, including alcoholism, depression, and divorce. More than a quarter-century ago, the child-bereavement specialist Erna Furman put her finger on one of the key differences between losing a parent in childhood and adulthood: "An adult distributes his love among several meaningful relationships—his spouse, parents, children, friends, colleagues—as well as in his work and hobbies. The child, by contrast, invests almost all of his feelings in his parents. . . . Only in childhood can death deprive an individual of so much opportunity to love and be loved."

Yet, as we have seen, those who do rebound from the loss are fully capable of living satisfying, and even distinguished, lives. Several men I interviewed said their experiences with an early father-death had made them particularly grateful for the gifts in their adult lives, especially their own families. And a 1978 study actually found a link between the early death of a parent and future career success. The study focused on 699 eminent persons throughout history and found a higher than average incidence of early parent loss.

Among the notables who lost fathers in childhood: U.S. presidents George Washington, Thomas Jefferson, James Monroe, Andrew Johnson, James Garfield, and Herbert Hoover; writers Mark Twain, Bertrand Russell, and Herman Melville; U.S. General Omar Bradley; and India's liberator Mahatma Gandhi. As the author of the study theorized: "If feelings of insecurity, inadequacy, emptiness, and, especially, guilt can inhibit functioning" after an early parent-loss, "then the mastery of these feelings may be a springboard" for success.

Among the sons I spoke with for this chapter, such "mastery" was almost always hard-won. In the beginning, what they needed most was outside help: as much stability as possible, the loving guidance of both women and men, and the safety to explore their thoughts and emotions related to the loss.

Some sons got all that and more, and by adulthood, had emerged from the tragedy, often with special strengths. In most cases, however, the man who grew out of the boy had to finish his mourning in adulthood, identifying the legacies of the loss in his life, addressing disruptive behavior patterns, and finding a way not to banish the memory of his father but to settle it, gracefully, within himself.

Michael Jordan

—∿—

In June of 1993, Michael Jordan's career was soaring.

At thirty years of age, he had just carried the Chicago Bulls to their third consecutive NBA championship. For the seventh straight year, he'd averaged more than thirty points a game, winning three Most Valuable Player awards in the process. During the 1992–93 season, Jordan had earned $4 million playing hoops, and $30 million more endorsing shoes, cars, hamburgers, cereal, and underwear. He had a movie deal, book proposals, video offers, and online opportunities galore. He was, in short, the hottest commodity in a commodity-obsessed society.

And then on August 3, just six weeks after the Bulls clinched that third championship, Jordan's father, James, was found shot to death in a creek in rural South Carolina, the victim of an apparently random roadside robbery. Michael Jordan—who had grown up playing sports with his father, sought his father's guidance throughout his career, and recently described his father as "my best friend"—went into seclusion with his family. When he emerged two months later, it was to announce the unfathomable.

He was leaving the NBA.

At a press conference broadcast live around the world, Jordan was flanked by his wife, coaches, teammates, NBA brass, and corporate executives. He declared that "the desire was not there" any longer to play professional basketball. "I don't have anything else . . . to prove," he told the assembled throng. He had thought about quitting before his father's murder, he said, but made the decision after. He'd learned from the death that the future "can be . . . taken away from you at any time." And he added, "I guess the biggest positive thing that I can take out of my father not being here today is that he saw my last basketball game, and that means a lot."

It also meant a lot that James Jordan had, before he died, urged his gifted son to retire from basketball and become a professional baseball player. The elder Jordan had played pitch and catch with his son throughout the boy's childhood, and believed Michael could be a baseball star.

At first, Michael had resisted his father's urging. But after the death, he decided to honor his dad's memory by living out the older man's dream for him. In December 1993, four months after his father's murder, Michael Jordan began training to become a major-league ballplayer.

As Bob Greene writes in *Rebound*, his account of Jordan's baseball career: "Overcome with grief and uncertainty, Jordan made the instinctive decision to do what few men and women in adult life ever do: to start over. He tried to turn himself into who he had been before all the renown and all the privilege and all the adulation—to find out, as a kind of medicine for his grief, if he could do it all over again."

He couldn't. The next fifteen months would be, for Jordan, a major disappointment. After a frustrating spring training with the Chicago White Sox, he spent the 1994 season with the Birmingham (Alabama) Barons of the Class AA Southern League— two long steps from the major leagues—bouncing in a pink-and-purple-splotched team bus through Tupelo, Memphis, and other points of the erstwhile Confederacy. He struggled at the plate and in right field. After his early season twelve-game hitting streak, opposing pitchers found Jordan's soft spots, and his batting average sunk below .200 for most of the year.

But if he couldn't make contact with the ball, at least his new career allowed him to remain close to his father. As he told Greene: "I think about him every day. Every single day. I think about him when I'm worried, and I think about him when I have a decision to make. I think about him when I have a bad problem. I think about what advice he would give me, what he would say to me. So on my drive to practice in the dark every morning, he's with me, and I remember why I'm doing this. I remember why I'm here. I'm here for him."

Despite his discouraging first year, Jordan was not ready to give up on his father's dream. In February 1995, he rejoined the White Sox for spring training. But then fate, in the form of a baseball strike, intervened. Jordan was asked either to cross the picket line set up by major-league players or leave the White Sox. He chose the latter. For the next couple of weeks, as millions of fans wondered what would be next for Jordan, he huddled with his family. And then he answered those fans with a resounding two-word press release:

"I'm back."

It would take another fifteen months for the Bulls to win their next championship. But after the 87–75 win over the Seattle SuperSonics in the game that clinched it, Jordan lay on the parquet floor of the United Center in Chicago, hugging the basketball to his chest, his eyes shut tight against his tears.

The victory, on June 16, 1996, had special significance for Jordan. It capped his remarkable comeback, proved his domination of the sport, and ended a season in which the Bulls compiled the best record in the history of the NBA.

Appropriately, the victory came on Father's Day.

My father died just as I became an adult. . . . It's a tough thing
because you've kind of known this guy as a child and then,
just at the point where you start to understand
where he's coming from, he's gone.
—ACTOR JOE MANTEGNA

Chapter 2

TOO SOON

Ages 18 to 32

I T WAS AN HOUR into the visitation, and Alfred Freeman was getting restless. He'd already said his good-bye. As the organist played her seamless laments, Alfred had risen from the folding chair in the mortuary's small chapel, stepped up to the coffin, and leaned his face into it. There, instead of kissing his father's cheek as his mother, sisters, and brothers had done, Alfred found himself searching the old man's eyelids for a quiver or a twitch. Finally, satisfied that his father was indeed beyond recall, the gangly twenty-one-year-old college junior returned impatiently to taking condolences from the stream of "family acquaintances, third cousins, and aunts with cigarette breath . . . telling me how I had to be a man."

Then came his opportunity for escape. It arrived in the form of an old high-school friend, an energetic, round-headed, former football player named Roger. Roger had surprised and pleased Alfred by showing up early at the visitation, and as Roger rose to leave the chapel, he whispered to Alfred: "I've got some . . . hash in my car. Wanna join me?" To which Alfred had replied, simply, "Yes."

The ten-minute ride through the residential Toledo, Ohio, neighborhood, in Roger's black 1960 Chevy Biscayne, transformed Alfred's mood, and he was able to return almost cheerfully to his condolence-taking duties. But the ride also marked the first step of Alfred's descent into addiction.

Alfred had smoked marijuana before. It was 1973, after all, and pot-smoking was prevalent at virtually every American university. He'd even stashed away a small plastic bag of marijuana a friend had given him. But in the past, he could always take it or leave it. Not anymore.

In the weeks after his father's death, Alfred began to smoke with increasing frequency. Within two months, he was getting stoned every day. Within four months, he'd quit engineering school and taken a job at a factory. As his marijuana use became protracted, Alfred grew so paranoid that he rarely left his apartment except to go to work. "At the time, I had no idea that any of this was related to my father's death," Alfred recalled more than twenty-five years later. "I felt: This is the way it is. He's seventy-three years old, he's been ill, he's died, and we go on. . . . Now, I realize that for me, it came too soon."

Too soon. The phrase resounds through the lives of sons who lose their fathers in young adulthood. Men between the ages of eighteen and thirty-two—the "novice stage" of life, in the words of sociologist Daniel Levinson—enjoy most of the legal prerogatives of full adulthood. But, by their own admission, they still are works in progress. Most sons I talked with who'd lost fathers in early adulthood said that, at the time of the death, they had still been dependent on their fathers—for guidance, money, and emotional support. In addition, they said, they almost always had unfinished business with their dads: resentments unexpressed, affection unacknowledged.

The death of a father during a son's young adulthood—which happens to approximately one in five men—tends to sever a vital relationship before it's reached fruition, before the son has completed the key task of Levinson's novice stage: to shift his center of gravity from his family of origin to his own home base. Given this, it is no surprise that the immediate impact of the death of a father is often as devastating for young adults as it is for children.

Young adults do understandably have some advantages over children in the recovery after the initial blow. When they know the death is coming, young adults tend to prepare themselves better for it. My survey showed that young-adult men are more likely than children to be involved in the father's medical care, to say good-bye to the father, and to talk with him about the death. By the time of the father's death, 80 percent of young-adult sons said they felt resolved with the older man, compared to just 51 percent of children.

Nonetheless, more so than middle-aged and older sons, the men I spoke with who lost fathers in early adulthood faced formidable threats, including substance abuse, social withdrawal, and ongoing battles with self-doubt.

For Alfred Freeman, the immediate peril was marijuana addiction. By the time he'd quit school, a few months after his father's death, Alfred was engaged "in a full-blown habit," he told me. He craved the euphoria that marijuana offered him, and spent his days riding the ups and downs of the drug's effect. When the pain of his father's death threatened to overwhelm him, he simply smoked another joint. "It was," he told me, "a case of extreme denial."

At a certain point, however, as is the tendency with most addictive behaviors, the euphoric effect of the habit started to ebb. For Alfred, this began about eighteen months after his father's death. By that time, he recalled, he was beginning to see the damage of his chronic use of marijuana. He felt physically depleted and ashamed. "I realized I was nothing like the person I had been, and certainly nothing like the person I wanted to be," he recalled.

His greatest incentive to quit marijuana was his fear of becoming "a washout." Growing up in the 1950s and 1960s, part African-American, part Native-American, Alfred had received messages from the dominant white society (and even his father at times) that he was destined for failure. Now, in his early twenties, the possibility that he might fulfill that destiny began to haunt him. For the first time, he could imagine himself trudging through the decades ahead, his ambitions and dreams strewn behind him.

So Alfred did what many other addicts are unable to do: He discarded his drug paraphernalia, along with his drug-using friends, and struggled to take charge of his life. He "backslid" a number of times, he recalled, but after about a year, he was off marijuana for good.

It helped that the pot experiences had begun to inspire as much paranoia as euphoria. It also helped that his girlfriend, who would later become his wife, supported his desire to get off drugs; she stopped using them too. And perhaps most of all, it helped when, about a year after he stopped smoking pot, his wife gave birth to a son, who would be their only child.

Through his subsequent experiences as a father, Alfred said, he was forced constantly to confront, and reevaluate, his relationship with his own dad. Early on, he found himself rejecting his father as a role model; he thought his dad had been too ill-tempered and critical. But as the years passed, Alfred gradually recalled his father's more positive attributes, especially his dependability and sense of humor. While Alfred could not remember ever crying over his father's death, he said that he managed, through this sorting-out process, to mourn the old man nonetheless.

When I spoke with Alfred, he was forty-seven years old. He held engineering and law degrees, was a high-ranking manager at a large corporation, and had the thin, muscular build of a man who worked out almost daily. His first marriage had ended after five years, but he'd been remarried—happily, he said—for more than a decade. After the divorce, he'd been granted custody of his son, who was now navigating the turbulent waters of young adulthood.

Not surprisingly, Alfred's immediate response to his father's death—using drugs to help manage his pain—was more common among young adults than any other age group. My survey showed that 21 percent of sons who'd lost fathers between eighteen and thirty-two acknowledged using alcohol or nonprescription drugs to help them cope in the first month after the death. That was nearly ten times the rate reported by sons under the age of eighteen, and more than triple that of adults over the age of thirty-two.

It was also not unusual, among the young adults I interviewed, for this short-term use of drugs to turn into ongoing abuse. Unlike children and adolescents, young men often lived away from their families of origin, frequently alone. Several told me that it was tempting for them to retreat inside their homes after their fathers died—and stay there. To keep thoughts of the death at bay, some of these men said in retrospect, they began or deepened addictive behavior patterns. Frequently, they told me, their emergence from such patterns became a pivotal struggle in their lives.

Seth Oakes was six years old when the man he now considers his father came into his life. Before that time, Seth and his mother had been mostly on their own; Seth's biological father had deserted his family when Seth was two months old. Nonetheless, Seth remembered his early years as happy. He had virtually all of his mother's attention, as well as the attention of relatives and neighbors who watched out for the single mother and her son.

When Seth was six, his mother remarried, and life got more complicated. At first, Seth resented the presence of his mother's new husband and clashed with him. Seth was also less than enthusiastic when a half-brother was born two years after the remarriage. Between the ages of nine and fourteen, even after Seth's stepfather had adopted him, Seth viewed the older man as "that guy who sat at the other end of the dinner table."

Then his mother got breast cancer and died quickly. In the grief that consumed the family home, Seth and his adoptive father battled angrily. For both, it was a relief when Seth went off to college. He kept a distance from his adoptive father during the next four years and drank heavily, he said, in part to submerge memories of his family life. After college, although he was smart and talented, Seth struggled in the working world. He had few goals and little initiative; he became the office cynic, openly critical of the corporations that employed him.

After he was fired from two jobs for "attitude problems," his adoptive father stepped back into his life. First, he apologized to Seth for having been so hard on the boy after his mother's death. Then he offered to foot the bill if Seth wanted to get psychological help.

Seth accepted both. He soon learned one reason he was so cynical and angry. As he told me: "I had this notion that I'd never be as happy as I'd been when my mother was around." Openly acknowledging this fear helped Seth begin to let go of it. Eventually, he felt safe enough to shed tears at a counseling session over the loss of his mother.

After eighteen months of therapy, a sense of optimism had returned to Seth's life. Not only had he mourned for his mother, his relationship with his adoptive father was flourishing. The two men were becoming friends. They had dinners together, traveled together. The rest of Seth's life was full too. He had a girlfriend, a new home, success on the job. "I was almost punch-drunk because everything was going great, everything was turning to gold," Seth said of the period between ages twenty-five and twenty-nine. "Everything I tried, I was succeeding at."

Then one day, his father summoned Seth to his home and broke some awful news. He had inoperable lung cancer. He'd decided against chemotherapy. He had less than six months to live.

In the weeks leading up to the death, as the older man sat wrapped in blankets in the easy chair in his living room, father and son talked at length about the past and future. Among the final words Seth heard from his father: "I'm not sure about your brother, but I know you'll be all right."

Seth appreciated the affirming words, but his subsequent mourning was agonizing nonetheless. Through the experience of grieving his mother's death, Seth had sensed after his father died that it would help him if he cried. So in the early days, he often lubricated himself with scotch and let his tears flow.

Nonetheless, the pain diminished little. "It was like I lost my compass. Dad was my toughest critic. When I was younger, I had a real hard time with it. But once I got to be about twenty-five or twenty-six, I knew how to tune out the negative and make it constructive." Now, without the loving concern of his father, Seth lost his motivation. "I don't really feel like an adult. I'm looking for someone to light a fire under me. But there's nobody there."

Not long after the death, Seth quit his job. He had begun taking business-school classes at night, and convinced himself he could get his new degree more quickly if he wasn't distracted by a regular job. He began living off the money his father left him. He spent most of his time alone. The only woman he dated was someone he'd broken up with a year before his father's death. The reconciliation was briefly comforting, but ultimately painful; this time around, she broke up with him.

In part to ensure that he'd be unattractive to other women, he told me, Seth succumbed to a tendency to overeat. Up to several nights a week, he said, he'd order a large pizza for dinner and eat it alone. Then he'd top off the meal with a few doughnuts. Within a year of his father's death, he'd put on thirty pounds. He added fifteen pounds more in the following two years.

I spoke with Seth twice. In our first conversation, three years after the death, he described himself as "an island. It's a solitary life I'm living. And I'm not happy with it. . . . I stay at home with my dog. I insulate myself. I'm waiting on the sidelines. I'm waiting for a sign that things will be all-clear."

Seth acknowledged that he feared becoming "paralyzed" in his "cocoon." But when we spoke again two years later, his fears had not been realized. Seth had finished graduate school, secured a good job, and had just been offered a better one. "A company I used to work for called me up out of the blue," he told me. "I'm getting a good-sized raise out of it, and we need the money. We just bought a new house, and there's the wedding coming up."

The wedding, ironically, would involve Seth and the same woman he'd dated before and after his father's death. Following the last breakup, they'd spent a year apart, dating other people, before getting back together for good. "We've always been compatible," Seth said, "but the timing had never been right."

When I asked Seth how he managed to emerge from his isolation after his dad's death, he told me the key was patience. "I couldn't rush it. Each day, I hurt a little less." Now, Seth said, instead of dwelling upon his father's absence, he generally looked to his father for guidance. Of his dad, Seth said: "He's still probably the single most important person in my life. With the wedding coming up, obviously I wish he was here. I'm disappointed, but it's not really that bittersweet. That's so long ago, and I think I've moved on. He'd want me to have moved on."

"Moving on" took Seth about four years, which may seem like a long time. But consider Seth's circumstances: His mother was already dead, and his only sibling, a half-brother, was an active alcoholic after their father's death. Seth had no immediate family with whom to share his loss. Thus, it's not hard to appreciate his need to pull back and take cover for a while, before reengaging the world.

Besides, compared to other young-adult men I interviewed, Seth's was not an abnormally long recovery. Walter Wang, for example, took considerably longer to come to terms with his father's death. Even with his wife and children living in the same home, Walter found a way, after his father's death, to isolate himself for more than thirty years.

Walter was a twenty-two-year-old engineering student at a Southern California university when he received a phone call from his sister saying that their father, a Chinese immigrant and small business owner, had died of a heart attack at the age of fifty-seven. It was crushing news to Walter, but he immediately moved into his "mechanical mode," shutting away all emotion as he concentrated on what he had to do next: plan the funeral and help his mother make the initial transition to widowhood. A couple of weeks later, with that accomplished, Walter went back to his old life as if nothing big had happened.

That old life included an upcoming wedding. In one of his father's last acts, he had blessed Walter's engagement to a fellow student. And three months after the death, the couple was married. Almost immediately, however, Walter and his wife began what would be a decades-long struggle: She would urge him to open up emotionally; he would fend her off.

As far as Walter was concerned, his mechanical style was the right one. It had been his father's style. And after his father's death, Walter had decided that "what was good enough for my father was good enough for me."

The father, who had come to California as a young man in the 1920s, certainly had a noble goal: educating his five children so they could move from the laboring to the professional class. He had succeeded. But his methods had been harsh. At the dinner table each night, the children were forbidden to speak unless spoken to. And often that speaking-to was a rebuke from the father. Walter recalled: "Once, when I was in the sixth grade, I had a report card that said, '[Walter] does not always listen.' You can bet I heard about that. It was brought up at the dinner table, and I was shamed in front of my brothers and sisters. It was rough. But the idea was to shame us in front of the family before we did something that shamed the family in public. Even as a kid, you carried a burden beyond yourself."

Walter was destined to pass that burden on to his own children. After his marriage, Walter took an entry-level job at a small engineering firm near Los Angeles and began working his way up. By the time he was thirty, Walter was a mid-level manager and the father of four. Everyday life consisted of an updated version of his father's existence: ten to twelve hours at the office followed by dinnertime conversation centered around what his children must do to get ahead. "When one of my kids would tell me he got an A in school, I'd ask, 'Why not an A-plus?'" Walter recalled. "I was hard on them." And he was no easier on his employees. "It was my idea that if I didn't have anything negative to say to them, they should believe they were doing fine."

By age fifty-five, Walter was by all appearances a successful man. His children had made it through college; he'd been married to one woman for thirty-three years; he was earning a six-figure income; and he had moved to within one slot of the presidency of the now

$20-million-a-year engineering company. That's when Walter's boss, the company president, announced his retirement and told Walter that he was ready to turn over the reins to him.

For the first time in his life, however, Walter balked at advancement. He had spent his career on the technical side of the business. There, his style had always been rigid; he was demanding and unforgiving. His attitude was: "If something didn't stand up structurally, it was no good." Up to this point, he had always been rewarded for this approach. But now, even he wasn't sure that this method would work once he took the role of top executive.

So Walter took a risk. A few years earlier, his boss had encouraged him to attend a management seminar designed to help him become more of a "people person." At the time, Walter had refused, believing that "touchy-feely" education was a waste of time. "I don't want anybody messing with my head," he recalled telling his boss. Now, as he struggled with the decision of whether to seek the president's job (and, as he approached the age of his father's death), he decided to attend.

The seminar began comfortably enough. For three days, the facilitators taught Walter and about twenty-five other participants the science of human behavior. Using research studies and case histories, they explained how people's needs and strengths changed over their life spans, and how managers in business might be more effective by taking these changes into account. Finally, on the morning of the fourth day, the participants were gathered in a classroom and asked to close their eyes and imagine being in a warm, safe environment. Then, working from the present day backward, one of the leaders talked them through a slow and careful review of their lives.

Walter could not remember the exact instructions. He did recall that when he reached the point in his life when his father died, a short and powerful burst came unexpectedly from his mouth. At first he tried to shut it off, but he noticed that the room was filled with weeping colleagues. So he let go. For several minutes, he cried for his loss of thirty-three years before and, he would tell me later, for the years of emotional holding back that had followed.

The experience changed Walter. Returning home, he did something he had never done before: He asked his wife for advice on a career decision. He also admitted to her that she'd been right about his emotional distance. After his father's death, he told her, he had adopted the old man's nose-to-the-grindstone approach to life. Walter acknowledged that his obsession with his career had helped him cope with the death, but that it had also shut her and their children out. Finally, he told her, he was ready to open up.

Her reaction: "It's about time."

Together, they decided that he would take the president's job. And for the next ten years, he told me, he worked vigorously to bring a more human face to his management style. He encouraged employees to state concerns about him. He sought input before making decisions. And he was willing to be persuaded. He also sat down with his grown children, told them about his seminar experience, and apologized to them. He had been a fool, he told them, and had lost his opportunity to be close to them in their childhoods. He wanted to try again in adulthood.

When I interviewed Walter, he was sixty-seven and retired. A lanky, energetic man, he said his relationships with his children had gradually improved over the previous decade. He said he still got frustrated with himself at times, when he slipped back into his mechanical way. But he was determined to keep trying: "For thirty years, I avoided intimacy. I wouldn't share my hurt. I screwed up. I could have been helped if I had just vented. But I didn't know how to vent. I thought venting meant weakness."

Walter was not alone among young-adult men in his reluctance to share pain with others. Many of the sons I interviewed in this age group believed at the time of their father's death that to depend on others for support would compromise their manhood at the very moment it was being tested. For these men, young adulthood was a time for "stepping up," as one man put it, for proving that he could weather hard times on his own.

And yet, one of the key lessons I took away from my conversations with men who lost fathers in young-adulthood was this: A young man's willingness to depend on others was often his greatest ally in rebounding from the loss. Depending on others did not necessarily mean crying on other people's shoulders, or allowing others to make important decisions. Rather, it often involved nothing more than a son accepting comfort or practical assistance from friends and family.

Lee Jones was twenty-five years old, married, and a Washington, D.C., real-estate agent when he was awakened at three o'clock one morning by a phone call. It was his sister, informing him that their father, who lived in Mississippi, had died suddenly of a heart attack at the age of forty-nine.

It was the end of an intimate father-son bond. As a six-year-old boy growing up in the rural South in the early 1960s, Lee was his father's "gofer" as the older man built a grocery next door to their home. After the store opened, Lee spent many afternoons stocking shelves while his dad rang up soda, candy, and other groceries. The family was active in the local African Methodist Episcopal church, and while his father employed corporal punishment with his children, Lee recalled, "I always felt I was respected. He was warm, friendly—and firm."

Lee entered adolescence in the late 1960s, and clashed with his father at times over racial politics. His father had seen the enormous progress of blacks during the previous two decades, and he cautioned his son not to push the white majority too hard. But the son was energized by the turbulent political climate and campaigned actively for voting rights and other civil liberties for minorities.

Despite these political differences, however, father and son remained loving. Lee's father expressed enormous pride when his son went off to college and wrote to Lee regularly during his college years. When Lee returned home for the holidays, his father was the one waiting at the bus stop, ready with a warm handshake. "What I can say about my father is I never had to look for him," Lee told me.

After college, Lee served a two-year hitch in the Army ROTC. Shortly before his military obligation ended, he spoke with his dad about his interest in the real estate business. He remembered his father's reaction: "That's a good business, son. You can do well in that." Within a few weeks, Lee had secured his first job in a real estate agency.

Then came the sudden death. Lee was devastated. "You feel you lost a part of yourself," he told me. But instead of facing it alone, he allowed himself to be supported.

The support began with his employer. A few hours after the death, Lee called his boss, a man his father's age, to say he'd be gone a few days for the funeral. The boss told Lee: "Take all the time you need. And if you don't have the money to get home, I'll help." Lee stayed for a week in Mississippi, assisting his mother in her transition and spending time with his siblings recounting the story of their father's life. In the ensuing months, he would talk on the phone for hours at a time with a brother or sister as they shared their memories of their dad.

When he returned to Washington, D.C., Lee said, his wife gave him the combination of space and support that he needed. Lee remembered being emotionally erratic during this period, but, he said, "She didn't judge. She was just there. She had lost her dad as a junior in college, so she knew what I was facing. She talked with me when I wanted to talk, and left me alone when I didn't. When I wanted to go out with my male friends, she didn't complain."

His friends in church were important too, as was his relationship with God. He had a core belief that his father was in heaven. "Even though I was pretty upset at the funeral, I knew [my father] was in a better place. He had lived a good life. He was a deacon in the church. I had the faith that he was with God." Still, the event shook Lee's spiritual foundation. "It was a [question] of why. Why now? . . . Dad had struggled for years. He was in the best part of his life." Eventually, Lee reached this conclusion: "That's not my department."

When I spoke with Lee, in the office of the real estate agency he owned, he was forty-five. Muscular and soft-spoken, he said he still looked to his father for guidance in his actions. If he believed his father wouldn't approve of something, he tried to avoid doing it. He also said he had attempted to pass along his father's ethical values to his two children.

But like most other men whose fathers died young, Lee still felt the loss keenly at times. He told me he noticed twinges of pain when he saw a man of about seventy, the age his father would have been when we spoke. And he could count on May 28 being a wistful day. That was, and to Lee, always will be, Dad's birthday.

In addition to the support of others, Lee Jones was aided in his mourning period by the sense that he'd had a healthy, positive relationship with his father. "I just know at the time he died, we were on good terms," Lee told me. Because of this, Lee was able to experience his sadness about his father's death without also being burdened with regrets.

Many sons who are young adults when their fathers die are not so fortunate. Twenty-five percent of such sons I surveyed said they still were angry at times with their fathers, sometimes decades after the death. And 64 percent, the highest among all age groups, said they had regrets about things they had or hadn't done in relation to their dads. After the death, many of these sons had to grapple with that anger and regret, as they looked to finish the father-son relationship on their own.

Sons often accomplished this "finishing" in imaginative ways. Craig Chabot was nineteen years old, in his freshman year at a large California university, when his father died at age fifty-two after a long battle with heart disease. To Craig, his father had been a virtual god: a French bombardier during World War II and a superb athlete who also had earned a doctorate in English literature. The father had met his future wife while stationed in the United States during the war and married her after it ended. Over the next two decades, the father worked at, and eventually took over, his father-in-law's printing company.

Craig told me that as a young child, he often felt awestruck in the presence of his father. This was exacerbated in adolescence as Craig began to mature in his sexuality and realized that he was gay. Craig said: "I was always thinking I was not the kind of son he wanted. I felt like there was this big gulf between us."

Craig especially cherished one memory of his dad: A few weeks before his father's death, Craig had been home from college on winter break and visited his father at the hospital. Sitting beside his father's bed, Craig informed the older man that he'd gotten straight A's in his first semester at school. The father replied: "I don't want you to feel I'm pushing you to get good grades. I'm already proud of the way you've turned out." It was the first time Craig could remember his father ever directly expressing his pride.

Craig returned to college soon after and did not make it to the hospital again before his father died. The son was surprised by the power of his own initial reaction: "I felt abandoned. I wasn't ready. I wasn't prepared at all. I thought I still had years to goof off, to be irresponsible, to be a kid. Dad would be there tolerating me, until I finally grew up."

To calm himself in the first days after the death, Craig took Valium. (Three percent of young-adult sons in my survey took prescription drugs to cope with the death, more than twice the rate of any other age group.) It was during this time that Craig also made a radical decision: He decided to drop out of college indefinitely and return home to take over his father's role in the family business. Craig's mother tried to dissuade him at first, but the son insisted. "Maybe in the back of my mind, I was revisiting an old episode of *The Waltons*," he explained to me. "I was John-Boy saying, 'Don't worry, Mom, I'll take care of everything.' "

Craig stayed out of college for only six months. But more than two decades later, Craig remembered the boost of confidence he got after his decision to take a break. He told me: "To this day, that decision stands among the clearest, easiest decisions I've ever taken in my life: no room for discussion, no second thoughts, nothing. Just instant resolve."

Craig took the break from school because he was intuitively aware that he had some work to do before he could move on with his life. He felt he had to "complete" his relationship with his dad in order to let it go. This completion process began with long conversations with his mother. While working alongside each other at the printing company, Craig recalled his mother telling stories about his father that Craig had never heard before. Many accentuated the father's positive attributes. But what helped most, Craig said, were the many "very affectionate stories" that illustrated the father's insecurities and fears as well. This helped Craig begin to see his father less as a god and more as a human being.

Craig said it also helped to work at his father's desk each day.

Craig sorted through his dad's files, read his memos and mail, and inspected the notes his father had handwritten. Through this experience, Craig was forced to confront the memory of his father every day and also to see that his own abilities were quite possibly a match for his dad's. Craig told me: "I started to realize: 'Hey, I can run his company. I can step into his shoes.'" It was this realization that allowed him to go back to college and his own life.

Even after returning to school, however, Craig continued to stay connected with the memory of his dad. In a poignant decision, Craig switched majors from business administration to French, his father's native language. Craig learned the language and studied abroad in his junior year, just a few miles from his father's ancestral home.

After college, Craig returned to the family business and continued to work there, even after it was sold to a larger company. Through his twenties and thirties, he stayed connected with his dad through mementos; he'd frequently pull out his father's cadet-school yearbook, immigration papers, or photo albums. Most affecting, he said, were pictures he discovered of his dad in childhood. "In the earliest of them," Craig said, "he's just a scared little boy, the expression in his eyes the same one I'd felt myself for so long."

When Craig was in his late thirties, he was drawn to return to his father's homeland for the first time since college. Craig dedicated the trip to his dad. "He had never gone back. I went back for him." It turned out to be a bittersweet experience. "When I drove up on the little glen" that overlooked the father's hometown, Craig recalled, "I had to stop, I had to pull off the road. The feeling, the connection, was palpable. It was overwhelming." There, on the side of the road, Craig experienced what he called "a real catharsis." He told me: "I really felt something had been accomplished."

Returning from the trip, Craig felt stronger. And he made a decision that signaled to him that he had "come full circle" in his relationship with his dad. The decision was this: Upon Craig's death, his ashes would be spread in the village where his father had been born.

I talked with Craig when he was forty-three years old. While he told me he no longer felt sad about his father very often, he still had trouble seeing himself as an equal of his dad. His father, Craig said, always seemed "more competent, more moral, more upright" than Craig could ever be.

This struggle with ongoing self-doubt—sometimes subtle, sometimes overwhelming—was mentioned by many sons I spoke with who'd lost fathers in early adulthood. Dr. Calvin Colarusso, a California psychiatrist and author of *Child and Adult Development*, a book on the human maturation process, believes fathers often play an irreplaceable role in building the confidence of their young-adult sons.

In a son's *early* young adulthood—approximately ages eighteen to twenty-two—the father has the opportunity to be a "facilitator," according to Colarusso, assisting the son in getting established outside the childhood home. During this transitional period, a father might cosign a car loan or pay a security deposit on the son's apartment. Having the father in this facilitator/supporter role gives the son confidence that even if he stumbles, he'll have help getting up.

Following this period, in a son's middle and late twenties, a father often turns his focus from material support to "admiring and appreciating," Colarusso said, and "putting a major stamp of approval" on the son's decisions and accomplishments. The father may affirm the son's choices in his career, love life, and other arenas. When a son gets this kind of approval from his dad, Colarusso said, the son's confidence tends to rise, and he starts seeing himself as a full adult. Many sons I interviewed said that a defining moment in young adulthood occurred when they felt a sense of equality in relationship to their fathers.

The death of the father in a son's young adulthood can disrupt, or even abort, the progress of a son as he reaches toward this sense of equality with the father. In some cases, the son who loses his father in young adulthood finds a way to complete this maturation process on his own or with the help of father-surrogates.

But for a good number of the sons I spoke with, there remained, even decades later, an emptiness, a hole. It was in that emptiness that self-doubts often thrived. Even when sons were able to overcome these doubts, the yearning for connection with the father tended to remain. As one forty-six-year-old businessman told me twenty-four years after his father's death: "The thing I miss the most is not ever having been man-to-man with my father. I'd like to be able to go for a drink with him or go to a ball game as a couple of adults. . . . I don't really need really anything from him anymore. I just wish he could know me now."

Dylan Thomas

—⬥—

It is among the best-known English poems of the past century. One critic called it "a model of perfection." Another deemed it "one of the most moving tributes of a son to a father in all literature." It is curious, then, that the writer, the Welshman Dylan Thomas, never let his father read it.

The poem is known by its opening line: "Do Not Go Gentle Into That Good Night." Penned in 1945, it is a howling, haunting homage to a dying father. And its concluding exhortation remains a staple of American funereal liturgy: "Rage, rage against the dying of the light."

Thomas told friends that he concealed the six-stanza poem from his father because his father did not realize he was dying. But it's unlikely that his dad, known as D. J., was so naive. D. J. Thomas already had been forced by illness to give up his work. A schoolteacher renowned for his eloquent oral renderings of English poetry, he had been silenced by cancer of the tongue.

Perhaps it was the son who was in denial. In Dylan Thomas's

short life, no one had more influence on him than his father. To lose this man, as Dylan would when he was thirty-eight years old, was to lose his ultimate supporter. Some of the poet's biographers believe his father's death may even have triggered the son's demise; less than a year after his father succumbed to cancer, Dylan Thomas drank himself to death.

Throughout their lives together, father and son were at once intensely entwined and oddly distant. D. J. Thomas had wanted to be a poet himself. His meager means (and perhaps his talent) did not allow it, and he settled for the role of English teacher at a grammar school in Wales. He apparently never reconciled himself to his lack of literary success; his daughter-in-law once called him the "most unhappy of all men I have ever met."

But if the father felt bitterness, he did not overwhelm his son with it. Rather, he named the boy after a poet in the family lineage, then imbued him with a love of words and rhythm. Before Dylan could talk, he had heard through his father's voice many of the works of Shakespeare. The son would later say that his love of language seemed innate.

In school, Dylan excelled in nothing but English, and his father allowed him to drop out at sixteen to begin his writing career. By age twenty, Dylan had published his first book of poems and received his father's blessing to move to London. For the next decade, the two men visited each other regularly, and a fondness emerged. In the father's dying years, they lived near each other; when the poet was not lecturing out of town, father and son often spent hours at a time together, filling out crossword puzzles and drinking beer.

Despite their closeness, though, there was a formality, a reserve, that marked their interactions. Dylan's friend John Malcolm Brinnin spent a day with the poet and his father and detected something "unmistakably distant and wary between the two men." Another friend of the poet's, Constantine Fitzgibbon, also noticed the cautiousness, saying father and son had "a closeness that found only limited expression."

In his poetry, however, Dylan Thomas gave full freedom to his feelings for his father, never as passionately as when he bellowed sorrowfully about his father's demise.

> *Do not go gentle into that good night,*
> *Old age should burn and rave at close of day;*
> *Rage, rage against the dying of the light.*
>
> *Though wise men at their end know dark is right,*
> *Because their words had forked no lightning they*
> *Do not go gentle into that good night.*
>
> *Good men, the last wave by, crying how bright*
> *Their frail deeds might have danced in a green bay,*
> *Rage, rage against the dying of the light.*
>
> *Wild men who caught and sang the sun in flight,*
> *And learn, too late, they grieved it on its way,*
> *Do not go gentle into that good night.*
>
> *Grave men, near death, who see with blinding sight*
> *Blind eyes could blaze like meteors and be gay,*
> *Rage, rage against the dying of the light.*
>
> *And you, my father, there on the sad height,*
> *Curse, bless, me now with your fierce tears, I pray.*
> *Do not go gentle into that good night.*
> *Rage, rage against the dying of the light.*

Pop struggled to focus his eyes. He was trying to say something.
I leaned forward. "Colin," he whispered, pointing toward his head,
"there's nothing up there anymore." They were the last words
I ever heard him mutter. The following Saturday, he died.
The formative figure in my life was gone.
—GENERAL COLIN POWELL

Chapter 3

_____

THE BODY BLOW

_____

Ages 33 to 55

IN AUSTIN, Texas, Sandy Taylor was sweating out the week between Christmas and New Year's Day. Though only thirty-seven years old, and in fine health, Sandy was convinced that he would die before the first of the year. The countdown to this date had begun exactly eleven weeks earlier. It was then that Sandy's father, a retired military officer, succumbed to a heart attack at age sixty-eight. The death had followed by just three months the fatal heart attack of Sandy's grandfather. In the wake of the double loss, Sandy happened upon a photo of himself, his father, and grandfather. Staring at it gloomily one afternoon, he came to an admittedly irrational conclusion: All three men in the photo were destined to die in the same year. Now, as he endured his first Christmas season as the oldest man in his paternal lineage, Sandy's anxiety reached a peak. If his intuition was correct, Sandy, a radio disk jockey with a booming voice, was in his last 150 hours of life.

In Portland, Oregon, Christopher Nichols dug his spikes into the batter's box. It had been a month since two drug addicts had broken into his father's Florida home, wrestled a plastic garbage bag over the old man's head, and demanded he tell them where he kept his cash. Sick with emphysema, the seventy-four-year-old man suffocated in minutes. For Christopher, forty, a high-school math teacher, this was his first game back in the church softball league since the murder. The pitcher arced the ball toward him. Christopher swung, connected, and launched "a cannon shot" over the shortstop's head toward the gap in left-center field. There was no outfield fence, so Christopher was immediately thinking home run. He vaulted out of the batter's box toward first base and was strong as he headed toward second base. But as he touched it, a sudden tightness seized his chest. He tried to ignore the pain and keep his legs pumping. Rounding third, however, he was gasping for breath. He kept running anyway. Half-stumbling down the third-base line, he powered himself toward the plate, throwing his body into a headfirst dive. Then, as his belly made contact with home plate, his entire world went dark.

In Memphis, Tennessee, Jerrold Hartman settled on the couch to watch a rented movie with his wife and college-aged son. It had been a few months since Jerry's father had died after a long bout with Alzheimer's disease. Since then, Jerry, fifty-three, a tall, blond-haired insurance agent, had been stubbornly depressed. As the movie credits flashed, Jerry felt a sharp pain in his chest. His first thought was: *It'll pass.* But it didn't. He suffered a few minutes in silence. Then, when he felt the blood leave his face, he said aloud, "I think I need to go to the emergency room." A short while later, waiting for test results in a hospital bed, he thought: *I could be dying.*

Jerrold Hartman did not die. Nor did Sandy Taylor or Christopher Nichols. Rather, they were exhibiting, in particularly dramatic form, a concern common to middle-aged sons who lose their fathers: the fear that they are next. According to the FatherLoss Survey, a son who is thirty-three to fifty-five when his father dies is more likely than a man in any other age group—including those over fifty-five—to experience a rising concern about his own mortality in the couple of years following his father's death.

"Previously, I thought of myself as quite a young man," a forty-two-year-old musician told me after his father had died at age seventy-one. "I'm still possibly young," the son added, "but maybe three-quarters used up." A forty-eight-year-old college professor commented, a few months after his father had died: "Your parents are your buffer, they're running guard for you." With both his father and mother now deceased, this man observed: "I'm the end of the line. The next one is me. It's full-force."

Among the sons I interviewed who'd lost fathers in middle age, this heightened sense of vulnerability was experienced in a variety of forms. Some, like the men described above, endured actual symptoms of illness. (We'll revisit their stories later in this chapter.) Others became emotionally erratic for a time, or sought dramatic changes in their lives. Indeed, the death of a father, while generally less debilitating to the middle-aged man than to children and young adults, continues to have the potential for disrupting, and transforming, a son's life.

Max Halberg was fifty-three when his eighty-four-year-old father suffered a fatal heart attack. The day before the death, Max, a San Francisco lawyer, had talked by phone with his dad, who lived in a retirement community outside Phoenix. The father was having chest pains. He was in the hospital for observation. Max told his dad he was willing to fly down and be with him. But the father, always the stoic, insisted that there was no imminent danger. Less than twenty-four hours later, Max's father died.

Before Max's mother's death thirteen years earlier, Max had spent weeks sitting by her bedside as she lost her battle with cancer. It had been a crucial time of sharing appreciation and regrets, of closing the relationship. Even as she slipped toward a coma, Max recalled, "I could talk with her and I'd see her smile. No matter how bad she got, I could always recognize her teeth. . . . She let me comfort her."

Max had never had such connection with his father: A refugee from Russian persecution in the early 1900s, the father refused to let down his guard with anyone. Even late in life, he never asked Max or his two other children for help. A tradesman during his working years, he was always suspicious of his son's professional job. After the death, Max recalled painful moments in childhood when his father would deride him. Once, after Max expressed fear of a neighborhood bully, the father replied scornfully: "What's the matter? You're not able to take care of it yourself? You're not a man?"

Indeed, Max questioned his own masculinity throughout his life. He often felt as if he were caught in a trap. On the one hand, Max saw his father as hypocritical and uncaring, and Max was determined not to follow that example. Yet he also saw in his father a confidence and assertiveness—a faith in his own manhood—that Max wished he too could possess.

For the most part, Max told me, he'd failed to find the middle ground. In his efforts to reject his father's domineering way, Max ended up erring on the side of passivity. He allowed his wife, whom he'd married when he was twenty-three, to control their family life. And when his dad rebuffed Max's initial attempts to talk about their father-son relationship, Max backed off. He could not match his father's ferocious will.

In the years leading up to the father's death, Max mostly tried to ignore his frustrations with his dad. The death brought them back to his awareness. In the weeks afterward, Max brooded and drank more heavily than usual. He seemed to have a harder edge to his personality too, not unlike that of his father. He felt a rising anger toward his wife and began having strong doubts about their marriage. "Was this what I really wanted for the rest of my life?" he started asking himself. He saw his wife, more than ever before, as domineering and insensitive.

Mixed in with the anger was fear. He recalled his despair the day after the death as he went room-by-room through his father's home: "It was the emptiness of the apartment that brought it all home. There was no longer a wrist that went in his wristwatch. There were suits with no one to wear them. There was a fresh meal in the refrigerator, but no one to eat it." More than his mother's death, his father's convinced him of his own mortality. Max told me: "Taking in his death, I had to take in that I have a finite life, and I only have one life." If his time was indeed limited, Max told himself, "I'm not going to go through the motions. I'm not going to live a false life."

Rather than resolving on its own, Max's crisis worsened during the first few months following the loss. And it reached a climax two years after the death when he decided he would leave his wife after more than thirty years of marriage. On the morning he made the decision, he telephoned his three grown children to let them know that he and their mother would be separating. "I wanted to start over," he recalled. "The thought was that . . . if I got rid of all my [connections], I would find out who I was."

Before the end of the day, however, Max changed his mind. Faced with his children's anguished reactions to his announcement, he decided (like 7 percent of midlife men dealing with this loss) to see a counselor. The decision proved fortuitous. Almost immediately, Max came to see that his anger at his wife was largely misplaced. Max discovered that his real anger was toward his father for being so judgmental and uncompassionate. With the father dead, Max's wife, a strong-willed woman herself, had become a convenient target.

Gradually, in two years of twice-weekly sessions, Max began to reenvision himself, not as the weak man his father might have perceived, but as a son trying to live up to unreasonable standards of manliness. The therapy did not so much eradicate Max's negative appraisal of himself as it did give sustenance to a more positive, compassionate part of him. "I'll have this tendency to think or feel in the old way, and then I'll stop for a moment and remember what's really going on," he explained. "Therapy," he said, "helped me understand the irrational basis of my thoughts or actions. And then I could stop acting in self-destructive ways."

When I talked with Max, more than a decade after the therapy ended, he was retired and still not totally settled with his father. He could easily conjure up resentment. But he'd also begun to allow himself some positive memories of his dad. Max actually felt some compassion for a man whose precarious childhood in Europe certainly contributed to his hard-edged, macho stance in later life. Meanwhile, Max said his marriage was intact, and largely satisfying, as he and his wife approached their fiftieth wedding anniversary.

Max had to go to the brink of divorce before accepting the death of his father. And when it comes to marriage problems, he was not alone among men who lost fathers in midlife. Eight percent of the men I surveyed who were married or in committed relationships at the time of the father's death said their marriages or relationships worsened in the two years after the loss. A 1984 University of California study of the impact of parental death found an even higher rate of trouble.

In Chapter 8, I'll discuss more extensively the potential problems that can hit a man's marriage or relationship after he loses his father. I'll also address there (and here) a surprising survey finding: that overall, sons who lose fathers are more likely to experience an *improvement* in their marriage or relationship than a worsening. It seems that the loss can bring couples together by reminding them of their love and need for each other.

Kevin O'Keefe's whole life became richer after the loss of his dad. Kevin was single, thirty-nine years old, and a high-school teacher living near San Diego when his father died suddenly at the age of sixty-four. Kevin had always considered his dad a "flunky" and hadn't expected to react strongly to the death. The father, raised by hard-drinking Irish immigrants in New York City, had drawn a disability check for most of his life after suffering severe burns in combat in World War II.

In Kevin's childhood, he told me, his father's daily routine usually included a stop at a local bar. When the father finally made it home, he'd often "sit in the dark in the living room drinking a few beers before stumbling off to bed." The older man never hit Kevin or his younger brother, Kevin recalled. "He was just not involved. . . . He was ineffectual."

There was little progress in the relationship in the two decades after Kevin left home. Kevin recalled: "I even said to him once: 'The only time you call is when Mom's in the hospital. You never even send a birthday card.' He responded, 'You're right,' as if he'd been chastised." But then nothing changed.

Despite this history, when Kevin's mother called from New Jersey with the news of the father's sudden fatal heart attack, Kevin promptly broke into tears. "It was a shot to the chest, like someone cut through me. It just hurt so much," he told me when we talked eight years later. While still on the phone with his mother, Kevin recalled the few times he'd hugged his father, "the touch, the way he smelled, the way he felt. I missed it instantly."

The death turned out, in Kevin's words, to be "a match to a powder keg." Kevin had been seeing a counselor since he'd quit drinking two years before the death, and until this point, had skirted the subject of his father. Now, he began to focus on it. Two themes quickly arose. First, Kevin discovered that his powerful reaction to the loss was not so much about the father's death, but about the father-son relationship they'd never had. The death itself, Kevin explained, "made me aware of not having the dad I needed. I had to go through that sense of loss. I had to realize: He's gone. It ain't gonna come true now. I'm not gonna get what I want."

Secondly, Kevin began to realize that there were aspects of his father that he had indeed appreciated, especially his father's sense of humor, and—at least compared to Kevin's mother—the older man's generosity and gentleness. Kevin even recalled some warm memories, such as the day in 1962 when his father took him and his brother to a sold-out doubleheader between the New York Mets and San Francisco Giants.

Unlike Max Halberg, whose marriage suffered after his father's death, Kevin said his relationship with Angie, a woman he'd been seeing for a couple of years, improved after the death. During his months-long "sorting-out process," as he called it, she listened, empathized, offered insights, and was generally "right there with me on the path."

At work, Kevin was frustrated that he had to hide his loss. "People used to wear a black armband for a year after a death," he told me. "I wanted to do that. I wanted a sign that said, 'I'm grieving.' And I wanted other people to say, 'Yeah, it's hard.' It's the exact opposite of what we do. The attitude is: Deal with it on your own."

Kevin did manage to befriend a coworker about twenty years his senior, and the relationship somehow helped Kevin. He explained: "I was like a sounding board for him. He'd tell stories from the old days. Somehow, just hearing him tell the old stories was reassuring. I've always been mystified why I got anything out of [the relationship]. He'd tell the same stories over and over again. But I didn't begrudge him. I just thought, if this is all he has to give, I'll take it."

About six months after the death, Kevin's sadness began to diminish and was replaced by an unexpected urge: He wanted to be a father. Until this point in his life, Kevin had had no particular interest in having children. When he and Angie, who was also nearing forty, had moved in together a year earlier, Kevin had in fact been leaning against it. Now, however, he changed his mind.

Looking back, Kevin said that actively grieving his father's death "cleared me to see that I wanted to be a dad." Up until that point, he'd felt little compassion for his father, and this had made him question whether he wanted to be one himself. In the months after the death, however, Kevin gradually came to believe that his father had done the best he could. Kevin reasoned that his father, after the experiences of growing up in an alcoholic family, and of being wounded in combat, had been thrust into a culture where men were discouraged from talking about their problems. To cope, Kevin figured, the old man had turned to alcohol.

This reconciliation with the memory of his father became for Kevin "a real acceleration, a trigger point." Kevin married Angie, and at age forty-two, three years after his father's death, he became a father for the first time. As a symbol of his forgiveness toward his own dad, Kevin chose a traditional Irish name for his son: Patrick.

It had also been his father's name.

But though Kevin wanted to keep his dad's memory alive, he was determined not to carry on the older man's legacy of noninvolvement with his own children. In our conversation, Kevin, a trim, blue-eyed man with thinning blond hair, recalled a time when his son was a few months old, cutting teeth, and going through an intense few days of crying. "I remember that I'd rock him for hours," Kevin said. "I had a big feeling at the time: I'm doing for him what never happened to me."

———————

Both Max Halberg and Kevin O'Keefe reacted strongly to the deaths of their fathers and that was true of most of the sons I interviewed who'd lost fathers in midlife. But there was also a considerable number of men who appeared to absorb the death with little turmoil. At first, I wondered if these men might be suppressing their emotions. But after hearing their stories, I reconsidered. It was possible, I came to believe, that a healthy detachment from a father is possible, and that when it exists, it naturally softens the impact of the death.

Sometimes, the detachment between father and son emerges out of disappointment. One man I spoke with, a professor who was forty-six at the time of his father's death, told me that he and his dad, a building contractor, were never on the same wavelength. The son moved away from his family to go to college and never returned. He eventually transferred most of his paternal connection to his wife's father, he told me. His father-in-law, unlike his father, took a keen interest in the son's career, marriage, and other aspects of his life. By the time his father died, this son said, the two men had grown apart. The son told me he didn't cry at the death or react strongly in any other way. When his father-in-law passed away, on the other hand, he said, "I could barely contain myself."

Another man, a teacher, said that his father (who in late adulthood was diagnosed as clinically depressed) had always seemed to the son distant or preoccupied. The son recalled: "It was like he'd bought a book about being a person. He'd try to do it on the surface, but there was a lack of connectedness."

In young adulthood, this son lived in a variety of cities, most of which were hundreds of miles from his childhood home. He got married, started his own family, and enjoyed watching his kids relate to their grandfather. But he found in his young adulthood that trying to deepen his own relationship with his dad was "like banging my head against a door." During his thirties and forties, he said, he focused on his wife, children, and friendships, and let his family of origin fall away.

By the time of the father's death, when the son was forty-nine, he viewed the older man mostly as "a safety net." The son's most memorable reaction to the death was "that I was an orphan." When I spoke with the son, a stocky, red-haired man, five years after the death, he said: "Sometimes, I'll be sad that my relationship with my father and mother wasn't more complete. I didn't feel there was much I could do about it. It's too bad they couldn't have enjoyed me more. It's too bad I couldn't have enjoyed them more. I have those regrets, rather than missing someone essential to my life."

Sons who were emotionally distant, or estranged, from their fathers were not the only ones who had less-than-dramatic reactions to their fathers' deaths. I met several men who said they loved their fathers deeply and felt cherished in return. And yet, these men also seemed to respond to the deaths rather mildly.

Richard Johnson is an example. Richard was born in rural Alabama in 1932, when his father was fifty-two years old. Richard was the tenth and youngest child in the family. In their earliest years together, Richard didn't see his dad much; the older man, whose parents had been slaves, worked long hours farming eighty acres of peanuts, cotton, and other crops. The son's main connection with his dad in those early years was harvesting vegetables together and selling them door to door in a nearby town.

When Richard was twelve, his father retired from farming and started working part-time as a carpenter. It was then that a real closeness began to develop between father and son. Richard told me: "When he'd be doing something like fixing steps, he'd call me to be the hand-me-the-hammer, bring-me-the-saw guy. At first I thought he just wanted me to hand him things. But then I saw he wanted to talk with me." During Richard's high-school years, he and his dad formed a close connection. "He listened to me. He respected me. We had real conversations."

Father and son maintained their close bond after Richard left home to join the military. While in the service, Richard sent a portion of his monthly salary to his parents, who were living on Social Security and a small pension. With the money, his father opened a convenience store near their home and named it the Richard Johnson Grocery, after his son.

Richard remembered another relationship highlight from this period, the early 1950s. In the Army, Richard had taken up cigarette smoking, a habit of which he knew his father would disapprove. During one of his visits home on military leave, Richard continued to smoke, but did it privately at first, out of sight of his dad. A couple of days into the visit, however, talking with his father on the front porch, Richard got up his courage, pulled out a cigarette from his pocket, and prepared to light up. He also braced himself for his father's reproach.

It didn't come. Instead, the father looked at Richard, looked at the pack of cigarettes, and said: "Could I have one of those?" Richard laughed recalling the incident: "We sat there puffing cigarettes together. It was sort of a crowning point. We were both men then."

The relationship continued in a positive vein for several more years. Then Richard's father, at eighty-two, suffered a terrible stroke. Richard, then thirty, was working in Philadelphia and rushed home to Alabama to see his dad. "It was pretty bad," Richard recalled. "He'd lost his speech. He couldn't walk. He was paralyzed on his right side." The father began physical therapy and was making good progress before falling one day and breaking his hip. The trauma of the fall apparently caused another stroke, and his father was in a wheelchair for good.

The next five years were tough on the whole family. Richard would visit every few months. His father usually would be resting in an easy chair in a wide windowless hallway that he'd chosen as his sitting spot because it was near the coal-burning heater that warmed the house in the winter. In the summer, he stayed in the hallway because it was also the coolest spot in the house.

When Richard visited, he would pull up a chair and sit beside his dad. His father wasn't in physical pain, Richard recalled, "but he seemed lonely. He'd always been much involved in the community." Perhaps most dispiriting to father and son, the older man did not regain his ability to speak after the second stroke. Conversation, which had been the currency of their connection since those days handling hammers and nails together, was no longer possible. Occasionally, his father would attempt to form words. Richard recalled: "You could see the pain on his face when he'd try. He'd try so hard. Tears would flow down his face. And he wasn't a cryin' man."

When the death finally came, Richard, then thirty-six years old, was more relieved than anything else. While he loved his dad, he told me, "I really had begun to feel bad about him sitting there year after year, and not being able to do anything. . . . There was that mixed feeling. Overall, I felt that it was best for him" to die.

Richard took a week off of work to "savor the joy of the relationship." He was gratified that the funeral attracted a large crowd. While he was at his childhood home, he dug up photos of his father, made copies of them, and framed them for his siblings. He also spoke with relatives and friends about his dad's life, and chronicled their stories.

He recalled: "I'm not a journal-type guy, but I did make notes about my experience. I took time just to think about the enormous obstacles he'd had to overcome: being born just fifteen years after [the abolition of] slavery; having parents who were enslaved; living in Alabama, with all the bigotry and hatred. But he kept the family together, raised ten kids, sent all at least through high school, several of them to college. It was a great achievement. . . . How often do we recognize and honor the accomplishments of our parents, especially if we have moved ahead of them?"

After the funeral, Richard said he was "not immobilized in a serious way." Returning to his own life, he was glad that his father was no longer suffering. And he used the memory of his dad to inspire himself in a job he was starting up at the time. "He used to say: 'You can do anything you want to do. Put your mind to it,' " Richard recalled thirty years after the death. "I believed that."

Richard told me his relatively mild reaction to the actual death was largely the result of having so much time to prepare for it. For six years, he'd watched his father's painful decline. He'd had a chance to care for his father. He'd had a chance to say good-bye. In a way, while Richard's mourning was never overt in that period, much of it seems to have occurred in the hours he spent sitting beside the paralyzed, speechless old man in the windowless hallway of his childhood home.

Richard's sorrow after the death also was eased, he told me, by the sense that he and his father—despite the older man's inability to talk toward the end—had left nothing unexpressed. Richard assured me that he and his dad had their differences: the father was a deacon in his Christian church, the son an atheist, for example. But well before the end, their love for each other was no longer in question.

Many sons are not so lucky. Even into middle age, they remain unsure of their father's love for them—and often of their own feelings for their fathers. As we saw earlier in this chapter, some of these sons decide that the relationship is hopeless or not worth a struggle; they let go and move on. Others, however, cannot, or choose not to, let the relationship lapse. And in the years before the father's death, they may take considerable risks in their attempts to reconcile with their fathers.

Clay Heinson was nine months old when he was adopted from a Catholic orphanage. He came of age in a small town in southern Michigan, living most of his childhood within a few blocks of grandparents, aunts, uncles, and cousins. His earliest memories of his father were warm ones: playing catch in the backyard, reading books together, singing silly songs. But the two became more distant during Clay's teen years. While his father, a metalworker, loved to hunt and fish, the son was more interested in piano, art, and acting. "He encouraged me" in sports, Clay recalled, "but I felt I was a disappointment to him."

Clay recalled that at age eighteen, he did join his father and some other male relatives for a hunting trip. He found that he enjoyed being in the woods with his dad, "waiting, whispering, noticing so many little things about the forest." Clay didn't shoot anything, but said he "really got a sense of [my father's] connection to the outdoors. Dad showed me how to track, and to recognize footprints." Clay also enjoyed the other men, who "were so much more gregarious and funny, and so much more intimate, in that cabin than they were with the wives and kids back home."

Despite this connection, Clay's relationship with his father did not progress much during the son's early adulthood. A major sticking point was Clay's fear of telling his father that he was gay. "I thought it would be the total end of the relationship," Clay explained to me. After graduating from a Southern university in 1975, Clay started a public relations career in the South before moving back to the North in his early thirties. He continued a perfunctory relationship with his parents during this period, visiting or hosting them once or twice a year.

Then one day, a friend suggested to him that he would never feel at peace with his parents if he continued to hide his sexual orientation from them. The next time he saw his mother and father, Clay sat with them in the living room of his home, making small talk as he tried to get up the nerve to come out. Finally, he blurted: "I'm gay." It was, he recalled, "like jumping off a forty-foot platform, knowing you're going to hit the water and go way down."

To his surprise, when Clay came up, it was his mother, not his father, who seemed most disturbed by the revelation. His dad's response: "It's not going to change anything in our family. We're still going to love you the same." Then he added: "Don't expect me to be happy about it!" Fifteen minutes later, Clay's father was ready to go out for dinner as planned.

Clay was both uplifted and saddened after the conversation. "It made me look back on all those years, and wonder why I'd let them go by." Clay's mother took a year to adjust to the news, but his father almost immediately began asking about Clay's love life. "So he's an architect?" the father said during one of these conversations. "If he's a millionaire, I suggest you pursue him." And after educating himself about the incidence of homosexuality, Clay's father actually calculated how many people in his small town must be gay. Coming out "totally changed our family," Clay told me. "We went from a family that shares only the good things to one that shares everything."

That became particularly important three years later when the father, at age seventy-six, was diagnosed with prostate cancer. Clay recalled a walk on a beach with his father and the gist of the conversation that ensued.

CLAY: How do you feel about the possibility of dying?

FATHER: How's a guy supposed to feel? There are certain things you can't change.

CLAY: Are you afraid?

FATHER: I have a great life. I love my life. If I can be here for a few more years, I would like that very much. But if it's my time, I'm ready. I have nothing to do or say that I haven't already done or said.

The father survived that bout with cancer but three years later started feeling intense back pain. The cancer had spread. A tumor was lodged on his spine. Clay was in his dad's hospital room when the doctor shared the bad news that the father would likely die within a few months. Clay told me that after the doctor left the room, he started to cry. "Then I climbed up on the bed. I laid next to [my father] to weep. He stroked my hair. I was forty years old, but I felt like I was a little kid again. He kept saying, 'It's going to be all right. Don't worry about me. Don't be upset. Take care of your mother.' "

When Clay got up from the bed, he recalled, it was as if "I'd said good-bye to my childhood." For the next two months, as his father's condition deteriorated, Clay began to step into the role of family patriarch, acting as "an usher, a master of ceremonies," calling on his father's friends and relatives to come to the bedside to say good-bye.

On the day of the death, Clay received a call at his mother's house at 5 A.M. His father's nurse told Clay that his dad probably would not make it through the day. Clay awakened his mother, telephoned his sister, and they met in the father's hospital room.

"Dawn was just breaking, it was a beautiful spring day," Clay recalled. "The hospital preacher came in, and we prayed together. Then each of us said it was okay [to die] to my dad. I told him I would try to take care of the family. . . . He had really raspy breathing before the prayer. After the prayer, the breath became really calm." Then it stopped. Clay recalled, "One moment there was breath, the next moment, the absence of breath. It was really calm. There was a completeness about it." After about a minute of silence, the family hugged, and then Clay went house-to-house in his neighborhood informing friends and family members.

While he cried at the funeral, and occasionally thereafter, Clay said the overarching feeling has been one of satisfaction about his relationship with his father. By coming out to his dad, caring for him, and taking the opportunity to say good-bye, Clay felt settled by the time of the death. "We had gotten to know each other as adults," Clay told me.

The loss also taught Clay "the futility of running away from death. I'm conscious of the completeness of my father's life. That's my own goal now. Things I thought were small are now large. Like helping a friend. Being there for someone who needs you. . . . My career seems small to me now. Nobody on their deathbed says, 'I'm glad I got that 15 percent raise.' Meaning does not ultimately reside there."

One of the last things Clay and his father did together was to plant a tulip garden in Clay's yard. The father had always been a gardener; the son had never been one. Yet after the death, Clay told me: "I suddenly had this constant yen to be in the garden. It was such a communion with him."

Before his mother died two years later, Clay unearthed many of the perennials from his father's garden and replanted them in his own. When I spoke with Clay six years after the death, he said he often put on his father's flannel shirt and denim work pants, gathered his father's garden tools, and settled into his own yard. His garden, once a nondescript, untended landscape, now is known in the neighborhood for its lavish displays of color.

———

Psychologist Roger Gould once said that midlife can "slam us in the face like a steel door." Up until his early thirties, a man tends to see the world as virtually limitless. And then, sometimes suddenly, sometimes gradually, loss moves from being a virtual stranger to a regular guest. A man's friends and colleagues start dying. His children move away. His sex drive slackens. His career opportunities dwindle. Add to this the death of a parent, and the future of the midlife man can seem depressing and frightening.

This fear was apparent in the three men I mentioned at the beginning of this chapter, the men who experienced intense anxiety or physical symptoms after their father's death. Whatever happened to those men?

Sandy Taylor, the man who believed he would follow his grandfather and father into death between Christmas and New Year's Day, told me that when January rolled around, his fear mostly disappeared. Several years later, when I spoke with him, he laughed about it. "I'd probably seen too many Rod Serling movies," he said. But he also understood why he had become so frightened by the two close family deaths. "It was like two layers of protection had been peeled off. They were my line of defense." After surviving beyond the end of the year, he said, "I felt like a hurdle had been crossed. It was time to start trying to put the pieces back together." When I last spoke with him, three years after the death, Sandy was no longer preoccupied with it; his new passion was his first child, a daughter.

Christopher Nichols, the softball player, remained unconscious for a few seconds after sliding into home plate. Then he was taken to the hospital and diagnosed with severe asthma. I spoke with him three years later. He told me that he had not played softball since that first asthma attack and had in fact been forced to stop all forms of vigorous activity. "I can't run a hundred yards," he reported. Did he think the onset of his breathing problem was related to his father's murder? Absolutely, he told me. He reminded me that his father had been suffocated, a plastic bag placed over his head. The asthma, Christopher told me, was giving him a small taste of the same experience.

Jerrold Hartman, the man who fell ill as he prepared to watch a video with his wife and son, had his heart and lungs throughly examined at the emergency room, and was found to be in fine shape. He'd had no subsequent physical scares when we last spoke. But he was clear that his attitude about life had been changed by his father's death. "I kid that I'm next up on the firing line. I joke about it. But I'm much more conscious of my mortality."

The stereotype of the midlife man is that when he starts feeling the heat of his mortality, he buys a sports car and drives away. And yet, most of the men I spoke with who were middle aged when their fathers died seemed willing to face the loss. They called upon their own extensive resources, both internal and communal, to help them absorb the death—and in many cases, to launch a period of self-discovery and growth. I found midlife men willing to ask themselves the hard questions: What do I want to carry on of my father? What do I want to change? What do I want my own legacy to be? It was in the process of addressing such questions that most were able to move through their fear of "I'm next," to a more inspiring, "*What's* next?"

John Quincy Adams

—∞—

On July 4, 1826, one of the great coincidences of American history occurred. In the early afternoon of the fiftieth birthday of the Declaration of Independence, its primary architect, Thomas Jefferson, eighty-three, died at Monticello, Virginia. Five hours later, John Adams, ninety-one, who had led the debate in the Continental Congress to approve the Declaration, took his last breath in the bedroom of his home near Boston.

The nearly simultaneous passings of the second and third presidents of the United States—on the golden anniversary of the country they'd helped found—confirmed for many Americans the existence of "a divine hand" in the nation's business. It also plunged the country into grief. And perhaps no citizen felt it more intensely than the man then serving as president, John Quincy Adams, fifty-eight, the eldest son of John Adams.

Born in 1767, John Quincy had not known his father well in early childhood; the elder Adams spent most of his son's early life away from home, organizing pre-Revolution resistance to British rule.

This father-son relationship began to change in 1779, when John Adams invited his then eleven-year-old son to travel with him to Europe; the elder Adams was being sent overseas to help hammer out a treaty to end the Revolutionary War. For most of the next seven years, father and son traveled and lived together, forging an affectionate and respectful bond.

The two men also worked together in the federal government in the early years of the United States; as president between 1797 and 1801, the elder Adams appointed his son minister to Berlin. John Adams retired to Massachusetts after his presidency, and for the next two-plus decades, the son stayed in Washington, serving the government in a variety of roles. As secretary of state under President James Monroe, he made perhaps his foremost contribution to the young republic: He was the principal crafter of the Monroe Doctrine, which warned Europe against future colonizing in the Western Hemisphere.

Adams's ascension to the presidency in 1824 seemed almost preordained. But his administration collapsed quickly when he alienated congressional leaders early in his term. It was with some relief, then, that he left Washington for a trip to Massachusetts in July 1826 upon learning that his father was ill. John Adams died while his son was traveling home by stagecoach.

John Quincy stayed for three months in Massachusetts after the death, doing the nation's business in between writing remembrances of his relationship with his father. According to his journal, the news of his father's death at first "had no sudden and violent effect on my feelings." But entering his father's empty bedroom "was inexpressibly painful. . . . My father and my mother have departed. The charm which has always made this house to me an abode of enchantment is dissolved."

John Quincy had been willed much of his father's land and went into debt buying the rest from relatives. He decided that he would retire to Massachusetts after his presidency and compile his father's biography. As he wrote in his journal: "It is time for me to begin to set my house in order, to prepare for the church-yard myself."

But something happened on his way to the churchyard. Noticing the way his father had been lauded at his death, John Quincy prayed in his journal that the same would happen to him, that he would "die as my father has died . . . , sped to the regions of futurity with the blessings of my fellow-men." To accomplish this, he pledged "to live the remnant of my days in a manner worthy of him from whom I came."

It was a bold pledge. And it did nothing to save his presidency. Andrew Jackson ousted him from the White House easily in 1828. But after returning to Massachusetts, John Quincy made a decision that would change his legacy: He would run for a seat in the U.S. House of Representatives. His wife discouraged him, as did many politicians who thought it unseemly for a former president to return to public office.

Nonetheless, he was elected overwhelmingly, and at age sixty-three, Adams began his political career anew. For most of the next seventeen years, he worked strenuously, and with great political skill, to curtail the spread of slavery in the expanding United States. He was a passionate debater in the House on the right of citizens to petition the government against slavery. And in 1841, he addressed the U.S. Supreme Court in the *Amistad* case, arguing for the freedom of the fifty-three Africans who had revolted on the high seas and killed a ship's captain who was transporting them into slavery.

In 1848, at the age of eighty, Adams was still pushing the antislavery cause when he collapsed on the floor of the House of

Representatives after suffering a stroke. He died two days later. As he had prayed, the career he forged after his father's death enhanced his legacy. History now remembers him not primarily as a failed president, but as one of the most effective antislavery campaigners in the decades before the Civil War.

Pop's misery and Mom's suffering at life's end were, I now realize,
their final gifts to me. Their unhappiness made them want to die, and
painful though it was, it made me wish them on.
—JOURNALIST MAX FRANKEL

Chapter 4

─────

CLOSING THE CIRCLE

─────

Ages 56 and Up

THE MINISTER completed his account of the old man's life, delivered a closing prayer, and stepped back from the pulpit in the narrow, wood-paneled chapel. It was the signal for Dan Hammell, along with his wife, sister, children, and grandchildren, to rise together in the front-row pew. The family would file out first among the one hundred or so mourners, heading for a side room through an open door not far from where the coffin stood.

It had been three days since the death of Dan's father, at age eighty-five, following a series of strokes that, over two years, clouded his mind and ravaged his body. In those three days, Dan, who was sixty years old, had felt no strong emotions. Now, however, as he rose from his seat, a lump formed in his throat. He thought he was about to cry.

Dan swallowed the lump and followed his family on the slow-moving trek past the open casket, toward the side room. When Dan reached the coffin, he stopped and took in the peaceful face of the man in the beige sweater. He extended his hand and touched his father's arm. Now, he was sure he was about to weep.

And then it happened. Without knowing why, Dan lifted his gaze from his father's body. Through the doorway leading into the side room, he glimpsed his two-year-old granddaughter in her mother's arms. The girl watched him intently, seemingly curious what he would do next. For a long moment, Dan maintained his focus on her face. And then his sadness disappeared.

Dan did not look again in the casket. Instead, he stepped through the open door to the side room. Away from his father's body, and the crowd, he reached his hands toward his granddaughter. Her outstretched arms reached back to him. And for the next few minutes, he carried her against his hip, feeling a sense of happiness. Two years later, when I spoke with Dan in his backyard, he tried to explain what happened: "It's unfair to presume. . . . If I had to interpret it, I'd say that when I saw [my granddaughter], I had the sense that one life is gone, another is just starting, and that's just the way things are."

Among older sons, acceptance of the loss of their father appears to be the norm. My survey showed that sons who were over age fifty-five when their fathers died were least likely of any age group to cry over the death, to use drugs or alcohol afterward, to seek professional help, or to attribute ongoing problems in their own lives to the impact of the loss. Only 17 percent of older sons in the survey said the death of their fathers affected them more than any previous death—compared to nearly 80 percent among sons younger than thirty-three, and 58 percent among those thirty-three to fifty-five.

Not that older sons were unfeeling. Most of those I spoke with expressed genuine sorrow at their loss. And the great majority—

more than 85 percent—said they sought, or accepted, support from wives, partners, friends, or relatives in the aftermath.

But in the majority of cases, their pain was balanced by a recognition that the father had lived a long-enough life. Compared to younger sons, few in the over–fifty-five range said they felt cheated by the death or more concerned about their own mortality. One man, who was sixty-three when his father died of cancer, spoke for many older sons when he said: "I didn't consider my father's death a disaster. I really didn't. There was of course a sadness—sadness but not grief."

The story of Dan Hammell, the man who held his granddaughter at the funeral, illustrates one son's path to acceptance. In Dan's childhood, in a small Delaware town in the 1930s and 1940s, he and his dad rarely had much to say to each other. The older man, a toolmaker, was "quiet, unemotional, and not demonstrative." Most of Dan's interactions with his dad involved the father fixing things around the house while the son looked on. "Basically, he tolerated me," Dan remembered.

In his teens, Dan occasionally accompanied his father on fishing trips. They'd spend the days, mostly in silence, on a boat on a Vermont lake, and the evenings, quietly, in a cabin on the lake. Even in adulthood, after Dan got married, started a family, and began his engineering career, things between him and his father didn't change much. Through Dan's young and middle adulthood, he remembered, his mother compared their father-son moments to Quaker meetings. Dan recalled: "We'd talk a little about work. We'd talk a little about the house. Then we'd watch TV."

Finally, as Dan moved into his fifties, and his father into his seventies, the relationship began to change. Dan's mother, who'd had osteoporosis for two decades, was taking a turn for the worse. For the first time, Dan recalled, his father told him about dreams he'd once harbored to buy a boat and travel the world. The plans had to be scuttled because of the mother's illness. Yet Dan's father didn't seem to be complaining. Instead of traveling, he had developed other interests, including collecting antique tools, recaning chairs, and refinishing furniture.

When Dan's mother died at age eighty-one, Dan, who was then fifty-seven, saw his father's vulnerability for the first time. After the funeral, Dan's father confided in him. "I thought I was ready," the father told the son, "but I'm not."

Dan, it turned out, wasn't ready either. At the time, it had been thirty years since he'd experienced the death of a close relative. As his mother moved inexorably toward her end, Dan became exceedingly fearful and continued to resist the inevitable. "I had trouble letting her go," he said of his mother. "It was hard to imagine that I'd never see her again."

After the death, Dan said, he coped in part by transferring some of his "motherly attachment" to his mother-in-law. But then she died too. Dan said he cried openly at her funeral.

Though he was thrown off balance by the losses, Dan learned from them too. Upon reflection, he realized that his inclination to resist death, to fight against it, had probably added to his pain. Perhaps it would have been better, he thought, to have simply focused on making his mother and mother-in-law more comfortable in their dying days. Neither woman, he recognized in retrospect, had seemed afraid of death. His mother, in pain for so long, actually appeared to welcome it.

These realizations helped guide Dan when his father got sick soon after. Dan decided that his goal this time around would be not to save his father, but to deepen their relationship. Every other weekend during the last year of his father's life, Dan drove the two hundred miles round-trip from eastern Pennsylvania to his father's home in Delaware. There, Dan spent a couple of days helping his father with household responsibilities and taking him on long car drives. With Dan behind the wheel and his dad in the passenger seat, the two men visited family grave sites and other significant places from their pasts.

Between stops, the father—the same man who'd been so quiet for so many decades—rarely stopped talking. He recounted stories about his parents, aunts, uncles, cousins. He recalled his early man-ufacturing jobs, his years as a father to small children, his relationship with his wife. Dan said of those trips, "You could tell he was en-joying it, but it was melancholy too. It was as if he was in a dream state."

These reminiscences went on, visit after visit, until the father's deteriorating health forced him into a nursing home, where he died on Christmas Eve of his eighty-sixth year. When I talked with Dan, two years after the death, he described the loss as "sad, but not bad." After the funeral week, he told me, he'd sorted through his father's tool shed, and taken home many of the antique tools his father had collected. Later, Dan said, he used them to build an arbor in his own backyard.

I asked Dan what had helped him most in coping with his father's death. He said it was "all the contact" in the final months. "I was able to watch Dad get ready to die and even to help him some. He reviewed his life over and over again with me. He was at peace with himself. He was proud. I think he felt he had achieved his important goals and was satisfied. And if he was satisfied, I thought I could be too."

Dan continued: "Intellectually, I knew I couldn't stop the pro-cess" of the illness. "And I knew I'd get through it. I'd been through it before." His sadness over his father's death, meanwhile, was stained neither by resentments over long-ago slights, nor by regrets about what might have been. During sixty years with his dad, Dan had been able to work through, or simply let go of, these concerns.

In this way at least, Dan was typical of older sons. According to my survey, sons who were over fifty-five when their fathers died were about half as likely as younger sons to harbor ongoing regrets after the death. In more than nine out of ten cases, older sons reported that they'd resolved the father-son relationship before the death occurred. And in no cases in our survey did a son who was over fifty-five at the death attribute ongoing problems in his life to the impact of the loss.

This doesn't mean that older sons forgot their fathers. In my conversations with older sons, in fact, I found them particularly attuned to, and creative about, maintaining connection with the memories of their dads. More so than most younger sons, it seemed, older sons found that keeping the spirits of their fathers alive could bring them far more comfort than pain.

Alberto Sanchez hardly knew his dad in the first few years of his life. When Alberto was a toddler in Detroit in the early 1930s, his parents embarked on a bitter divorce, and his mother took Alberto to New York City, not telling his father where they had gone. The father, an autoworker in the early days of Ford Motor Co., managed to track Alberto down when the boy was fifteen and bring him back to Michigan. Alberto told me his father's loving concern for him in the three years that followed helped steer him away from trouble with the law.

Alberto was a slim, wavy-haired eighteen-year-old when he joined the Marines in 1945. He married three years later, and over the next four decades, worked mostly in civil service for the Indiana National Guard. Through it all, he maintained regular contact with his dad. Even in the early days, when he was stationed far from

Michigan, Alberto made it a point to visit his father whenever he could get away. Alberto told me he looked forward to the storytelling and laughter that often occurred when he and his dad spent time together.

It was around Alberto's sixtieth birthday, after his retirement, that he realized rather suddenly that his relationship with his dad was nearing its end. The older man was in his late eighties, and though the father seemed healthy, Alberto felt an urgency "to get everything I could from him before he passed." Alberto started visiting his dad more regularly, driving about 650 miles round-trip. Alberto usually brought along a video camera, and at some point during the visit, he'd attach the camera to a tripod, set it running, and then launch into an on-camera conversation with his dad about the old man's life.

As it turned out, Alberto would have six years to review his father's life with him. When death finally took his dad, at age ninety-three, Alberto was sad but not distressed. "Yes, I had a loss, but not a painful loss. I was all right with it," Alberto told me. "Dad lived a good life. . . . We knew eventually that this was gonna happen, and we moved on."

But moving on from his father's death did not mean leaving the old man completely behind.

A couple of years after the death, Alberto decided to write a history of his family. And for the next four years, his father was a regular presence in Alberto's life. Working out of a small, crowded home office—outfitted with a high-powered computer, large-screen monitor, color printer, phone, fax, scanner, radio, TV, and VCR— Alberto reviewed the videotapes he'd made of his father and tracked down scores of family members, in the United States and Mexico. The result was a hardback, 333-page history book with more than two hundred family photos, some of which dated back to the nineteenth century.

When I talked with Alberto six years after his father's death, he had just finished the book. He was stocky now, with a wispy gray beard. A lung condition required him to remain hooked to an oxygen tank, but he remained energetic and laughed easily. On one shelf to the right of his computer, two books stood side-by-side, alone: a brown leather copy of the Bible, and *Meditations for Men Who Do Too Much*.

Even with the genealogy project completed, Alberto told me he would never fully let go of his dad. He shared with me a ritual he'd conducted daily since his father's death.

Each morning, after he rolled out of bed, Alberto went to one of the venetian blinds in his room, twisting it open to let in the light. Then he approached a wall of family photos that included one of his beaming dad at about age ninety. "Good morning, Dad," Alberto always said to start the day. And then he usually added some other appeals. "Watch over me today," he might say. "Walk with me. Guide me. Help me." After he finished talking to his dad, Alberto would flip on his radio, then open the other venetian blind in the room, and begin his normal day.

If he happened by the photo later in the morning or afternoon, Alberto might "stop and chat a little," he told me. Or it might be nightfall before he repeated the ritual of the morning, in reverse. After readying himself for bed, Alberto went to the venetian blind he'd opened last that morning, and closed it. Then he'd look into his father's face again. "Good night, Dad," he'd say. He might share a few highlights of the day. Then he'd turn off the radio, close the other blind, and crawl into bed.

"It's no big, long thing—maybe fifteen or twenty seconds. But it makes me feel good," Alberto said. And then he added: "An interesting thing is that I recently gave my son a picture of my dad. I told him [about the ritual]. I told him, 'This is what I do every day.' And I gave him the picture. Well, I went to his house Saturday to eat over there, and I looked into his bedroom, and by golly, there's the picture of Dad."

Coming away from my conversations with Dan Hammell, Alberto Sanchez, and other older men, I almost always found my spirits lifted. These men offered me hope that as I age and move closer to my own death, I will become less afraid, more accepting. To these men, most of whom were in the final season of their lives, it seemed mortality was less a catastrophe-to-come than motivation to enrich what time they had.

I did meet up with some older sons who'd been quite shaken by the loss of their fathers. One social worker, who was fifty-eight when his dad died at age eighty-five, told me he went through a few months of wrenching fears about his mortality. Like 8 percent of older men in my survey, he also started questioning his religious beliefs. A lifelong Christian, he acknowledged for the first time that he was unsure whether there really was a heaven and hell. "Not knowing what's going to happen [after death], I'm a little scared," this man told me. "But there's nothing to do about it. I just have to take [death] as a way of life."

Another man, a retired car dealer who was sixty-six when his father died at age eighty-nine, said that he started feeling guilty a few weeks later. His dad, a tobacco farmer, had lived 150 miles away from the son for most of their lives, but the son had rarely visited. "I could have found time," the son told me thirteen years after the loss. "I just didn't. I regret it. It took his death to teach me." While older sons were least likely of any age group to be regretful after the loss, one in four still reported having regrets.

Rather than simply suffer the regrets, however, this son took action that served to ease them. After the father's death, he began making the three-hundred-mile round-trip drive to his hometown that he had failed to make during his dad's lifetime. When I spoke with this man, he said that twice a year for the previous decade—once around Independence Day and a second time around Christmas—he climbed into his Ford van and made "the big loop" to his dad's hometown.

The loop usually took him about eight hours, and he did it in a single day. After navigating the twisting roads of West Virginia in the morning, he usually stopped first at his father's grave, tidying up the site and saying a prayer. Then he'd drop in at the homes of old friends. Later, he'd drive past the white, two-story farmhouse his dad had built in the 1940s and the old tobacco warehouse where the older man had sold his crop at auction. Sometimes, before dark, the son said, he'd stop by one of the fields his dad used to farm, where he might "actually see" the image of his father in the field, a lone, muscular figure walking behind a wooden plough and a single horse. "It brings back good memories," the son said in explaining the bi-annual trips. "I get an internally good feeling."

If the death of a father tends not to disrupt the lives of older sons, it still occasionally has the effect of stimulating meaningful changes. More than 40 percent of older sons in our survey said they experienced notable shifts in their relationships with siblings, children, mothers, and spouses, as well as at work or in their religious convictions.

Ethan Harris, a college philosophy professor from Southern California, was sixty-three years old when his father died, at age ninety-one after a five-year battle with Alzheimer's disease. Father and son had struggled in their early relationship—Ethan remembered his dad as a man with "almost a dog trainer's view" of discipline—but had reconciled, gradually, during Ethan's middle age.

When I spoke with Ethan, a tall, slender, white-haired man, it had been nearly three years since his father's death. He said he'd had no major problems related to it, but he did mention that there had been a couple of meaningful changes in his life that he connected to the loss.

The first change had actually begun the year before his father's death and centered on Ethan's religious practice. In childhood, Ethan had spent Sunday mornings at a Christian church that emphasized an embracing, comforting God—a God who knew and loved the heart of each person. His mother, who died when Ethan was fifty-eight, had embraced this God and even seemed to embody it, Ethan said, by being unconditionally loving herself. In his teens, however, Ethan did not feel connected with this God. He eventually left the church, and remained outside any religious community into his mid-life years.

In his forties, Ethan joined an interdenominational congregation, mostly to provide a community for himself and his teenaged son. Leaders in this church did not require members to believe in God—rather, they encouraged spiritual exploration—and Ethan was inspired to examine religious and ethical issues outside of a traditional Christian context.

Ethan was satisfied with this exploration until his father's last months of life. Then one Sunday, listening to a sermon about Martin Luther King, Jr., Ethan was moved to tears. What brought them on was the explanation of King's theology, which—not unlike that of Ethan's childhood—stressed a belief in a God who takes care of "his children."

For the first time since he was a boy, Ethan longed to know this God. In the year after hearing the sermon—during and after his dad's final days—Ethan awoke early on most mornings to sit quietly alone, meditate, and reach out for contact with "a God who will put his arm around my shoulder and say: '[Ethan], it's all right.' " The experience was rich. Praying in this way, he became more aware of the gifts in his life, he told me. But he did not make contact with the God he sought.

Eventually, he stopped the daily meditations, but not his spiritual explorations. Two years after his father's death, he presented a talk at his church in which he called on church leaders to "convene a commission to investigate the personal god—the one who listens to you, who responds to you, who loves you, who comforts you—and find out why he, she, or it is so aloof."

When I spoke with Ethan, a year after that sermon, he said he saw "an overlap" between his spiritual longing and the deaths of his father and mother. While neither death overwhelmed him, he told me, together they represented "a real loss of an era in my life." It was an era in which he had access to an unconditionally accepting mother and a powerfully protective dad. Who could replace those two icons in his life?

No one, perhaps, but God.

The other change that followed the father's death involved Ethan's relationship with his own son. Before Ethan's father had died, Ethan often wished he and his father could talk more openly about their life struggles. However, when Ethan brought up a problem or apprehension, his father usually started trying "to fix me," Ethan recalled. He'd slip into an "it'll-be-okay, problem-solving format." What Ethan really wanted was to hear about the kinds of issues with which his father struggled. Since his dad didn't offer that, Ethan eventually stopped bringing up his own concerns.

After the death, however, Ethan began to notice that when relating to his own thirty-year-old son, Carl, Ethan often acted much like his father had: unflappable. Ethan said of his relationship with his son: "In general, though we'd spent time a lot of time together and shared a lot, I had a continuing need to be kind of a perfect parent." Ethan recalled how unattractive this had been in his own father and decided that he no longer wanted to relate to his own son in this way.

Carl had already expressed an interest in hearing more about his own teen years, so Ethan took his opportunity. One day, he sat down and told Carl about specific mistakes he thought he'd made in raising Carl. One example, Ethan said, was that at times, in his quest for female companionship after his divorce from Carl's mother, "I would take care of my own needs first. I wasn't always totally focused on him, and doing whatever's best for him."

Ethan thought his son might get angry when he heard these confessions. Instead, Ethan recalled, "He was so thankful. He said, 'That's what I've been missing, the human-being quality.' " Tears came to Ethan as he recounted this moment. "All during [my son's] life, I've purposely tried to be open. But maybe with Dad's death, we reached a new level."

A year after the conversation with his son, Ethan said their relationship had continued to deepen. "I am more relaxed and revealing," Ethan told me, adding, "It's maybe another step toward being a couple of humans relating to each other, rather than somebody in the role of son and somebody in the role of father."

Thomas Lynch, a funeral director, poet, and author of *The Undertaking*, a book of essays on dying and death, told me that in his experience working with older men, he'd noticed a particular strength: "They've learned to let go." Throughout most of our lives, Lynch believes, men tend to focus on *performance* at the expense of *meaning*. But as men move into their fifties and sixties, Lynch said, "Meaning begins to win out. And when it does, [men] begin to turn things over. The list of what's out there that God takes care of gets longer. The list of what they have control over gets shorter. . . . They affirm their right to simply be."

Lynch's observations seem to echo those of the psychoanalyst

Carl Jung, who in the 1940s noticed that as men and women pass through middle age, they seem to trade dominant characteristics. Women become more aggressive and competitive, while men become more nurturing and empathetic. A quarter-century later, psychologist David Gutmann confirmed Jung's observations in a major study of late-adult development, noting that men become "more pacific" in later life.

How does this shift affect a man's handling of his father's death? Lynch, who was in his late forties when we spoke, said older men are less "reactionary" in their grief than younger men. "At sixty," he said, "the best you can do is have a good cry, have a good laugh, and say thanks."

Part 2

———————

REBOUNDING

FROM FATHERLOSS

Mahatma Gandhi

—∞—

How a son interacts with his father in the period leading up to the father's death can forever affect the son. Mahatma Gandhi, the leader of India's independence movement, never forgave himself for his actions on the night of his father's death. Even forty years and a lifetime of political struggle after his father's final breath, Gandhi would insist that his greatest sorrow was what he considered to be his abandonment of his father in the older man's hour of need.

Gandhi, known as Mohandas in his childhood, grew up in a village in west India during the 1870s and 1880s. He was the fourth child of his father's fourth marriage, and he viewed the older man as wise and moral, though sometimes aloof.

The incident that most bonded father and son occurred about a year before the older man's death. Mohandas was fifteen at the time and was struggling with a heavy guilt after stealing money from his brother to pay off a debt. In an attempt to clear his conscience, Mohandas decided to confess his misdeed to his father, who was bedridden, suffering from an infected wound he had received in a stagecoach accident.

As the son recalled in his autobiography, he wrote out his confession on a piece of paper, handed it to his father in bed, and waited to be beaten or rebuked. Instead, the older man sat up, read the confession, "and pearl-drops trickled down his cheeks, wetting the paper. For a moment he closed his eyes in thought and then tore up the note. . . . Those pearl-drops of love cleansed my heart, and washed my sin away."

If the confession was the highlight of Mohandas's relationship with his father, the low point came a few months later. The father, who was approaching sixty years of age, had not been able to shake his infection, despite a procession of priests, doctors, and other would-be healers. Near the end of 1885, the father's brother was called in from a neighboring village to help Mohandas and his mother nurse the failing man.

For months, the son had spent hours each day by his father's bedside. He'd mixed his father's medicines, dressed his wound, and massaged him each night. Mohandas, who by tradition had been married off at age thirteen—and whose teenaged wife was then pregnant—would later admit that "whilst my hands were busy massaging my father's legs, my mind was hovering about [my wife's] bed-room."

One night, as Mohandas was tending to his father, the father's brother offered to take over. Mohandas gladly accepted the respite and returned to his room, where he awakened his wife for sex. In the midst of their intimacy, a servant knocked on the door. "Get up. Father is very ill!" the servant shouted. Mohandas composed himself quickly. But by the time he reached his father's bedroom, the older man was dead.

The boy's remorse was immediate. For having missed his father's dying moments, he later wrote, "I felt deeply ashamed and miserable." What's worse, when his wife gave birth to their first child a few weeks later, the infant lived just four days. "Nothing else could be expected," Gandhi wrote, blaming himself for the child's death.

To the end of his life, Gandhi referred to the loss of his father and son as "my double shame . . . , a blot I have never been able to efface or forget. Although my devotion to my parents knew no bounds and I would have given up anything for it . . . , it was weighed and found unpardonably wanting because my mind was at the same moment in the grip of lust."

It is perhaps noteworthy that two decades later, in his mid-thirties, Gandhi gave up sex. He remained celibate for the last four decades of his life.

It was only at that moment that I realized how much I really loved
and needed him, and I had never told him. Just before he died,
I said, "I love you, Father." He heard me, because he looked up
at me and smiled. Then he died.
—HUMPHREY BOGART

Chapter 5

PREPARING FOR FATHERLOSS

E VEN IF A FATHER has been on a long, gradual decline, the
news of his actual death—so decisive, so irrevocable—tends
to hit a son hard. It can take months, or years, for him to
fully absorb the blow. But even if a son can't feel the full impact of
his father's death in advance, there are ways that he can prepare for
the day when the death occurs.

For many of the sons I spoke with, the most valuable preparation
for a father-death was one over which they had no control: previous
experience with loss. Sons, especially middle-aged and older ones
who had been through major deaths prior to the loss of their fathers,
tended to know what to expect, from the situation and themselves.
The mystery of death had been partially unveiled. Perhaps most importantly, these sons seemed to know their own limitations. As a
forty-five-year-old engineer told me: "When my mother was dying,
I kept trying to fix the situation, to keep her alive. By the time my
father got sick, I knew . . . to let go."

For younger sons, particularly those under the age of forty, a father's death often is their first major loss. They're negotiating new terrain. It turns out, though, that even among these sons, preparation is possible.

For Gary Isikoff, a union official from Chicago, preparation involved getting cozy with death. At age thirty-seven, while his father was still healthy, Gary became a Hospice volunteer. When I talked with him a decade later, Gary couldn't recall exactly what inspired him to enlist in Hospice. But he remembered well his six months of duty, keeping company with a half-dozen people in the last days and hours of their lives. Mostly, he said, he sat at their bedsides, making small talk with them, holding their hands, applying cool cloths to their foreheads.

Gary described his Hospice experience as "transformative." He explained: "Death is something we tend to avoid . . . until it's thrust upon us. These people were dying. I knew they were dying. They knew they were dying. And it's something we'll all experience. The whole context was profound. . . . Doing something like this—a familiarity comes. I got accustomed to death."

This acquaintanceship with death, Gary said, made it easier for him to cope with his father's kidney failure five years later. As his eighty-year-old dad lay dying in the hospital, Gary remembered the Hospice concept of "a good death," with family present and the dying person made as comfortable as possible.

In his father's final days, Gary sat by his bedside for hours at a time, massaging his feet and swabbing his lips to keep them from cracking. "That was hard," Gary told me five years after the death. "But I wouldn't have traded it for anything. Being able to see him out of this life, being part of that process. . . . He took care of me, I'm taking care of him. There was that mutual, 'coming-full-circle' aspect of it."

In the weeks before the death, Gary also prepared for it by reading the *Tibetan Book of Living and Dying*, which, he said, taught him a Buddhist perspective on death. He had received the book as a gift two years earlier, he recalled, "but I never cracked it. Now I grabbed it." As a teenager, Gary had doubted the life-after-death teachings of his family's Christian religion, but had never explored alternatives. Reading how Buddhists viewed death as a "transition" made the loss of his father seem less tragic, he said. "I found it made a lot of sense. It felt right. If you see [death] as a natural thing, it takes a lot of the sting out of it."

Gary was helped by Buddhist readings; other men can benefit from spiritual texts in their own faiths. Christian and Jewish men tend to focus on the Psalms, and on biblical passages related to eternal salvation. Muslims read the Koran and the Hadith (the sayings of the Prophet Muhammad), both of which profess belief in the afterlife. Hindus have the Sutras (which describe rituals around death), as well as the death-related inspirational writings of Rabindranath Tagore and Gandhi. Other men said they found comfort in the poetry of Rainer Maria Rilke, Rumi, Emily Dickinson, and Walt Whitman, and the prose of Elisabeth Kübler-Ross, Stephen Levine, and Earl Grollman. Besides demystifying death, readings can provide a sense of community for many sons by helping them feel that they have company on a journey they've not made before.

Sons told me they also prepared for their loss by having direct conversations with their dads about the older man's death. Thirty-two percent of those in my survey said they talked with their fathers about the death before it occurred, and 83 percent of those sons said the talks helped them later in coping with the loss. These talks most often took place after the father had become ill. Occasionally, however, a father or son would bring up the prospect of death even when the older man was still healthy.

Luis Ramirez, a social worker who was fifty-nine when his father died, makes a strong case for such father-son conversations. When his mother-in-law died suddenly in the 1960s, she left behind a distraught family—and no will. The result was a nasty fight among her children, Luis told me, mostly over the family home. In the end, the siblings could not agree on what to do, and the home was repossessed by the bank. When I spoke with Luis more than thirty years later, he said that in his wife's family, "negative feelings persist even today."

Luis vowed to avoid a replay when it came time for *his* parents to go. It took him several years to get up the nerve to talk with his father, he said. But finally, Luis approached his dad by saying he wanted to carry out the older man's wishes after his death; to do that, Luis would need to know what those wishes were. To Luis's relief, his father was gracious and inviting. As the father's health deteriorated over the last couple of years of his life, the two men had several conversations focusing on three basic questions:

- At what point did the father want to end medical treatment?
- What did he want done with his possessions?
- How did he envision his funeral?

On the last point, Luis recalled saying to his dad: "We're a large family. When you die, what do you want? Because let me tell you, all six of us [children] are going to be fighting one against the other: 'Dad would like this, not that.' "

Luis's father, a retired sharecropper who had never learned to read or write, dictated to Luis what he wanted for his funeral service, as well as his wishes about his medical care and personal items. Luis then turned his notes into legal documents and, with a notary public present, asked his father to initial them. Finally, a few weeks before the death, Luis mailed copies to his mother, brothers, and sisters. "They were not all happy with what Papa wanted," Luis recalled of his siblings, "but they were all accepting."

When the death finally came, there were no significant family disagreements, Luis said. Meanwhile, Luis found it particularly affecting to carry out his father's funeral wishes; the older man had planned the event down to the price of the casket and the order of the hymns.

Luis, in the course of those conversations with his father, also came to appreciate the uniqueness of the older man's life story. And he decided to try to preserve a piece of it. His acts of preservation turned out to be another way of preparing himself for his father's death.

Luis's father had descended from Mexicans who had lived for generations in what later became the State of Texas. Early in the twentieth century, Luis's father had worked the cotton fields, cornfields, and other fields in the region. He'd also traveled throughout the United States as a migrant worker in the 1930s and 1940s. "This was my roots, and I didn't want [them] to disappear," Luis told me. So in their last visits together, the son brought along a tape recorder, and he and his father conversed, in Spanish, about the older man's life adventures.

When I spoke with Luis, three years after his father's death, the tape was still making the rounds of his siblings. Luis said that knowing that his father's life, and voice, were still accessible gave him "a sense of assurance [and] a connection to my father and my past."

Videotape was another powerful tool for remembrance and preparation. One son told me he asked his father, a few months before the older man died, to lead a tour of the Ohio farm on which he'd grown up and lived his entire life. The son videotaped the tour. Another son, who videotaped his dad telling stories of his life, reported "something special" about watching the tapes after the death. "You see him in the flesh. You see how he moved, the little mannerisms."

One of the other benefits of talking intimately with a father is the opportunity for a son to see that his father can accept his own mortality. Luis Ramirez, the sharecropper's son from Texas, discovered in the process of audiotaping his father that the older man was not afraid of, nor resistant to, dying. This helped Luis be more accepting as well. Luis told me: "My dad . . . was a devout Christian. He had no negative thoughts about dying. It was not a dastardly step. He'd say, 'Not to worry.' "

Another son, a mechanic who was thirty-six when his dad died, also benefited by hearing firsthand how his father felt about death. The older man had suffered for years with emphysema. In his final months, the father related to his son a premonition he'd had in which, after dying, he would go through a "doorway" into eternal love and acceptance.

The son said of his father: "When he died, I was sad, yet I felt a sense of peace knowing that he wanted us to let him go into that doorway. . . . He looked forward to [death], not in a fatalistic, suicidal way, but as more of an adventure into the great beyond. . . . His final words to me were, 'I love you son, but I have to sleep now.' I said good-bye, knowing that I had to let him go."

Not all sons who try to talk about death with their fathers succeed; some fathers simply refuse to engage. One son I spoke with, a middle-aged physician, said he brought up the subject of death with his terminally ill father on several occasions. The older man changed the subject each time. "I tried to get him to see the forest for the trees. But there was a vociferous denial that this was [happening]. He was immortal," the son told me about a year after the death. "If he could have written his epitaph, it would have said, 'I don't deserve this.' "

For sons like these, action can replace words as a way of preparing for the death. And when the action involves caring for the father in his terminal stage, it is often just as beneficial for the son as a conversation. Among sons I surveyed whose fathers needed late-life care, 56 percent said they were at least somewhat involved in that care. Not surprisingly, involvement increased with age, with three out of four sons over fifty-five being involved, compared to just one out of six sons under the age of eighteen. Among all sons who were involved in a father's care, 93 percent said it helped them in coping with their loss.

The form of care varied widely in style and duration. Frank Hernandez offered perhaps the most comprehensive care among the sons I interviewed. He took his father into his house for the last two and a half years of the older man's life.

Frank was thirty-two years old at the time, recently divorced, the father of four, and less than thrilled to be opening his home to a man he had not known well for most of his life. The son felt an obligation, he told me, because in the Hispanic culture, it is traditional that young people provide for elders in need.

For Frank, the job of caring was not a major burden at first. But after a few months, as his father's emphysema worsened, Frank became responsible for feeding, medicating, and even bathing his father each day. There were many times that he resented his responsibilities. However, when I met with him at his suburban St. Louis home eight years after the death, Frank said he had no regrets: "It was an important period because I had been away for a few years. I'd kind of lost fellowship with my father. He was more of a stranger than a father. . . . It was a time for me and my dad to get to know each other again. I value that time we had."

Shawn Martel also found value in caring for his dad. Shawn's father had battled prostate cancer for many months. It was in the last thirty days of the father's life that Shawn, then a forty-seven-year-old college administrator, began visiting his dad almost daily at the hospital. In his father's last twenty hours, Shawn and his older brother stayed at the bedside, moistening their father's lips, wiping his forehead, reminiscing about his life.

Shawn's father was comatose at the time. But, as the brothers told stories about the father's intense work ethic, his offbeat vacation destinations, his fear of flying, his love of fishing, and other memories, Shawn sensed that the dying man was enjoying himself, "and wasn't ready to go while the stories were good."

Shawn said he was with his father until just moments before the end. "I always had worried how I would react in the face of death, but I was surprised at the calming effect it had," Shawn recalled. "I lost some of my own fear in the process. He died quite peacefully, as far as I saw. I felt at peace, and I was very, very content that I had been there."

In the weeks after the loss, to comfort himself, Shawn would remember moments from those last days in the hospital: "I'm very happy about the fact that at one point in his illness, I kissed the top of his head and told him I loved him. We didn't exchange emotions very readily, but I'm glad I had the opportunity. That was very satisfying and healing. I would regret it if I hadn't obeyed that impulse."

Gary Isikoff, the union official who volunteered at a Hospice, also enjoyed a new kind of affection with his father in the final days.

Gary recalled: "My dad was not a hugger. The most physical contact we would have was a warm handshake. A real blessing during that last month in the hospital was that we both felt more free to display affection. It was unspoken. I would kiss him on the forehead. I massaged his feet with lotion. He liked that and so did I. That helped me make a healing connection to my dad that had been missing since I was a small child."

Gary had the advantage of living near his father; he could care hands-on. Other sons, not in daily contact with their fathers, had to find less direct, but nonetheless meaningful, ways of caring. Some oversaw the father's finances; others researched nursing-care alternatives.

One man recalled, five years after his father's death, a satisfying contribution he had made to his father's care. This son, who was in his late fifties at the time, traveled a thousand miles to accompany his aged father on a visit to a doctor at a health maintenance organization. The son recalled of the doctor: "He was starting his exam. I couldn't tell if his heart was in it. So I did something that might seem extreme. I took him aside. I spoke with him very quietly, respectfully, and I said, 'You know this man here?' He said, 'It's your father.' I said, 'No. It's *your* father, let's say. I wonder how you would look after him.' And he gave me a wonderful look. And he gave my father very careful attention and admitted him to the hospital for a surgical procedure, which was something they brushed off the time before."

Another man, a middle-aged psychologist who also lived far from his widowed dad, arranged for home health care as his father began suffering from dementia. The son, who flew in for regular visits over the last few years of his father's life, told me that his involvement helped because he was "able to grieve along the way. Each time I saw him, another hunk of him was gone. We had our chance to gradually say good-bye."

A forty-seven-year-old musician had a much shorter time to care for his dad. But he made the most of it. The father, who'd appeared in robust health at seventy-seven years of age, suddenly suffered a massive stroke. The son lived in Ohio, and traveled, upon hearing the news, to his parents' home on the West Coast. By then, doctors had determined that the father was brain-dead and would never regain consciousness.

A couple of days later, the son, along with his mother, sister, and grandmother, agreed to take the father off life support. In the hospital room, the four family members kissed the stricken man good-bye just before he was to be removed from the respirator. The three women then left the hospital room. That's when the son thought: Dad shouldn't die alone. He pulled up a chair beside his father's bed. And as the older man's heartbeat gradually slowed during the next twenty minutes, the son sang the first verse of "Amazing Grace" over and over again.

If conversations between a father and son about the father's death, and late-life care by the son, can help a son in the aftermath of the death, so too can a direct good-bye. Among the men I surveyed, 40 percent reported saying good-bye to their fathers in some way; 82 percent of these sons said the good-bye helped in coping with the loss. Younger sons were least likely to say good-bye to their fathers, often because they were kept away from their dying dads or even shielded from the knowledge that he was desperately ill. While almost half of adult sons reported saying good-bye to their fathers, only 18 percent of sons younger than eighteen did so.

Dr. Robert Kastenbaum, author of *Death, Society and Human Experience*, offered me his opinion about why these final conversations between fathers and sons are so important: "Many of us would like to have a blessing, or at least an acquittal [from the father]: 'You did all you could. I love you. I'm not dying because you didn't eat your spinach. It's not your fault.' I think people need that so they can release themselves" from any guilt they might feel about the loss.

Indeed, among sons I spoke with who didn't have an opportunity for a last conversation or good-bye, I noticed that many struggled afterward with a sense of regret. Here are some examples:

A Mississippi historian who was thirty-seven years old when his father died of a heart attack: "Dad and I were very close, in a male sense. We could communicate, but we were never really demonstrative. I now wish I'd said some things. I wish I'd said how much I appreciated the sacrifices he made. I know there were sacrifices that maybe I didn't realize at the time, him working to put me through college, things like that. I never sat down and said: 'Thanks for making that choice.' "

A Tennessee landscaper who was thirty-six when his father died in a car accident: "Before [the death], I thought: 'Dad's being a real turd. We'll just let him be an old turd. And one of these days, my life will slow down, and I'll be able to deal with him, things will cool off and we'll talk. . . . We'll make some sort of reconciliation, and I'll feel better and he'll feel better. There's time, right? We'll do this tomorrow.' Now I'm coming to the realization that there is no tomorrow."

A New York department store manager who was thirty-nine when his father died of cancer: "So much was left unsaid. Maybe because of the culture, the male-dominated culture. We did not have a model to show us how to break the line, so we did nothing. . . . There seemed to be nothing between 'stoicism' and 'overly expressive.' The last time I saw him, I didn't hug him. I didn't tell him I loved him. I didn't tell him thanks."

Expressing appreciation. Clearing the air. Showing affection. They seem like simple acts, but fathers and sons know how difficult they can be to carry out. Many of the sons I spoke with said they were trained in a communication style that avoided the personal and emotional. They were more comfortable talking with their fathers about *things*—work, sports, politics—than about relationships, especially their own.

Yet the most common piece of advice from the 376 men who contributed to this book—advice to men who still have living fathers—was this one: *Make peace with Dad, in the best way you can.*

The participants in the survey made this point in a variety of ways:

- "Say what you have to say before it's too late."
- "As quickly as you can, resolve those old issues and sore spots and unfinished business."
- "If you have any conflicts, clear them up before you go to sleep that day. Do not wait until the next day; you never know if he will be there."
- "Show him love and understanding with your whole heart, and try to resolve your misunderstandings."
- "If you have any scores to settle, I would say do that."
- "Try to patch [things] up."
- "Nobody is perfect, so you have to forgive him and yourself for the mistakes that both of you have made."
- "The best way is not to hold back anything, for crying out loud. Say it, get it off your chest, even if it hurts."
- "Get rid of any hard feelings or grudges."
- "Make peace with him before he goes."

Peacemaking looked different to each son I interviewed. Stan Halstead, a motorcycle mechanic, offered an olive branch in the form of a letter. He and his father had been at odds in their early relationship. The father had been authoritarian and occasionally violent in Stan's childhood—not to mention too poor to help send Stan to college. Stan was very resentful as he moved into full adulthood.

In Stan's late twenties, however, about a decade before the father's death, the relationship began to change. A major precipitating factor was the decision by Stan's wife to leave him with two young children. Stan was dazed and depressed after the divorce. That's when his father inserted himself into the scene, offering financial support, and more importantly, showing Stan's children the kind of affection that Stan had always wanted as a child. Rather than being jealous, Stan was elated.

Four years later, while his father was still in good health, Stan wrote him a letter. "Dear Dad," it began, "I understand you did the best you could. All I want to do is say: Thank you for being my father." Later, Stan's dad told him: "When I got that letter, I felt like I'd graduated as a father."

Ed Warshak needed no words—written or spoken—to make peace with his dad. Like Stan, Ed remembered that his early relationship with his father had been marked by disappointment. Ed felt his dad was penny-pinching and too quick to anger. For a long time after Ed had left home, he clung to his resentments.

Then, when Ed was thirty-seven, a curious incident occurred. Ed was living in upstate New York, and teaching at a small college. On the last day of a visit home to his parents in Wisconsin, the son was about to say good-bye: "We'd been sitting in the living room talking for a while. And it got time to go, and I walked out to the kitchen and I hugged my mother. In the past, I would have hugged my mother and shaken my father's hand. Somehow, spontaneously, I began to reach for his hand, and hugged him instead. He hugged me back. And we both cried. We looked at each other and cried. We didn't say anything. There was perhaps no need for words."

When I met with Ed twenty years after the incident, and a decade after his father's death, tears came to his eyes as he told the story: "I can still feel his body, me hugging him, and his whiskers. . . . And then there was just this melting. I don't recall ever again resenting him."

Don Page, a civil engineer who was thirty-nine when his father died, did not so much need to reconcile with his dad as express his appreciation. As his father endured the advanced stages of prostate cancer, Don contacted about seventy of his dad's relatives and friends, and asked each to send a photo, memento, or story about his father. Then Don compiled these in an album and presented them to his dad at an eightieth birthday party in his honor.

"There was a sort of stunned reaction, but he spent a lot of time looking at it," Don recalled. "It was very important as a way of saying how much he meant to me, as a way of showing respect. It was like a memorial while he was still alive."

Among the men I interviewed, most said their fathers were open, accepting, and even visibly moved when a son reached out to them in appreciation or reconciliation. But there were exceptions. One son, who was thirty-nine at the death, said that in the months leading up to the death, he tried to talk with his dad about resentments he had. The son said: "He wouldn't let me unburden myself. He would leave the room. 'Time to go.' He'd change the subject." The son soon gave up. "I wasn't forceful. I could see it wasn't going to do any good."

Another son, a pharmaceutical salesman, remembered his father as absent or distant through most of his childhood—and as a violent drunk when he was around. Father and son remained estranged throughout most of their adulthood together.

As he neared age fifty, however, the son started attending

meetings of Adult Children of Alcoholics. He decided he wanted to forgive his father and reconcile before the older man died. The son explained to me what happened when he visited his father next: "I sat down and tried to tell him how I felt, how I wished we could have a relationship. I was just sobbing getting this out. He was not moved at all. He just said: 'You know, you really didn't have it that bad.' "

When the father died four years later, the son was angry at first. However, when I spoke with him six years after the death, he was satisfied that he'd done his best. In addition, as the son learned more about his father's background—the older man had been in an orphanage until age four, and later, served in numerous combat situations in World War II—he came to believe that his father also had done his best.

As we've seen, sons who help care for a father, who talk with him about his upcoming death and who say good-bye before the death, usually benefit afterward. These options, of course, are more available to sons who know in advance that their fathers are dying than to those whose fathers die suddenly. Thus, it was no surprise that sons in our survey whose fathers died suddenly— about 42 percent overall—reported being more affected by the death in the short-term than those whose fathers died after an extended illness. They were more likely to cry over the death, the survey showed, and in interviews they often focused on their guilt or regret.

Still, sons who lost fathers gradually, especially when the dying process took years, also spoke of hardships. And my survey found that they were just as likely as those whose fathers had died suddenly to experience ongoing problems as a result of the death. Several of these sons reported feeling helpless and angry as they watched their dads deteriorate slowly—and then guilty about wishing that the end would come more quickly.

One son described his father's two-year-long deterioration after a stroke a "nightmare." This son, who was forty-three at the death, said his family squabbled over medical decisions that the father could no longer make. He also said there were severe tensions among siblings over who was spending how much time at the hospital.

Another son told me about his struggle watching his dad die of Alzheimer's disease over an eight-year period. The family had first noticed the older man's memory problems as they prepared for a celebration of the parents' fiftieth wedding anniversary at the son's house. The son told me: "Dad came over to help fix something, and I needed something from the hardware store. So I sent him to get it. He never came back."

The father did make it back to his own home a couple of hours later, but things quickly worsened. Soon, the father began hallucinating and accused the son of stealing things from him. The son said: "He eventually didn't know how to turn on a light switch, and here was a man who had been an electrician. That just cut through me." Toward the end, the son recalled, "I would tell people: 'The dad I know has died.' I had this shell of Dad walking around."

Even after being the primary caretaker for his dad, this son felt regrets about how he had handled that role. He told me three years after the death: "I would love to apologize to [my father]. Being the caregiver, at times I was very impatient. I can see where it was understandable, but I also see where it would have been ideal if I had not gotten that way. . . . Getting him dressed, I might [yell]: 'Get this shirt on!' That would hurt his feelings."

One way I have prepared for my own father's death is by researching and writing this book. Like Gary Isikoff, the hospice volunteer mentioned early in this chapter, I've steeped myself in the topic of death. I've read about it and talked about it at length with researchers, therapists, and others. Spurred by these conversations, I've altered my relationship with my father; I've expressed gratitude more directly and broached the subject of his wishes upon his death. While I am far from serene about losing my father, there's been a gradual lessening in my fear and confusion about it.

Of course, no matter how thoroughly I might try to prepare for my father's death, I cannot mourn this loss in advance. I agree with the psychotherapist Therese Rando, who says it is a "fallacy" that there is "a fixed volume of grief to be experienced" and that grieving before the death automatically reduces the grieving afterward. More than anything else, among the sons I interviewed, consciously preparing for the loss seemed to take the hard edge off the pain to come. In the vast majority of cases, however, the death itself launched the son on a new and considerable journey.

Dwight D. Eisenhower

—◆—

Even when a father's death is deeply felt by his son, the son's immediate circumstances can mute his emotions. When Dwight Eisenhower's father died in March 1942—just four months after the Japanese had bombed Pearl Harbor—Eisenhower was so busy with war planning that he was not able to go to the funeral. To his family and fellow officers, he showed little emotion. But a few poignant lines in his diary, published nearly forty years later, reveal his profound sorrow.

Eisenhower was fifty-one at the time of his father's death. He was the third of six surviving sons of David and Ida Eisenhower. The couple had been a hardworking team in turn-of-the-twentieth-century Kansas, with David employed at a creamery and Ida overseeing a brood of children and a small family farm. The parents were fundamentalist Christians who taught their children to be self-reliant and to respect others as children of God.

The methods of such teaching could be harsh. When Dwight was twelve, one of his younger brothers skipped school. The father's reaction was to beat the child so hard with a leather strap that Dwight felt the need to intervene. Nonetheless, in later years, Eisenhower said his father's action in that case had been justified, and he always spoke highly of his father.

For many years, Dwight was the least successful among his brothers. From 1911, when he began his military career at West Point, until early 1941, he was not well known outside the circle of soldiers and officers with whom he worked. During the summer of 1941, however, his effective planning of the largest peacetime maneuvers in U.S. history caught the attention of the military brass in Washington. After Pearl Harbor, he was summoned to the nation's capital, and assigned to the War Plans Division with responsibility for the Far East.

It was a desk job, and Eisenhower worked fifteen hours a day, seven days a week. It was at his office, on March 10, 1942, that he learned of his father's death. His diary notes: "Father died this morning. Nothing I can do but send a wire."

The next day, his emotions began to seep out on the page. "I have felt terribly," he wrote. "I should like so much to be with my Mother these few days. But we're at war. And war is not soft, it has no time to indulge even the deepest and most sacred emotions." Later that day, Eisenhower wrote that he was quitting work three hours early, at 7:30 P.M., because "I haven't the heart to go on tonight."

The following day, his father's funeral was held in Kansas. In honor of the event, Eisenhower decided to "shut off all business and visitors for thirty minutes, to have that much time, by myself, to think of him." Then he wrote his personal reflections of his father's life.

"He had a full life," the remembrance began. "He was undemonstrative, quiet, modest, and of exemplary habits—he never used alcohol or tobacco. He was an uncomplaining person in the face of adversity, and such plaudits as were accorded him did not inflate his ego."

Eisenhower's reverence for his father was great. He wrote on: "His word has been his bond and accepted as such; his sterling honesty, his insistence upon the immediate payment of all debts, his pride in his independence earned for him a reputation that has profited all of us boys. . . . I'm proud he was my father. My only regret is that it was always so difficult to let him know the great depth of my affection for him."

Eisenhower finished his entry with an inscription: "David J. Eisenhower 1863–1942."

Then he went back to the war.

Seeing him, outstretched on the embalming table . . . with
the cardiac blue in his ears and fingertips and along his distal
regions . . . , I thought, This is what my father will look like when
he's dead. *And then, like a door slammed shut behind you, the tense*
of it all shifted into the inescapable present of This is my father, dead.
—POET/MORTICIAN THOMAS LYNCH

Chapter 6

———

THE FIRST DAYS AFTER

———

CHARLES GARTEN took a ride on a cable car. Ed Warshak took a walk in the park. Aaron Delfino took a trip to his liquor cabinet. Stan Halstead drove to a secluded lake. Kip Nielson visited a doughnut store. Seth Oakes listened to Beethoven. All had just heard the news that their fathers were dead.

Predicting how a son will react to such news is virtually impossible—even for the son himself. Many men I spoke with said that before the loss, they had no idea how they would handle it, and were ultimately surprised by what they said or did.

Several men who had not cried for years said they did so upon hearing the news of the death. "Right there on the phone, I wept," recalled a manufacturing-plant manager who was forty-seven at the time. He said it had been more than thirty years since he'd last shed tears. He told me he cried because "I felt like an orphan. My first thought was: Nobody else is going to care about me as much as he did."

Another man, a psychologist who was forty-nine at the death, also let tears flow immediately upon hearing the news. This man and his dad had been at odds for much of their early relationship, but had reconciled before the death. The son told me: "At his death, I walked to a park, alone, and cried. And I was grateful that I cried. Maybe I didn't know whether his legacy would be his anger or his love. There was gratitude that I felt the sadness. To not have felt it would have meant I was still holding on to the bitterness."

Other men who cried were less accepting of their tears. A college professor who was thirty-four at the death described his feelings when his brother telephoned him with the news: "I was very calm at first. I hung up. Then I came upstairs and collapsed for a short moment on the floor in the kitchen. I just sort of curled up. I cried my head off for a few seconds. I thought I was going to hold it together. And I sort of did."

One reason to "hold it together," this man went on to say, was to appear strong in front of his ten-year-old daughter. She apparently heard her father's initial collapse and came running from another part of the house. She arrived in the kitchen as her father was getting back to his feet.

Sixty-one percent of the men in my survey said they cried in the month after their father's death, including 19 percent who said they cried a lot. But 39 percent of men reported that they did not cry at all in that first month. Most often, it seemed to me, these men, like the college professor mentioned above, held back tears as a way of appearing strong for family members who they believed needed their support.

One man, who was eighteen when his dad died, said he "gutted it out," keeping his tears inside, because "I wanted to be there for my mother." A thirty-three-year-old son, upon hearing the news of his father's fatal stroke, remembered "starting to cry, then holding it back" because he wasn't comfortable letting go in front of relatives. "The mechanism to [hold back]," he told me, "was so powerful that later, it was hard to reverse." A third man, who was forty-three at the death, confessed: "For the first few days, I would wake up in the middle of the night, and think of my dad and cry. But I was quiet about it. I didn't want to bother my wife."

Another reason sons went without tears in the first days was because they didn't have any strong feeling. This bothered some men, who felt that they *should* be more emotional. One thirty-six-year-old son told me he thought it was "inhuman" for him not to cry. Eventually, he tried to force the issue. He dug out his favorite photo of his father, and sat staring at it. "I was trying to summon up deep emotion," he said. "It didn't work."

For children, the struggles around crying were often even more confounding. One son, who was thirteen when his father died, told me that in the first days after the loss, no tears came. He thought that was fine—until his relatives started coaching him that it was "okay to cry." When I spoke with this son more than thirty years later, he said: "What I never heard from anyone was that it was also okay *not* to cry."

According to my survey, children were not significantly more or less likely to cry in the month after the death of their fathers than were young adults or midlife sons. Older men were least likely to cry; fewer than one in three sons who were over fifty-five when their fathers died reported shedding tears in the first month, including just 4 percent who said they had cried a lot.

Race, region, and education level all had no apparent effect on a son's likelihood to cry. But the manner in which a father died had an impact. When the death was sudden, 70 percent of sons reported crying in the first month; when the death followed an extended illness, the figure fell to 56 percent. Several sons whose fathers died gradually told me they had cried before the death, either upon learning of the terminal diagnosis, or as they witnessed the father's deterioration. "I was cried out" when the death came, one son said.

Perhaps the survey's most interesting finding on the subject of crying—and one that may surprise some grief counselors—was this: Shedding tears had no apparent impact on whether a son experienced long-term problems due to the father's death. According to the FatherLoss Survey, 10 percent of sons who cried after their father's death reported problems in their current lives that they related to the death. Among those who didn't cry, the percentage of reporting problems was 11 percent. Statistically, that's no difference.

Sons who did not cry over the death often reacted instead by doing something that connected them with the memory of their fathers in a positive way. Upon hearing the news of his father's death, a thirty-three-year-old lobbyist immediately exited his San Francisco apartment, walked to a cable car stop, and rode the trolley across town. It was something he'd done with his father when he was a kid. "I remember walking around [on the day of the death] thinking: 'How can the world go on in a normal way? Don't you realize my father just died?' "

Another son, a thirty-nine-year-old lawyer, immediately sought solace at a doughnut store. It wasn't because he was hungry. "As a child, many Sunday mornings, my dad would get doughnuts to eat while drinking coffee and reading the paper," this son said. "Since I was informed of his passing on a Sunday morning at six A.M.," the son immediately thought of getting doughnuts. About this response, the son told me: "I would say it was honoring his memory."

A twenty-seven-year-old social worker from California tried to make contact in a more direct way. His dad had died of a heart attack while fixing the roof of a barn on the family farm. The son said that after leaving the hospital following the death, "I headed down to the farm to be with my mom. I got there around 1:30 A.M., and went up to the barn where it all happened. I climbed up on the roof and it was littered with his reading glasses, a pencil, and bunches of those yellow butterscotch candy wrappers. He was a big fan of that candy. It was a really crisp fall night with billions of stars in every direction I looked. I sat there for a good hour and tried to find my father somewhere in that universe. But he was nowhere to be found."

Other sons acted in ways designed not so much to connect with their fathers as to release an initial surge of emotional energy. A thirty-year-old graduate student told me he took a "furious walk" right after learning of his father's death from a heart attack. The son said of the walk: "It wasn't very long, maybe a mile. But it was brisk. I couldn't sit still."

A mechanic, who was thirty-six at the death, said that after he heard the news, he took "an anger run" on his motorcycle, riding at high speed along winding roads in the hills near Phoenix. Five years after the death, he recalled the ride in detail: "I went past this little pond. There were mountains behind it. I stopped at this turnoff, and looked for a little bit. There was this beautiful sunset, this red sky, the clouds, the mountains, and the light reflecting off the pond. It was just such a beautiful, breathtaking view. I stood there and enjoyed it for a little bit. I felt a sense of release in that the day had a very beautiful end."

Other sons simply sought to blunt the force of the blow by distracting or numbing themselves. "That first night, I got hammered drunk," said an architect, who was fifty-four years old at the death. He was among numerous sons who told me their first response to the news was to pour a drink.

Many sons I spoke with said they felt like they were spinning during the first few days after hearing of the deaths of their fathers. Some needed to make flight reservations, arrange bereavement leaves at work, and travel great distances. Most were helping with funeral arrangements and tending to the needs of other family members.

During this period, one important question for sons was whether or not to view the body. In my survey, among sons eighteen to fifty-five at the time of the death, 85 percent said they viewed their father's body before it was buried or cremated. And more than 75 percent of those men reported that seeing the body was helpful later in coping with the death.

A disk jockey who was thirty-seven when his dad died told me the viewing brought a sense of closure. He recalled his experience in the hospital room after the death: "I put my hand on my father's shoulder. There was a realization that this was the last time I'd ever have any type of intimate contact with him. . . . It was sort of like a threshold, a crossing over. It was a very black-and-white, concrete, tactile moment. Looking down into his eyes—his eyelids were partially closed—it was confirmation for me that this was actually happening. Something went from Dad to me. It felt like a passing of something. Inside, I was like: 'This is real. There is no possibility that this could not have happened.' "

Several sons told me that seeing the body brought them to tears for the first time. And some used their visits with the deceased father to say good-bye, fix the image of his face in their minds, or perform a personal leave-taking ritual.

A man whose father had died suddenly when the son was twenty-seven said he spent a few minutes with his dad just before visitation opened to the public. The son recalled: "I had provided the undertaker with a string tie engraved with a bear's head that I had given my dad. . . . They had put the tie on him. I slipped a twenty-dollar bill, his pocket knife, my picture, and my business card into his sports coat jacket. It was important to me to do these things just because I felt these were things that represented his life and should go with his body in death."

When I met this man, it had been four years since the death. He told me: "Strangely, as time has passed, it gets harder and harder to remember what he looks like, and my memory focuses around the string tie. I visualize it on him in the casket, and then I am able to see his face and body."

Some of the sons who chose not to see their father's body said they preferred to recall their dads in life rather than death. Others just didn't feel very connected to the older man; seeing his body wasn't important. Those who had reported in the survey that they'd had a negative relationship with the father in childhood were, not surprisingly, less likely to see the body than those who had reported a positive relationship.

Sons who had watched the father deteriorate up close in the final weeks or months of a long illness said they needed no further evidence that the older man was really dead. This seemed especially common among sons who were over fifty-five at the father's death; these men, the survey showed, were less likely than other adults to view a father's body.

Occasionally, a son who chose not to see the body came to regret his decision. A journalist I spoke with, who was a young adult at the time of the death, said he was told by an uncle that his father's body was not in good enough shape to view. When I spoke with this son twelve years later, he said he wished he had ignored his uncle's words. "I remember walking behind the casket being pushed out the door [of the chapel]. I remember thinking, well, I'll get a chance to see him later. Of course, as soon as we were out the door of the chapel, the mortuary guys whipped him into an elevator to send him down to the garage to load him into the hearse. Of course, he was in a box, in a hearse, and in the ground, six feet of dirt covering him, and there was no opportunity. It was the ultimate procrastination. 'Oh, I'll get to see the body later.' Well, only if I have it exhumed."

Another man I spoke with didn't have a choice about seeing his father's body. When the son was thirty-six, his dad had died in a traffic accident in a foreign country. Five years later, the son told me: "All I got was a police report of the accident and his ashes. . . . I need concreteness." Occasionally, the son said, he wonders if his father's really dead.

A few studies have measured the effect of viewing a loved one's body and generally found that it helps survivors in their grieving process. Many grief counselors recommend it. Stephen Levine, author of *Who Dies?* and other books, is emphatic about the value of seeing the deceased. He contends that when the body of a deceased person "lies in its own bed," and family members can pay respects, "the departure of a loved one becomes real. There is a wholeness about it."

According to my survey, sons who were under eighteen were least likely to say that viewing their father's body was helpful. Several who did see the body after death told me they were frightened by the experience.

University of Michigan psychologist Albert Cain, a child bereavement specialist, told me that when it comes to the viewing, a surviving parent should be very attentive to the messages sent by the child. "Unless the body is in a particularly mangled condition, most [grief therapists] are agreed that the child should be *free* to see the parent in the casket—but that's very different from saying they *must.*" Even recognizing that some sons may later regret *not* seeing the body, Cain said, "Clearly, you don't want to force them."

For young sons who do choose to see the body, Cain added, it's often helpful for them to pick a possession—a symbol of something they shared with their dad, such as a letter or a gift from the father—to place in the casket. "It gives them a sense that they've done something," Cain said, "that they've participated."

A young son's attendance at his father's funeral should be handled with similar sensitivity, Cain said. Adults should offer surviving sons the chance to attend the funeral, but "should not drag them kicking and screaming." Some boys may choose to attend only the memorial service and not the burial itself. That should be permitted, Cain said.

When the boy does choose to attend, Cain added, it's usually helpful for the surviving parent to assign a friend or relative—someone the child knows and trusts—to stay with the child throughout the event for those times when the surviving parent is emotionally overwhelmed or pulled away from the child to receive condolences or perform other duties.

My survey showed that 78 percent of sons who were under eighteen when their fathers died attended a funeral or other service, and 74 percent of those who attended said it helped them in their subsequent grieving.

One such son, who was ten years old when his dad died of a heart attack, told me that at first he didn't want to go to his dad's funeral: "I guess I was afraid. I didn't want to deal with it." His mother, however, encouraged him to attend. When I spoke with the son more than two decades later, he was glad he'd gone. "The value was mostly in seeing how many people loved my dad. He was a high school teacher, and the room was over capacity."

A son who was sixteen at his father's death told me the funeral helped him accept the loss. "I'm a believer to some extent in ritual. It means something. This was it. It wasn't a dream. Here I was in church. And here was my dad, dead, in front of us. And that wasn't going to go away. It really solidified it, finalized it. 'This is it. There's no turning back.' "

More than 90 percent of the men in our survey who were adults at the time of the death attended a funeral or other death service for their father, and 84 percent of these men said it helped them cope with the death. Funeral attendance was not affected by the frequency of a son's attendance at religious services; nonreligious families tended to replace religious services with secular ones.

One son, who was thirty-nine when his father died several months after being diagnosed with cancer, said he had a feeling of closure during his dad's funeral. "As I sat there, I realized that the pain, the suffering, the worries, were gone for him and us. I'm not going to say it was a relief, but there was an easing."

Many sons told me the funeral helped by bringing them together with family and friends who shared a love for the father. One thirty-seven-year-old son said that people who came to the funeral "expressed the fact that they were going to have to feel this too. That helped a great deal. I was kind of caught up in: 'This is happening only to me. It's just me and my family. Nobody else has been through this before.' "

While some sons appreciated it when their fathers made their own funeral arrangements before the death, others said they gained from planning it themselves. James Haddad, who was forty years old when his father died, told me he took great care in picking out a casket in which there was "a lot of warmth to the wood." James's father had been a tradesman, and James wanted a casket with "a degree of workmanship that honored him." James added: "I wanted to make sure he had a very special funeral. I wanted to have some very beautiful flowers, to represent Dad's love of paint and color. This particular funeral home encouraged you to bring personal items from home. I just went hog-wild. I brought his guitar, his paintings, an easel, lots of photographs. We did a sort of storyboard."

While recounting this memory, James, a soft-spoken man with large brown eyes, allowed tears to fall. He continued to talk through them: "I wanted people to know there was more to him than anybody knew. He wasn't just a guy at a store. He wasn't just someone you saw at church. It was my chance to expose my dad in a positive way. There was a lot of pride."

It was also important to James to have a "proper church service with all the elements," one that honored the family's Lebanese Christian heritage. Even though James was no longer an adherent to his dad's religion, he told me he felt good about having the funeral where he and his father had worshiped together. "I'd been raised in the church. I'd sung in the choir. I was very involved until about [age] twenty. There was a sense of continuity."

Another son I spoke with chose a somewhat less traditional way of honoring his father after the death. This son, who was sixty-three when his father died, had his father cremated and then put off the post-death rituals for six weeks to plan "an appropriate celebration."

The celebration took place at the farm in Minnesota where the son's father had lived before retiring to Arizona. There, the son and his relatives engaged in a lively croquet tournament modeled after the ones the father had often organized. The tournament even included the father's traditional trophy to the winner: a giant green zucchini.

The following day, the family gathered again to feast, tell stories about the deceased, and build a wooden bench in his honor. Three generations worked together on the bench and placed it near a lake on the property. Then, in a simple ceremony, they spread the father's ashes beside the bench. The two-day memorial gave the son "a sense of completion, and a lot of joy."

A few men told me that the biggest benefit of the funeral was gaining a greater appreciation for their father. Hearing the stories of other family members, friends, and the father's work colleagues helped sons understand the older man better. One son, who was thirty-four when his dad died, said that a phrase from the eulogy continued to echo years after the death. The phrase was a description of the father: "He never said a mean word about anyone." Since hearing those words, the son said, "I've tried to adopt this in my life. I try to enjoy other people as best I can. I try not to judge other people."

This man said another moving moment occurred at the burial site. There, he and other family members placed items on the coffin before it was lowered: a tomato to symbolize the father's love of gardening and a handball glove to signify his love of sports. Then, after the coffin was lowered, the family, which is Jewish, participated in the traditional burial ritual of putting the first few shovelsful of soil on top of the casket.

I asked the son why shoveling the soil was meaningful. He responded: "Well, I suppose the ritual gives one the sense that one is putting the dead away as opposed to having the dead taken from you. I should say that I don't know if I ever had that thought until this moment."

Seventeen percent of men in our survey said attending their father's funeral was not helpful. Funerals were least valuable, sons told me, when they failed to reflect the father's real spirit. One man said he felt resentful as he listened to a series of glowing accounts of his father, whom the son had experienced as abusive. Another son said the minister at his father's service spent too much time talking about a theology in which neither the father nor the son believed. Not surprisingly, our survey showed that sons who attended religious services regularly were more likely than those who attended rarely or never to say the funeral helped them cope with the death.

When the funeral and burial services were over, several sons said it was important to release the tension of the experience. After the burial, one man recalled, the family came together for dinner. "That night," he added, "we sat on the front porch until it was dark, telling stories. We laughed a lot."

Another man, whose father had emigrated from Mexico, said: "When we got home [from the funeral], we had a celebration. This is common among older Mexican folks. We had two hundred people, a full sitdown dinner. We'd rented a place. We had music, dancing. It was a good way to bring a nice closure to a life."

Fifty-six percent of adult sons in our survey who went to the funeral also participated in it in some way. Once again, the vast majority of these sons—86 percent—cited their participation as helpful in coping during the aftermath. One forty-nine-year-old son explained the importance of giving a eulogy at his father's funeral: "It was a time for me to express my gratitude, and hope others felt gratitude as well. It was a time for praise. I wanted to honor him. I wanted to tell his story in an honoring way."

Thomas Lynch, a funeral-home director and author of *The Undertaking*, a book of essays on dying and death, told me that in his experience, adult children tended to benefit from what he called "large muscle involvement" in the post-death rituals of their parents—activities such as carrying the casket and giving eulogies.

When his own father died, one of the most meaningful tasks Lynch performed, Lynch told me, was to embalm his dad.

About 10 percent of the sons in our survey said they didn't attend a funeral or other service for their fathers. Among the least likely to attend, understandably, were sons who reported having had a "negative" relationship with their fathers in childhood. One man I interviewed said he hadn't talked with his father in fifteen years before the death. The man's mother had died prior to the father, and the son hadn't stayed in touch with his father or siblings. He stayed away from his dad's funeral, he said, because he didn't want to open up old family wounds and because he felt it would have been "hypocritical" to attend.

According to my survey, sons who claimed the western United States as their home also were less likely than other sons to attend a father's funeral. More than 20 percent of Westerners said they did not attend, while just 2 percent of those from the Northeast, 4 percent from the Midwest, and 13 percent from the South reported not attending. This may in part reflect the greater distance some sons had to travel to reach their childhood homes.

Distance from the funeral site was an issue for one son I spoke with, although it involved more than just a cross-country trip. This son, who was twenty-three at the death, said he missed his father's funeral in India because he was studying at the University of New Mexico when his father died. I spoke with the son a year after the death. He had not yet been home, and said he continued to feel guilty and "incomplete."

In a couple of cases, sons reported that there was no post-death service for a father. One man said that both his father and mother were adamant that none be held: "This seems a bit cold, but we knew this philosophy for years before their deaths. They died, their bodies were taken away, and about a week later, we were given death certificates and boxes with their ashes. No one in our family seemed the lesser for this way of doing things."

But Frank Hernandez found that he was not comfortable forgoing a funeral service for his dad. When circumstances ruled out the possibility of a communitywide service, Frank went solo.

Frank is the man from the previous chapter who was thirty-two when he took his father, suffering from emphysema, into his home for the last two-plus years of the older man's life. During those years, as the father's condition worsened, Frank's responsibilities grew. Frank filled prescriptions and dispensed medication. He prepared all of his father's meals. Late at night, on occasion, he even served as his father's confidant. His dad would sometimes call to him in the wee hours, half dreaming, to review incidents from his past. Once, the older man asked Frank to help end his life. Frank said he couldn't do it.

Death finally came to Frank's father at a particularly awkward time for his son. Frank, a radiology technician, was scheduled to fly one morning from his home in St. Louis to San Francisco to take three days of recertification tests; without them, he couldn't continue to perform his job. On the morning he was to leave, however, as he was dropping off his father at a VA hospital to be cared for, the older man suffered a heart attack and died.

Frank was devastated, but he could not cancel his trip. So he informed his siblings of the death, arranged for cremation, and caught his flight to the West Coast.

Frank had spent forty-five minutes with his father's body, in a hospital room, after the death. On the plane trip west, he was emotionally upset and restless. Fortunately, his father had a connection with Frank's destination; the older man had been based in San Francisco during World War II. About a decade earlier, in fact, Frank and his father had spent a couple of days together in that city, walking the streets and reminiscing about the father's wartime experiences.

When Frank landed in San Francisco this time, he had several hours before his first exam. So after checking into his hotel, he began strolling the same streets he had with his father all those years earlier. "I felt good walking around where I knew he spent time," Frank told me. "Real or imagined, it felt like a spiritual connection." Frank kept walking until he reached Fisherman's Wharf, where he bought a bouquet of flowers.

Frank still had time before his exam, so he purchased a ticket for the next ferry to Sausalito, a small town just north of San Francisco, a couple of miles from the Golden Gate Bridge. When he reached Sausalito, he started hiking the steep streets back toward the bridge. It was a long haul. But Frank now felt he was on a mission. When he reached "the dead center" of the bridge, as he put it, he looked out over the San Francisco skyline, prayed a few words of remembrance about his dad, and flung the bouquet of flowers into the sea. Then Frank returned to the city to take his exams.

"I'm not sure what drove me" to carry out the ritual, Frank, a burly man with close-cropped brown hair, told me eight years after the death. "It felt really good to do it. . . . I felt like there needed to be some gesture on my part. I'd had a relationship with my dad for two years. It was a very personal, one-on-one thing. I didn't share it with anybody else. I was honoring that."

In the United States, these kind of self-created rituals appear to have been on the rise toward the end of the twentieth century. They have in many cases replaced traditional memorial services, which have declined along with the drop in religious participation and the rise in social mobility. But it's unlikely that death rituals will ever go out of style. Archaeologists have determined that they go back at least fifty thousand years. Margaret Mead wrote: "I know of no people for whom the fact of death is not critical, and who have no ritual by which to deal with it."

Thomas R. Golden, a Maryland grief counselor who specializes in working with men, told me that rituals are most effective when they connect the bereaved to the deceased and permit an opportunity for some form of emotional expression. Golden added that men and women sometimes have different ideas of what "emotional expression" means. Women tend to see it as talking or crying; men often move toward action.

When Golden's own father died in 1994, he and his brother ritualized the loss by designing and building an urn to carry the father's ashes. In the week preceding the funeral, working in the father's workshop, they made the urn out of wood their father had set aside for special projects. Golden told me that men who showed up at the family home during the week tended to be drawn to the workshop to witness the urn taking shape. "[The workshop] felt safe to us. If we had been sitting in a group and facing each other in a circle of chairs, I'm sure we . . . wouldn't have known what to say. We would have felt awkward."

The urn-building ritual, Golden said, helped him through the acute pain of his loss, as did the subsequent funeral and burial services. But these rituals did not end his grief. The same was true for most other men I interviewed. While funerals, memorial services, and other rituals often brought a son "to the brink of grief," in the words of one man, they rarely took him all the way through it. Before closure could occur, the son usually had to return to his home, school, job, family, and regular routines. Then he could begin to see the shape of the mourning that was still to come.

Ted Turner

In July 1998, Ted Turner stood, repentant, before a gathering of the Television Critics Association. It had been just days since CNN, his flagship TV station, had aired an alarming report—that U.S. troops had used nerve gas against American deserters during the Vietnam War. Shortly after the broadcast, CNN had retracted the report; the evidence, the network belatedly concluded, did not support the explosive charges.

Now, facing the TV writers, it was Turner's intent to offer a personal apology. He called the CNN fiasco "the most horrible nightmare I've ever lived through," and declared that he was "very embarrassed, very sad." Then he added a cryptic comment about the damage to his network's reputation: "Nothing has upset me more, I think, in probably my whole life . . . , [including] the death of my father. This ranks with one of the great catastrophes . . . in my life."

It's hard to imagine a catastrophe greater than his father's death. Ted was just twenty-four years old at the time, a brash, sailboat racing, former Ivy Leaguer who had recently taken a job as a salesman for his father's billboard company. The father, Ed, had started Turner Advertising Co. in Cincinnati during the Depression. Hard-driving and hard-drinking, he'd managed to build it into a thriving company, proving himself among the most impressive businessmen of his era.

Ed Turner was also, according to close observers, an erratic father. Some biographers have posthumously labeled him a manic-depressive. He reportedly beat Ted regularly; Ted's mother would later tell an interviewer that nearly all of the arguments she had with her husband were over his harsh treatment of Ted.

But if Ed Turner could be ruthless, he could also be generous. When Ted was about ten, his father bought him a sailboat; subsequently, father and son enjoyed many hours on the water together. They were close enough that Ed Turner stood as his son's best man when Ted was twenty-one. And after Ted was expelled from Brown University for breaking dormitory rules, his father gave him a full-time job as a junior salesman for Turner Advertising. Years later, Ted would describe his father as someone who "could be the kindest, warmest, most wonderful person in the whole world, and then go into a bar, get drunk, and get into a fistfight with the whole place."

As a young adult, Ted was desperate to prove himself to his father and worked long hours at the billboard company. He began almost immediately to generate his own ideas for the future of the company. The result, at times, was ferocious disagreement between the two men. One of the worst arguments occurred in the late months of 1962, when Ed, then fifty-three, leveraged his business and personal fortune to buy his biggest competitor. After inking the deal, however, he got scared. Rather than risk everything to pay off the enormous debt he'd taken on, Ed decided to backtrack and sell off the new acquisition.

Ted fought vehemently against this retreat. He believed that the acquisition had been a good one and that he could lead the company if his father no longer wanted to. Ted later told a biographer that he and his father "had terrible, terrible fights" over the issue. It was while this father-son discord was in full bloom that Ed Turner finished breakfast one morning, retired to his room, and shot himself to death.

Ted was devastated. And at the reading of the will, Ted suffered a second setback. He learned that his father already had put into motion—apparently irrevocably—the sale of the billboard business. In essence, his father was saying from his grave that Ted did not have what it took to lead the company without him.

Ed Turner was wrong. Within days of the suicide, Ted was back at the office, threatening court action to stop the sale of the company he now owned. He was, he told his adversaries, prepared to take the witness stand and say that his father had been depressed, deluded, demonic—whatever it took to keep control of the company. Eventually, Turner got his way.

And, for the most part, he's been getting his way ever since, in a now legendary business career. In the 1960s, he successfully managed the debt on the billboard business. In the 1970s, he parlayed a weak UHF television station in Atlanta into the still-flourishing TBS SuperStation. Later, he bought the Atlanta Braves at a bargain price and built it into a perennial winner, both on the field and the bottom line. In the early 1980s, he started CNN, the first all-news cable station, and built it into an international empire before merging his company with Time-Warner Inc. in 1996.

Turner's success also extended into sports. When he wasn't navigating his various enterprises, he was racing sailboats. He became a world-class yachtsman, victorious at every level of the sport; in 1977, he won the America's Cup.

In all of these endeavors, Ted Turner played from a foundation of high risk. The father-and-son biographers Robert Goldberg and Gerald Jay Goldberg believe Ted was "perversely eager" to court danger, "to test himself against all challenges in the crucible of risk. His father, after all, had failed just such a test."

Even today, the memory of his father's life and death is always nearby. Of his father, Turner once told *60 Minutes*: "If I had one wish for something that would give me personal joy and satisfaction, it would be to have my father come back, and to show him around. I'd like to show him the whole shooting match. I really would. I think he'd really enjoy it."

I had vowed not to cry. This was another test of my manhood,
another in a series of tests I was constantly giving myself for no other
reason than to prove my manhood.
—WRITER LEWIS GRIZZARD

Chapter 7

MEN'S STYLES OF MOURNING

WITH THE FUNERAL OVER, the father's body conse-
crated, and the shock wearing off, a surviving son often
feels pressure to finish his grief and become "normal"
again. After a brief bereavement leave, the son may be encouraged
by his employer to return to his pre-loss productivity. Colleagues
and friends may stop asking about the impact of the death. Even a
man's loved ones, who have depended upon him for stability and
security in the past, may start to lean on him again.

These external pressures combine with an almost universal male
urge to "get over it, already." Many sons I spoke with expected
themselves not to "lose it," even over a loss this great. After the
death, they moved with urgency to try to recover whatever psychological equilibrium they might have possessed beforehand.

Eventually, most regained their balance. But not always so fast.
In what might be called the "active grieving" period—usually the
several weeks or months following the loss—most sons I spoke with

adapted only gradually to the new circumstances, and new psychology, of their lives.

The method of adaptation was varied, but sons tended to fall into one of four basic styles of grieving. Not that the styles were mutually exclusive. The majority of sons seemed to rely primarily on one style, and then mix in aspects of the others. The styles they chose—or that chose them—depended largely upon the son's personality, the circumstances of the father's death, and the son's previous relationship with his dad.

About one in five men I spoke with could best be labeled as *Dashers*. These were the sons who sped through mourning; many hardly noticed it. Dashers tended not to cry, but rather to create, almost immediately, an intellectual framework to help them manage the loss. The father was old, or out of his misery, they told themselves. Or, "that's life." In essence, Dashers *thought* their way through their grief. Emotionally, they were settling down even as other men were just beginning to feel.

Edwin Hunt was sixty-three when his father died of heart failure at the age of ninety-three. The son, a bespectacled biologist, had gotten along well with his dad ever since childhood and had watched him gradually lose his physical and mental agility over two decades. When the death came, the son heard the news, flew with his wife to attend the funeral, and then returned home—all with little commotion.

"His death and the funeral didn't really have much of an effect," Edwin told me when I spoke with him five years after the death. "I accepted it. I don't even know what happened to him after we left the funeral home. He was in an open casket, and I saw him there. I remember going over and looking at him, and he looked the same as I last saw him. . . . I don't really remember having grief about my father's death."

The death of Edwin's mother, a decade earlier, had a much different impact. After that loss, Edwin recalled, he was depressed on and off for a year. In the months after his father's death, however, he was philosophical: "I had a realization that he'd had a complete life, and I guess I appreciated that. Other than that, I didn't dwell."

A cattle farmer who was sixty-three when his dad died was similarly undisturbed. The man's father, aged eighty-five, had deteriorated in his later years, and the son was expecting the phone call with the news of the death. After the funeral, "I just went back to my life," this son told me. "I couldn't bring him back. I couldn't push him further. I couldn't turn him over. . . . I saw to him the last part of his life. I'm happy with that."

As with these two men, many Dashers are older men. Experienced with loss, they are less often shocked, or knocked off balance, even by such a significant death.

Not only do older men have experience with loss, they are more likely to have taken action to prepare for the father's death. My survey showed that sons who lost fathers after age fifty-five were most likely to be involved in the father's medical care, to have talked with their fathers about the impending death, and to have resolved their relationship with their dads. In my conversations with these older men—most of whom were born before the middle of the twentieth century—there was also a high premium placed on traditional male stoicism. One seventy-eight-year-old man told me: "I don't believe I shed a tear. Men keep those things within their bodies."

Dasher status, however, was not reserved exclusively for older men. Several middle-aged and younger sons also told me their mourning was quick and nonchaotic. Most of these men had watched their fathers die gradually. Like the older men, they had accomplished some of their grieving in advance. Religion often played a part as well.

Patrick Bryan and his father, who had Parkinson's disease, spent many hours together in the father's last months. Patrick, who was forty-six at the time, sat at his dad's bedside while they talked about their lives and read a book called *Steps to Peace With God*. Three years after the death, I met with Patrick, a well-dressed man with carefully combed dark hair, in the office where he was a pastoral counselor.

When I asked him about the period immediately after his dad's death, he said: "The grieving process was pretty short. There wasn't a weeping and moaning and sobbing and gut-wrenching kind of reaction to it. I remember a couple people in my family talked to me: 'Seems like you're not reacting much.' I began to evaluate myself. I believe there was a reality that I knew he was in a better place. The Scriptures talk about we'll have a new body. He's with God and he has a new body. . . . That's what I kept thinking about."

This son added: "Here was a man who lived out the years he was supposed to live. If I felt sadness at all, it was for my mother because they had been married for almost sixty years, and she had never spent a night alone."

A college administrator, who also spent a lot of time with his father in the last month of the older man's bout with cancer, said his grieving was muted. This man, who was forty-seven years old at the death, explained: "I did not have terribly strong emotions. There was some sadness, some relief. . . . My father's mother had died as a result of his birth. My religious beliefs are strong, and I thought: 'Well, I hope Dad finally is having an opportunity to get to know his mother.' "

———

Another group of men who tended to be Dashers were those who had never formed close bonds with their fathers during adulthood. They often lived at a distance from their families of origin and saw their fathers only occasionally. They rarely connected with their dads in an emotional way, positive or negative.

Mark McGhee's father was an Army drill sergeant who became a public school teacher after retiring from the military. Mark recalled that his dad generally adopted the role of "instructor and critic" with him, rather than mentor or supporter, even in Mark's adulthood. Even when they embraced, Mark recalled, there remained a distance between them. "Think of Russians hugging with big fur coats," the son suggested.

After Mark became a father himself in his thirties, the tensions began to ease between him and his dad. And in the years before the father's sudden death, which occurred when Mark was forty-seven, the two men concluded their phone calls and letters with expressions of love. That helped Mark let go of any lingering anger after the death, but it didn't create a strong emotional attachment. When the death came, Mark said, there was no intense mourning. Mark told me: "I had resigned myself years before that it wasn't going to be like in the movies, a big catharsis. . . . I would have liked for things to have gotten better sooner. I would have liked to know: 'Has your opinion of me changed?' But things were about as good as they were going to get."

A writer, who was forty-six years old at his father's death, had moved away from his home in Michigan in his early twenties and had gradually disconnected from his dad. While he saw his father at least once a year, their talks skimmed the surface of their lives and thoughts. The father sometimes expressed racist attitudes, which made the son angry. But mostly, the son told me, he didn't engage his dad. The son said he was saddened when his father was diagnosed with Alzheimer's disease, but the progression of the disease only increased the distance between them.

The father died at age seventy. I talked with the son a few months later. He said: "I didn't feel much grief. I didn't have that much real affection for him anymore. . . . We had grown far apart."

This man, as well as several other Dashers I spoke with, acknowledged that they were not entirely comfortable with their lack of emotion after the father's death. They wondered whether they were suppressing their own strong feelings. As it turned out, some sons who originally seemed like Dashers, experienced the impact only later. They represented a second style of mourner: *Delayers.*

Among the men I interviewed, about one in five could be categorized as a Delayer. That was about equal to the percentage I considered to be Dashers. Like Dashers, Delayers did not betray a powerful reaction to the death in the short-term. But months, years or even decades later—often after they had built a community of support or had come to understand themselves better—these sons experienced mourning symptoms related to the father's death.

In Chapter 2, we met the prototypical Delayer. Walter Wang was the man who lost his father at age twenty-two, then buried his emotions through the funeral, his wedding three months later, the entire childhoods of his four children, and his passage into midlife. Finally, at age fifty-five, at a management retreat, a facilitator encouraged Walter and his colleagues to meditate on various eras in their lives. When he reached the point when his father died, Walter wept over the loss for the first time.

When I talked with Walter twelve years after the retreat, he told me he regretted holding in his emotions for so long, but added that he came by his stoic disposition honestly: "I was following the example of my father. I never saw him break down." Walter added:

"I was doing what I believed to be right at the time. Someone needed to be the strong one. Everyone in my family was falling apart."

Ray Hyatt also felt like he needed to hold things together after his father died of a heart attack while the two were playing basketball. Ray was twenty-seven at the time. His father had a history of heart trouble, and as they played one-on-one at a park near their home, Ray recalled, his dad suddenly "turns around, swoons, and falls. . . . It was almost like someone pulled an arrow out and shot him. You could hear the gasp."

Ray recalled kneeling by his dad, rolling him over, and accidentally bumping his father's head on the concrete. Then Ray yelled for help. About five minutes went by before an emergency squad showed up; by then, Ray's father had stopped breathing. Twenty years after the death, Ray told me: "The part I hold myself responsible for is that I never attempted mouth-to-mouth resuscitation because I didn't know how. It seems like I should have known how."

Ray cried a little in the days that followed, but "by and large, I took a man-of-the-house attitude." Looking back on the months following the death, he recognized that he had begun suffering from symptoms of posttraumatic stress: nervousness, sweaty palms, muscle tension. It was not until fifteen years later that his grief was expressed in a direct way.

Ray was seeing a therapist to deal with what he thought were unrelated issues when the "watershed" event occurred. Ray described it: "I remember leaving the therapy session. We'd been talking about my dad. It was a rainy day. I was driving home. And I was just sobbing. It was like I was in synch with the rain. The rain was pouring down. My tears were pouring down. And it was clear what I was doing. I was grieving the death of my father. And I was grieving in a way I'd never grieved before. That unabashed grief, accompanied by loud sobbing noises and tears. And since then, it's been more fluid. I haven't been blocked. . . . I'm more open to hard [to deal with] feelings."

In the first years after the death, Ray regularly drank beer to numb himself to his pain. Heavy use of alcohol and other drugs was a common trait among Delayers. According to the men I surveyed, sons between eighteen and thirty-two were at least three times as likely as sons in any other age group to use alcohol or nonprescription drugs to help them cope in the first month following a father's death. By using substances, these men often succeeded in burying their immediate pain, only to experience it later. It's one reason that young adults so frequently turned up in the Delayer ranks.

Stanley Meyer, for example, lost his father when he was twenty-five; two years after that, his mother died. After each death, he went into "my iron-man mode," during which he papered over his emotions with marijuana and booze. He also used sex, he said, to blunt the pain of his losses.

As if to underscore his delaying tactics, Stanley refused to complete probate on his mother's will for nine years. When he was finally threatened with heavy fines, Stanley finished the paperwork. Not surprisingly, that's when his grief surfaced over the deaths. Stanley told me: "It was like I was disinterring my parents. I had to bring them up to bury them again." During this period, he cried over the deaths for the first time. The mourning went on for several months, he said. It was difficult but, he reported, it ultimately "showed me my own strength."

For Walter Wang, Ray Hyatt, and Stanley Meyer the death of the father was the first major loss of their lives. This was another common trait among Delayers. Sons who lacked experience with major losses seemed more likely to bury—consciously or not—the immediate pain of a father's death.

Marvin Russell was fifteen years old when his father died in a car accident. I talked to him seventeen years later. He told me that in the first months after the death, he felt little sadness, anger, or other emotion. He recalled having no interest in talking about the death, looking at pictures of his father, or spending time evaluating their relationship. While he was curious about his lack of emotion, he didn't worry about it.

Then, five years after the death, following the suicide of his brother, Marvin's mourning for his father began. He explained how it happened: "My father came into my dreams. A recurring theme was that he wasn't really dead but just hiding from the tax department. [In the dreams,] I felt an overwhelming urge to hug him. I was so glad to have him back and didn't want to let go. I wanted to be with him for the rest of my life."

The dreams, Marvin continued, "started the mourning process. Actually, they *were* the mourning process. They made me think about him, wonder about him, miss him. . . . My mother had always portrayed my father as a negative, impulsive, uncaring person. After these dreams, I think I broke free from this view of my father and started to thread together little pieces of objective information. It was like I used to see the world through my mother's eyes, and now I started to use my own."

Marvin was thirty-two years old, and a stay-at-home father of two, when we spoke. He still considered his dream life to be the chief avenue of mourning for his dad. Interestingly, over the dozen years that he'd been dreaming about his father, only one major change had occurred in the content of those nighttime visions. Whereas in the early dreams, his father had resisted Marvin's attempts to embrace him, in the more recent ones, the older man warmly accepted them.

———

While I characterized the sons we just met as Delayers, these men, and most other Delayers, generally also carried qualities of the last two major types of mourners, *Displayers* and *Doers*.

Among the sons I spoke with, Displayers were about as common as Dashers and Delayers; they also represented approximately one in five men. The primary trait of Displayers was a powerful, acute emotional reaction to the father's death. In the first weeks after the loss, these men often felt flooded, or overwhelmed, by sadness, fear, anger, or guilt. They tended to experience their grief as happening to them; they were not in control of it.

Here's how some Displayers described their process:

A psychologist who was forty years old at the time of the death: "Death has always been hard for me. I don't know why that is, but it is. After Dad died, I was just really devastated. I cried all the time. Getting up in the morning, in the shower, on the way to work. Listening to music, watching a movie, I'd come to tears. My mental capacities began to suffer, and I found myself . . . forgetting things, getting confused, with a lower attention span. It's constitutional. I'm a sensitive person, someone who feels things easily and doesn't defend against it. I often wonder how other people do it. There's a guy at work who lost both parents. I watch him. There's no difference in his behavior. How can he do that?"

A real-estate agent who was fifty-three when his dad died of Alzheimer's disease: "I thought the grieving would all be over after the funeral. But it didn't stop. . . . I cried a lot. I even cried with my sons. . . . I was very close to my mother, very close. But dad's death was more of a shock. I feel like it's the male connection. I could always depend upon him. 'Dad, the hot water heater went out. What do you think I should do?' . . . In the beginning, my business slid. I couldn't concentrate. I'd go over to the cemetery to talk with Dad. I think the whole grieving process will go on the rest of my life."

A business consultant who was thirty-nine: "What's helped the most are all the tears. At times I've felt embarrassed that it's such a tender spot for me. But I eventually just added that to the reality that this go-round in life, I have my feelings close to . . . the surface."

A mechanic who was thirty-six: "I had a real sense of despair. What's it all for? We live, we die, and what's left? My father had made a good salary for most of his life; he was an important person at the church. By the time he died, he had nothing. He left me a car that I sold for fifty dollars. . . . If it hadn't been for my kids, I might have just stayed in bed. I had this feeling about life—that I got up, went to work, came home, ate gruel, went to bed, and did it all over again. I kind of felt like I was waiting for it all to end."

For all of these men, the months after the death were emotionally erratic and draining. They felt the sadness of the loss powerfully, and could not, or preferred not to, avoid that feeling.

While sadness was the dominant feeling among the Displayers I spoke with, it was not the only one.

After his father's death, Ned Keith became extremely angry. Ned lost his father when he was forty. The father had abandoned him and his mother when Ned was five. His father was gone from Ned's life for a quarter-century, then had sporadic contact with him in the last decade of his life.

After the death, Ned told me, "I put up his picture on the wall. I couldn't walk by it without yelling, 'You son of a bitch!' " This went on for about six months before Ned's anger began to ebb. It helped that Ned got to meet a half brother who had grown up with the father. The half brother told Ned that their father was "distant even when he was there."

Another man I interviewed also had a powerful anger reaction—one that turned into violence—after his father died when the son was in his mid-twenties. The son had to quit graduate school after the death and took a low-wage job to help pay family bills. This frustrated him, and one of his sisters felt the brunt of his anger a few weeks after the death. The son recalled: "I told her not to get on me in the first five minutes after I got home [from work]. One day, she did. I had a jacket over my arm. I struck her across the face with it."

The last category of mourners was the largest: Doers. Among the sons I spoke with, about 40 percent seemed to fit most suitably into this category. Most of these men were deeply touched by the father's death, but unlike Displayers, tended not to be overwhelmed by their emotions.

What set Doers apart was their focus on *action*. In the last chapter, we saw how some sons took action—walking, driving somewhere, retracing steps of a trip with their dad—in the immediate aftermath of the father's death. For Doers, long after this initial shock, action continues to be their primary way of processing the loss. Most often, this action involves doing things that consciously connect them with the memory of the father. It is as if Doers believe that they can begin to let go of their dads only after they first connect more closely to them.

The Doers I spoke with chose a variety of creative methods to make a connection with the lost father. Perhaps the most common was to spend time with physical reminders: photos, tools, books, medals, and other mementos. According to my survey, 72 percent of men (including some who were not primarily Doers) used mementos to help them cope in the aftermath of the loss.

Several sons I spoke with placed great importance on their fathers' clothes. One thirty-four-year-old son, whose father had died at age seventy-two, sorted through his dad's closet after the death and took home shoes, jackets, shirts, and ties. "One brother was too big [to fit into the clothes]. The other brother was too small. I was his size, exactly," the son recalled of his father. He added, "There were times I was completely dressed in his clothes. It was a very positive thing." I talked with this son four years after the death, and he said he had thrown out, or worn out, most of his dad's clothes. But he still had a jacket that he wore on days when he planned to meet one of his brothers.

Frank Hernandez, the man from the last chapter who had taken his father into his home, also kept most of his father's clothes after the death. He kept other items too. On a small wooden table in the corner of his den, Frank placed the folded pajamas and reading glasses his father had worn during the time he'd lived with Frank. Next to those, Frank set a photo of his dad as a young man and a commemorative plate from the father's hometown. Finally, Frank placed on the table the ivory urn containing his father's ashes. "I put [the shrine] in a spot where maybe it was out of the way. I thought it might have unnerved some [visitors]," Frank recalled. Frank liked to spend time at the shrine himself, sometimes only fleetingly. "I took time to reflect for a few moments, and then went on. It was a way to give honor and respect."

Of his father's clothes, Frank said: "I put them in boxes, and kept them" after the death. "Over the next few years, I moved five times. Each time, I'd give some of the clothes away. The last time I moved, I gave the last box to Goodwill."

Gary Isikoff, the one-time Hospice volunteer from Chapter 5, kept his father's wallet in the drawer of his desk at the union office where he worked. Gary, who was forty-three when his dad died, reported: "Sometimes, when I'm filing away a medical form, or pension check stub, I'll pull my dad's wallet out and look inside. I'll open up one of the scraps of paper he kept in there, maybe a note about a part for the dishwasher, and look at the neat printing or writing, and just imagine my dad writing it."

Gary also saved the .22-caliber rifle that his father had taught him to fire and clean, a few tools, and a copy of one of his father's favorite books of poetry. Gary had placed another copy in the father's casket.

In addition to using physical items to connect themselves with their deceased fathers, Doers also used places. In the months after his father's death, for example, Gary occasionally visited the attic in the home where he'd grown up. It gave him a chance to remember the summer of his twelfth year, when he and his father worked together refurbishing the upstairs room.

They had never completed the job. But sitting in the half-finished space after the death, Gary "got a rich feeling" as he remembered "that summer of no bedtimes, and the smell of sawdust and Old Spice." Gary recalled the summer well: "My dad was almost tender in the way he would show me how to drill, or have me complete some task. I really wasn't much interested in the actual work, or how things were done mechanically. I was just happy to be with my dad, to be in close physical proximity, to admire his muscle and be part of a man's job."

A construction worker who was forty-one when his father died took a road trip—from his own home in Wyoming to the Florida home in which his dad had last lived. Along with his two brothers and a nephew, this son "threw a few sleeping bags" into a van with no backseats and drove more than thirty hours straight. The son recalled: "When we got to my father's house, we loaded everything up. Then we took our time coming back. Four days on the road." Years later, the son remembered the road trip fondly: "I sure do miss those pancake houses."

Sal Pierce had to go only as far as his backyard to create an extraordinary connection with his father. Sal, who was sixty-four when I spoke with him, was fifteen years old when his father died. On the night of the death, he recalled, he cried by "the roots of a monstrous elm tree until my grandma came out to sit and comfort me." That was the bulk of his grieving until nearly three decades later. As Sal approached the age of his father's death, he told me, he used birthdays and death certificates to calculate a particularly poignant moment in time. "Then," Sal said, "when that hour arrived, I remember sitting in a chair by the pool, thinking 'this is the exact moment. I'm as old as Dad was when he died.' " Sal couldn't pinpoint the benefit of this act, but felt he was "honoring" his father by carrying it through.

The concept of *honoring* was repeatedly mentioned by Doers as their inspiration for their actions. One man I interviewed was a college English teacher; he always found a way to work into his curriculum one of the books his father had loved. Another son took over his father's company after his dad had died. A third set up a foundation to combat the disease that had killed his father. A fourth, whose father had taken his own life, became a volunteer suicide counselor.

An accountant who lost his father at age twenty told me about an act of honoring he had performed soon after his father's death. The man's father had been a professional baseball player in the 1940s. When the father died, the son was a collegiate player, and the season had just begun. The younger man was deeply shaken by the death, but also felt that "my father would want me to get back on the field." So he returned to the lineup a week after the death. Two decades later, the son told me: "I can remember standing at home plate on my first at bat [after the death], with my knees shaking, and hitting the ball at the pitcher. He caught the ball and I was out, but it didn't matter. I knew my father would have wanted me to [play]."

Why does honoring the father and connecting with his memory help sons in their mourning? Maryland psychotherapist Thomas Golden, a specialist in men's mourning, sees grief as an accumulation of energy in the body; the purpose of mourning, he told me, is to release that energy. Generally, Golden said, men are less comfortable than women with dramatic release, preferring "to slowly, deliberately chip away" at the grief. Masculine mourners will often intentionally suppress their sadness during certain times, then consciously bring it up at a later time. Golden calls this practice "sampling;" other psychologists have referred to it as "dosing."

Golden, himself a Doer, has written a book on the masculine approach to grief, *Swallowed by a Snake*, and frequently writes about his father's life and death. Golden is not alone among Doers. According to my survey, about 25 percent of men wrote about their fathers, or to their fathers, after the death.

Sometimes writing offered a son a chance to crystallize his thoughts at a difficult moment. Jesse Hefner, whose dad committed suicide when Jesse was thirty-six, wrote a letter to his father a couple of days after the death. Then he placed it in his father's casket. Three years later, he shared a copy with me. It read, in part: "It's been three days since you shot yourself, and I still don't understand. I know how much you loved us all. You showed that through your whole life, especially the last few weeks, trying to finish up things. But if you loved us so much, how could you have done this, knowing what pain it could cause us? . . . Why couldn't you just say, 'I need help?' "

Jesse told me that writing helped him articulate his greatest fears.

"I'm just like you," he said in the letter, "and that scares me so much right now. I hear those voices of worthlessness too. What am I going to do?" One thing Jesse did was get help; he joined a suicide survivor group.

Researchers at State University of New York and North Dakota State University recently found that writing can have a therapeutic effect, at least in some circumstances. In a 1999 study of patients with asthma and rheumatoid arthritis, the researchers found that those patients who wrote in a journal about the most stressful experience they'd ever undergone showed marked improvement in their disease state; those who wrote for the same amount of time about something mundane or innocuous, showed no improvement at all.

The authors of the study suggested that releasing emotion around a stressful incident, through writing, may boost a person's immune system. No studies have been conducted to see how this works with the bereaved, but Paul Harris, one of the men in my survey, found that writing helped recapture a dramatic memory and jump-start his mourning.

Paul was forty-three when his father died after a long illness. Upon hearing the news by phone, Paul recalled, he got up from his easy chair, poured himself a glass of whisky, and remarked to himself: "This should be momentous. Why doesn't it feel momentous?" It was, Paul remembered, "as if I was in a trance."

Until this time, Paul had always thought of himself as coming from "a pretty bland, suburban, boring family. . . . My parents were churchgoing people. Both of my grandfathers were ministers." Paul recalled that generally, he and his father fought in high school, often about politics (it was the 1960s), and sometimes about the father's assessment of the son as irresponsible. Paul was glad to leave his father's home at eighteen.

Through his twenties and thirties, Paul struggled in his career as an artist. He earned little money, which fed both his and his father's image of Paul as inept. Paul maintained a perfunctory relationship with his mother and father during this time, but felt it necessary to ask them for money to help support himself, a young wife, and their first of two children.

The father began a ten-year physical deterioration when he was sixty-seven and Paul was thirty-three. During this period of decline, the two men didn't communicate much. After the death, the son's indifference continued for some time. When he thought of his father, there was only a vague feeling of disgust. But when marriage problems arose at about this time, Paul started writing in a journal each day as a way of sorting out his thoughts. It was in this daily writing that he came upon a crucial revelation.

One day, words poured off his pen that he did not intend to write and that held no apparent meaning at first. The words were: "Hit me again, motherfucker!" As they appeared on the paper, Paul recalled, a terrible tremble shook his body.

A few days later, on a trip to New York City, Paul shared the journal entry with his younger brother Anthony. It struck a chord with Anthony too, and soon, over dinner, the two men were piecing together the outlines of a violent childhood both of them had substantially repressed. "We talked until the sun came up," Paul recalled. "We had never talked honestly in our lives. We had never compared memories. . . . The next morning, the world had changed. I had an awareness that there was a reason for much of the way I felt and [how I] dealt with my life."

The revelations from his writing spurred Paul to more action. First, he initiated conversations with his mother, who acknowledged that the abuse had occurred and that she'd felt powerless to stop it; the father had beaten her too, she said. Paul then contacted other relatives as well, who suggested that the father might have learned his abusive behavior from his own dad. Paul's grandfather, it turned out, had been so violent that one of his sons had run away from home in the middle of the night. Paul also joined a men's group, at which he was encouraged to unleash any rage he felt toward his dad.

When I met Paul, a self-reflective man with shoulder-length brown hair, it had been three years since the death. His anger toward his dad was diminishing. He told me: "The compassion I have for my father is [that] we share a similar childhood"—each had been beaten by his father. Paul said he could "see the energy being released" by bringing up his old memories of abuse. And he added: "Now I just think, God willing, as I plow through this, the rest of my life will be great."

Most of the Doers I spoke with took action that was in some way connected to their fathers. But in a few cases, sons told me they were helped by doing things that diverted their attention from their loss and memories.

A maintenance man who was twenty-three when his father died of cancer said that in the weeks after the death, he spent an hour or two a day drawing designs on paper. The designs did not directly represent his father, he said. Rather, since his teens, he'd found that he "could draw for a while and the negative feelings would pass. It would take me away from the situation for a while. It got me through hard times."

I talked with this man three years after the death and asked him if he thought he might have been avoiding deeper emotions by drawing. He didn't think so. He said he felt sad a lot in the weeks after the loss and that cartooning helped him when he was overwhelmed. "It relieves stress," he told me. "It's instead of smoking or drinking."

Another man I spoke with, a retired machinist who lost his father at age forty-one, told me he coped with the death in part by going fishing every day. "I fish on the Missouri River. I'm a hundred percent out there with nature. I really enjoy that. Me and the fish and nature." Mostly, this son said, fishing helped him "forget about everything." Occasionally, however, he'd think about his father, with whom he did not get along for most of his life. "I have forgiven him for a lot of bad stuff he did in my life, a-settin' out there."

Several men told me that going back to work was valuable in helping them through the loss. One man, a social worker who returned to work after a three-day bereavement leave, said: "I enjoy helping." His daily contact with disadvantaged people, he said, reminded him that "there are a lot of serious things happening other than my own problems."

The Canadian psychologist Philip Carverhill has found that working can be helpful for men in grief, in combination with other forms of emotional release. Work, Carverhill wrote in a 1997 article on men's grief, may "serve as a setting in which the bereaved male feels that he has some semblance of control during a very uncontrollable time."

Few men fit neatly into just one of these four categories of grievers. If I had met Paul Harris—the man who discovered his abuse while journaling—in the weeks immediately after his father's death, I might have labeled him a Dasher, not a Doer; he betrayed no emotion at the time. A year after that, as Paul started remembering his father's abuse, he had strong emotional reactions. At that point, he may have fit the definition of a Delayer.

What matters, of course, is not whether a man can label himself, but whether he can understand, and accept, his particular style of grieving. Drs. Terry Martin and Kenneth Doka, coauthors of *Men Don't Cry, Women Do: Transcending Gender Stereotypes of Grief*, have found that men are more likely than women to be intellectual, action-oriented mourners, but that the important task for a member of either sex is determining one's own style. Doka told me: "We experience grief differently, we express grief differently. The key to successfully dealing with a loss is to recognize your own adaptive strategies and use them effectively."

For example, a man who tends to feel a lot of emotion after a loss, but suppresses it because he doesn't want to appear unmanly, may be risking his health. "That's the one you hear about who five years down the road has ulcerative colitis, alcoholism, is extremely depressed, and quits his job," Martin told me. On the other hand, Martin added, if a man doesn't feel a strong sense of loss after a death, it doesn't automatically mean that he's suppressing his real feelings.

Some people would label as "crippled" a man who doesn't feel losses intensely. But Martin, who is a psychology professor at Hood College in Maryland, contends that emotions are sometimes over-rated in American culture. "The whole emphasis has been that feelings are the real key" to a full life, Martin said. "Frankly, playing with a great idea for me is as rewarding as being stirred emotionally."

Martin believes there are reasonable explanations for the masculine tendency toward emotional reticence, and they have their roots in men's longstanding social role as protectors. He explained: "If you're out there defending the walls from the barbarians, after the initial attack, you can't afford to look around at your dead companions and start grieving. You have to pull it together for the next wave."

Ultimately, Martin and Doka say, grieving for most men and women tends to involve a mixture of emotion, thought, and action—a mixture that varies with each individual. One grief counselor I spoke with said he tries to remind himself, and his clients, that "there are as many ways to grieve as there are people in the world."

Christiaan Barnard

—⚬—

On December 3, 1967, an ambitious and charismatic South
African surgeon named Christiaan Barnard cut out the diseased
heart of a grocer and replaced it with a healthy one from a twenty-
five-year-old woman who'd died hours earlier in a car accident. It
was the first human heart transplant, and with it, Barnard
demonstrated concretely that the death of one person could
improve the lives of others left behind.

It was a lesson that Barnard had learned, in a far more personal
and subtle way, when his father had died nearly a decade before.

At that earlier time, Barnard was a thirty-five-year-old father of
two, married for ten years to a nurse named Louwtjie. Throughout
their marriage, Dr. Barnard had been focused on his career. He
had just come back to South Africa after two years in the United
States, most of it spent without his family. Upon his return, he'd
found Louwtjie bitterly angry. "Why did you come back?" he
later recalled her asking. "Why didn't you stay in America and

never come home again? . . . We have ceased to exist for you."

The marriage at that point was close to ending. But then Christiaan Barnard experienced what he called "one of life's cruelest events," the death of his father. On the day of the death, from stomach cancer, Christiaan got a message at the Capetown hospital where he worked, telling him to come quickly to his father's home. The older man lived several hours away by car, and Christiaan sped to reach him. But he was too late. When he heard that his father had called out for him in his last moments, the son was overwhelmed with guilt.

"I could stand no more and went into the bedroom alone," he recalled in his autobiography, *One Life*. "[Family members] wanted to come in and comfort me, but I did not want them. I was beyond help. I wept for my father, and I wept for myself and how I had failed all those who wanted more from me than I could ever give them."

The next day, at the funeral, Christiaan sat beside Louwtjie. He later recalled that the tension between them began to soften. As a letter from Christiaan's father was read, Louwtjie took her husband's hand. And at the graveside, they listened together to the words Christiaan's father had selected for a reading: "This is my commandment: Love one another as I have loved you."

It was on the long drive back to Capetown that the reconciliation with Louwtjie seemed complete. Christiaan described the scene in his autobiography.

> *Louwtjie sat close to me, and for awhile we said nothing. Then a truck bore down on us and I was almost forced off the road.*
> *"Are you all right, darling?" she asked.*
> *"Yes."*
> *It had been years since she had called me darling.*

"I loved your father," she said.

"Yes."

"He was like my father—more than my father."

Then she said: "Is it all right if I sit close while you're driving?"

"Come closer."

She lay her hand on me and we joined hands with palms touching.

So it happened that my father in his dying left . . . [the] gift of understanding through love. Within it, he had returned Louwtjie to my side.

The reconciliation, like the South African grocer's new heart, did not last forever. The heart recipient, Louis Washkansky, lived eighteen days before pneumonia claimed him. The Barnard marriage continued on for a decade beyond the father's death, then went into a downward spiral soon after the Washkansky transplant.

In 1969, after twenty-one years of marriage, Louwtjie filed for divorce.

I became a man the day my father died. Nothing in my life gave me more clarity and a stronger sense of responsibility. I've become a better lover, a closer friend and a kinder stranger.
—ACTOR MATTHEW MCCONAUGHEY

Chapter 8

HOW SPOUSES HELP

IN THE 1989 MOVIE *Field of Dreams*, Kevin Costner plays Ray Kinsella, a seemingly levelheaded, thirty-six-year-old family farmer who is tending his Iowa cornfield one summer day when he hears a disembodied voice: "If you build it, he will come." Ray takes this cryptic comment as encouragement to plow under his lush corn crop and replace it with a baseball diamond. Still, the voice is not satisfied. Soon, Ray is motoring his Volkswagen van to Boston to meet a reclusive author, then heading off to a small town in Minnesota in search of an obscure ballplayer from the 1920s. Through all these adventures, Ray knows his strange behavior has something to do with his deceased dad. But only as the movie moves toward its conclusion do we learn the importance of Ray's "field of dreams": It is both the location for a reunion with his dad, and the symbol of Ray's declaration of independence from a father who, according to Ray, "never did one spontaneous thing" in his life.

Ray's quest to make peace with his father is the central theme of the film, which was nominated for an Academy Award for best picture. But no character in the movie seems more heroic than Ray's wife, Annie, played by the high-spirited, raspy-voiced Amy Madigan. Skeptical when Ray first broaches the subject of "the voice," she gradually becomes her husband's most ardent ally as he faces tests of will, stamina, and faith.

In one early scene, after helping her husband mow down their cornfield, Annie surveys the project alongside Ray. "I have just created something totally illogical," Ray says with wonder. Annie responds: "That's what I like about it."

A few scenes later, Ray tells Annie that the voice has returned. She's sarcastic at first: "You don't have to build a *football* field now, do you?" But ultimately, even as their farm's solvency is threatened, Annie continues to encourage Ray in his drive for closure with his dad. In the movie's poignant final scene, Ray is seen tossing a baseball with the ghost of his father as dusk falls over his magical field. When darkness threatens to end the game of catch, it is Annie who flips on the floodlights so the two men can continue to play.

As *Field of Dreams* demonstrates, losing a father can be a formidable challenge for a son. And it can be just as challenging for the son's spouse or partner. Following the death of his father, a bereaved son may become tearful, fearful, angry, aloof, confused, impulsive, or all of these at once. He may have a sudden interest in sex or become averse to it. On rare occasions, he might even question whether he's chosen the right person with whom to share his life.

Like Ray and Annie Kinsella, however, the vast majority of couples survive intact. According to my survey, sons who were in committed relationships when their fathers died were twice as likely in the two years afterward to experience an improvement in their relationships rather than a worsening. One reason for this may be the psychological growth that so many men go through after the death of their fathers. Nearly 40 percent of men in my survey said they felt more mature in the two years after the loss. Along with this rise in maturity, in many cases, came a realization of how precious their love relationships were.

But there was another, perhaps more compelling, reason for improvements in marriages and committed relationships after the death. Eighty-nine percent of men I surveyed said that on the whole, their spouses or partners were helpful to them during their reemergence from the loss of their fathers. Men told me that, like Ray Kinsella, they felt accepted and respected during their mourning—and that this support from their partners translated ultimately into a closer, stronger bond.

The men highlighted three areas of partner support that seemed to be most beneficial.

The first could be called *Holding Down the Fort*. Especially in the period just before and after a father's death, the son's regular routine was often disrupted. Some had to leave town abruptly or spend many hours at a hospital. Sometimes the emotional impact of the event left a son temporarily immobilized. In these cases, a wife or partner often helped most by, quite literally, taking care of business.

One college administrator told me he visited the hospital nearly every day for a month as his father died of cancer. During that period, he said, his wife handled the shopping, cleaning, and virtually all other routine household duties. The administrator said of his wife: "She didn't lay any expectations on me. I knew she would do anything, and would anticipate my needs. And she was flexible about what we had to do, where we had to go."

This man, who was forty-seven at the time of the death, had been married for nearly twenty years. His wife's assistance during his dad's final days, he said, "allowed me to concentrate on being there for my father."

Another son, a department store manager, who was not living near his father during the last days, depended on his wife on the evening his mother called with the news of the death. The father had suffered from cancer, and the end had been expected. But in the first hours, the son was dazed and unable to act.

His wife of eighteen years took over. As the son recalled, she was up until 3 A.M. that first night, making arrangements to transport the family the thousand miles to her husband's family home. To obtain the bereavement fare, she had to first secure a copy of the death certificate, then fax it to the airline before booking the flight. The son had regained his wits by the time they reached his hometown, but throughout the first week, he recalled: "A problem would come up, and she and I would look at each other and say: 'Who can take care of it?' We were a team."

For couples who had kids, holding down the fort often meant temporarily taking over primary responsibility for parenting. Jesse Hefner, who was thirty-six when his father committed suicide, felt he needed to focus on his mother on the day of the death. She was so traumatized by her husband's suicide that she fled to the basement and didn't emerge for thirteen hours. At the same time, however, Jesse's seven-year-old son was reeling. Upon hearing the news, the boy got on his bicycle and rode back and forth, back and forth, for three hours in front of the house.

"The most important thing [my wife did] at the beginning was to see what kind of help we needed for our son," Jesse told me. The boy "was trying to make sense of this totally nonsensical thing. . . . I was torn. I wanted to be with him. But I was trying to keep Mom from going completely under."

Beyond taking over extra parenting and household duties, many partners took on another supporting role: *Anchoring*. Several men I spoke with actually used the word "anchor" to describe their partners in the period just after the loss. It was during this time that the man was most likely to lose his psychological equilibrium.

Most often, anchoring was accomplished nonverbally. Here was how some men described it:

A store manager who was thirty-nine years old at the death of his father: "She was in my corner, so to speak, trying to make the best of a terrible situation. She was a major comfort. At times like this, a real good hug means more than words. I know this sounds kind of trite, but that hug and holding meant more to me than I can say. Maybe it was . . . the feeling that you know you are not in this alone. Your loss is being shared."

A psychologist who was forty-nine when his father died: "I remember returning to the church after the eulogy. At that point, [my wife] touched my arm. It was a very light touch. But the message was she was with me. . . . Grieving is always at least to some degree solitary. This didn't make it wholly solitary."

A musician who was forty-four when his father died: "I think the most helpful thing [my partner] did after Dad died was to take bereavement leave, fly down to California [from Seattle], and just be with me. We went through the Christmas holidays together, and with my family. It helped keep a sense of normalcy——that whether or not my parents were gone, he and I would go on."

A real-estate agent who was fifty-three at the father's death: "She accepts me where I am with my emotions and my grieving. Initially, I'd be at work. I'd call her to make contact. I'd immediately tell what kind of day I was having. The littlest thing would trigger grief. Initially, after trying to disguise it in a manly way, I know now that I can tell [her] that this has triggered something and I'm upset. She doesn't push it aside or say, 'Oh, get over it.' She's lost both of her parents. She's just there. She doesn't have to say anything. I just know that she's in sympathy with me."

When a man feels anchored, when he's secure that all of his life is not in turmoil, he's usually more willing to accept the next dimension of partner support: what I call *Sorting the Deck*. Most men I interviewed wanted to talk with their partners about their fathers and their loss. But the manner in which such conversations were carried out—and especially the way they were initiated—was a major factor in determining whether they had value for the man.

One son told me there were a number of tense moments between him and his wife in the first weeks after his father had died of a sudden heart attack. "We'd be just tooling along in the car and something would trigger me," recalled this man, who was thirty-seven at the time. Sometimes he heard a song on the radio that reminded him of his father or saw a man who looked like him. "I'd go silent, withdraw. And she'd start asking: 'Are you okay? What are you feeling? What's wrong?' "

The questioning was too insistent, the son remembered, and he'd sometimes tell his wife that he didn't want to talk. She'd then act hurt or refuse to back off. "She'd keep prodding, forcing it out." Rather than helping him, the son said, the prying became "an irritant."

Another man, who was thirty-five and was struggling in his marriage at the time of the death, had a similar experience with his wife. "The way things are phrased has always been a big deal" in their seven-year relationship, this son told me. "It either puts on the pressure, or not. . . . Sometimes she would say to me: 'You can't keep it inside forever.' " When he heard that, the son told me, "I turned away."

The difference between these approaches and ones that encouraged men to open up was, according to several men I spoke with, the difference between an *invasion* and an *invitation*. When a partner prodded or pushed, men tended to pull back. When the partner offered an opportunity to talk, most said they were willing to take it.

One son who had struggled with his wife at first on this issue, said he was much more open after she "got over the idea that she could make things better. She realized that she didn't have to try to control my emotions. She stopped trying to steer me. She started to say: 'If you want to talk about it, I'll be here.' And sometimes I would talk to her."

Another man said of his wife: "She gave me space. If I wanted to talk, or she did, we would. But there was no pressure. She'd ask: 'Do you want to talk about your dad?' That usually was the starter. For me, the less pressure to talk, the easier it was."

Once a conversation began, some men were very interested in what their partners had to say. In the weeks after his loss, one sixty-three-year-old son told me, he was "wrestling a little about not having a strong reaction. There were few tears." His wife of fifteen years sat with him and helped him sort out his thoughts. "She reminded me that [my father] had been sick [for five years], and I had been grieving for a long time. . . . She was a centering influence. She was very good at offering suggestions, and balancing my remarks."

The majority of men I interviewed, however, told me they were helped not so much by what their partners said, but by partners who listened to them. "On the first date with my wife, I'd fallen in love with her because she listened," a minister, who was twenty-two when his father died, said of his wife. "Most people I know are not good listeners." After this man's father died, whenever he wanted to talk about it, his wife was, he said, "a ready ear."

Another son said he received "total empathy" from his partner, a man with whom he'd been in a committed relationship for more than twenty-five years. When the son's father died, the partner happened to be tending to his own terminally ill mother in another city. The son said he and his partner spent hours on the phone during the first nights after the death. "Funeral arrangements, nursing home [issues], encounters with the family—this is what we talked about," he said. "We probably sounded like two consultants. But that's what we needed."

Weeks later, after the couple was together again, the son I spoke with said his partner listened well. The son told me: "He has a marvelous ability to let me babble. We'd be sitting there. I'd go on for an hour or so [about the death], and then I'd wake up and say, 'You just let me babble on.' He'd say: 'I enjoy hearing you talk.' "

About 11 percent of men in my survey said their wives or partners were not helpful in the aftermath of the death. A teacher, Henry Ravich, told me he sought support from his wife when his emotions around his father's death resurfaced after being buried for years.

Henry was twenty when his father died. He met his wife-to-be five years later and married her a couple of years after that. In the first decade of their marriage, Henry rarely mentioned his dad, but as he neared middle age, memories from childhood and adolescence began to surface. He tried sharing them with his wife. At first, she listened, but she eventually tired of the talk, Henry said.

When I spoke with Henry, it had been twenty-five years since the death. He spoke of his wife with sadness: "Sometimes I'll start talking to her about my father, telling a story. She'll get irritated, and say: 'I've heard that story. I've heard that story.' It's true that I do sometimes repeat them. But there are times I wish she'd just listen. Maybe there's a new wrinkle. Maybe I just want to talk."

Given the needs of some men after the death of their fathers, it was not surprising that relationships occasionally came under great pressure. Previous research has found that up to 46 percent of relationships undergo a crisis after one partner loses a parent. One researcher discovered that negative feelings that were previously reserved for the parent "can become suddenly and brutally projected onto the spouse." Another wrote: "People who are bereaved may be more likely to be ill, depressed, lethargic, anxious, heavily using alcohol, lacking sleep, or disorganized." Given this, he continued, it's no wonder relationship difficulties often ensued.

While many of the men I spoke with experienced relationship tensions after the father's death, my survey found that only about 10 percent of men said their relationship actually got worse during the two years following the father's death. Among the sons I spoke with, the relationships that struggled most tended to be those that were still fairly new or in which the partners were young.

In one case, a forty-six-year-old architect told me that after his father had died, his forty-something wife started to look like "an old woman" to him. He became angry with her easily and considered having sex outside the relationship. Before he actually had an affair, however, he saw that his new view of his wife might be related to his father's death.

"I was afraid of getting old and dying," he explained matter-of-factly four years after his father's death. His wife, he later decided, was "a mirror" for him; by pushing away from her, he was perhaps trying to push away from his own aging process. This man saw a therapist for about two years. When I spoke with him, he told me his marriage had survived the crisis.

In another case, a twenty-six-year-old man who had been married for three years, demanded a lot of space after the sudden death of his father. His wife did not object. But then the man began going to bars and having affairs. When I spoke with this man, fifteen years later, he blamed himself. "I was out of control, thinking I needed to grab for the gusto," he recalled. He added that he was not satisfied in the marriage before his father's death and may have used the event as an "excuse" to create a crisis. The couple was divorced a year after the death.

Several men told me they had experienced a heightened desire for sex in the first weeks after their father's death. For these men, sex acted as both an intoxicant—a temporary escape—and a sign that life could continue to bring pleasure as well as pain. Said one: "We had fantastic, life-affirming sex the day after Dad's death. The long pressure of Dad's decline was over, and I think we were acknowledging that we were still here and were joyfully connected."

James Haddad, who was forty years old when his father died, had just the opposite reaction. He had been married to his wife, Carrie, for fifteen years, and their sex life had generally been satisfying. Then, a couple of months after his father's death, he recalled, "My libido dropped off almost completely. It was difficult for me to function sexually. . . . Part of me wanted to have sex, but it felt like it was more work than it was fun. Then also there was the physical side of it. It was harder for me to get an erection. It was harder for me to maintain an erection. It felt like my body was mush. There was that ever-present sadness. Really, instead of having sex, I wanted to cry."

When I met James three years after the death, he said he knew the situation had tried his wife's patience. "She was worried I'd get stuck there." But she reacted with acceptance, James said. "The feeling I got from her was: 'I'm rooting for you to get over it. If there are things I can do, let me know.' . . . Sometimes, we just had physical contact. She made it clear that it didn't have to be shooting-stars sex. It could be fizzling-stars sex."

Interestingly, James said he was never afraid that his impotence was permanent. After previous deaths in his life, he'd noticed that he reacted more strongly than most men. He figured the symptoms of his grief would eventually end.

He was right. About a year after his struggles had started, they began to ease. It took perhaps six months beyond that before he was back to normal. Speaking of his wife, James told me: "She was very patient, very sweet. . . . We knew each other well enough so there was no threat to the relationship."

Among the nearly three dozen single men I spoke with, none entered into a permanent relationship in the first six months after their father's death. One man, who was thirty-one at his father's death, found a new girlfriend in another city soon after the death and spent thousands of dollars (from his father's life insurance) on gifts, trips, and loans to the woman. "It was a time of amazing possibility. It was one of the more emotionally intense times in my life," this man said. "I had this feeling: 'Don't put things off. Go for it.' "

The relationship lasted a year, then collapsed. Looking back a dozen years later, the man acknowledged that there was "a bit of a feeling of being on the rebound" after his father died. He added: "I guess there was an element of living large to avoid feeling small."

A public-relations man who was twenty-six and single when his father died, hooked up soon after the death with "a caregiver type. . . . I was putting out 'I'm hurting' vibes and she responded. But then she went back to workaholic mode and I wasn't getting anywhere near what I was looking for emotionally." The relationship ended after a few months.

Interestingly, while other studies have found that social support can be crucial for the bereaved, unpartnered men in my survey were no more likely to have problems dealing with the death than those with partners. It seemed that bereaved sons who lacked partners and spouses and wanted support sought it from other friends and relatives.

There was another tension that occasionally arose in the relationships of men who had just experienced the death of a father. In my survey, about half of the men said their relationships with their mothers changed after the death. Sons told me they often felt an extra responsibility to care for their mothers—to become the man of *her* house, now that her man was gone. This became a problem when the extra attention toward the mother left the man's wife or partner feeling abandoned.

Christopher Chen, an only child who was thirty-eight when his father died, visited his mother almost daily in the weeks after the death. She lived about twenty miles away, in a suburb of Philadelphia, in an old home with a big yard. Christopher's mother did not speak English, so he feared that she would become isolated; he knew she was depressed and afraid.

"I felt it was my duty to mow the lawn, fix things up at her house, keep her company—the stuff my father always did," Christopher said. For about three months, Christopher's wife, Deborah, said nothing about his frequent absences. Then she began objecting to them. If he was going to spend his evenings and weekends doing home maintenance, she told him, there were plenty of opportunities around their own place.

By then, however, Christopher's mother had become accustomed to, and even dependent upon, her son's regular visits, so she voiced concerns when he reduced his time there. Christopher attempted to solve the problem by hiring maintenance people to do the work he had done for his mom. That reduced the frequency of his visits, as well as the tension in his relationship with his wife. However, when I spoke with Christopher, six years after the death, he said, "I still cringe inside every time I have to tell [Deborah] I'm going to fix the toilet at my mother's house."

Another man, an only child who was thirty-seven when his father died, felt a similar pull between his wife and mother. "I was out in the DMZ," he said, referring to the alleged safe zone between warring armies. "Whichever direction [I went], I was going to take fire. It was a time that I thought I couldn't make a right decision."

There are, of course, no easy solutions to these tensions in marriages and committed relationships. Those relationships in which couples had built trust, and where the partners had strong communication skills, were understandably most resilient to the pressures that arose after a family death. The length of each relationship seems to have been a factor too in its ability to weather the crisis. According to my survey, the relationships of men over fifty-five were least likely to be strained by the loss, while the relationships of young adults— those between eighteen and thirty-two—were most likely to be threatened. Among the latter group, nearly one in five men who were in committed relationships said the relationship got worse in the two years after a father's death.

As we saw in Chapter 1, a son who is a child when his father dies may experience adult relationship problems that have their roots in the early loss. Conflicts around trust and emotional openness seemed to be most prevalent among these men.

One son I interviewed, who'd lost his father at age twelve, got married for the first time at age twenty-three. He said, in retrospect, that he was trying to re-create the family he'd lost when his father had died. The marriage ended quickly, he said, in large part because he was incapable of being open with his wife. When he moved out, he left behind a two-year-old daughter, with whom he has never reconnected.

A few years later, this son remarried. Though he was in his seventeenth year of that union when we talked, he recognized that the toughness and autonomy he'd adopted to help absorb his father's death continued to hurt him in his marriage. "The biggest complaint [my wife] has is my inability to let people help me. If I'm sick, put me in the bedroom and close the door." He said his father's death "made me an independent person, emotionally as well as in every other way. It's easy to say I'm on my own. But it's hard in a marriage."

Earlier in this chapter, I recounted the story of a man whose wife became frustrated when he repeated childhood stories about his father. She told him he was fixated on the loss and ought to get over it. That kind of reaction was rare among the partners of the sons I interviewed. More frequently, partners of men who suffered an early father-death saw it as part of their role to tend to the primal wound.

One example: Phil Bernstein, who lost his father at age eleven, met Dana, his wife-to-be, on the first day of college. At that point in his life, Phil didn't talk with anybody about his loss. That changed quickly with Dana: "One of the first times we went out, I told her about my father. I remember I was getting choked up because I really didn't talk about it much. The fact that I was even mentioning it meant something special was going on with this woman."

Soon, Phil learned that Dana had lost an eleven-year-old sister in an accident about a decade earlier. He found it curious that she didn't mind talking about the sister while he continued to feel edgy talking about his father. Gradually, though, he began to drop his guard. Dana helped.

Phil explained: "She wouldn't say, 'Let's sit down [and talk].' Something would just come up, and she'd unlock the door. She once asked, 'How did your father die, exactly?' And I could say only that he'd had a heart attack. But it made me want to know more. So I started asking questions of my mother, and that started a whole chain of people talking. We ended up having a lot of conversations where afterward you feel drained, but you're the better for having had [them]."

Today, about a quarter-century after the death, Phil told me he finds it "enjoyable" to talk about his dad.

More than anything else, what helped Phil was the empathy he felt from his wife. She'd been through a terrible loss herself, and he could trust her to understand his reactions to his loss. Commitment was important too. In words and deeds, Dana made it clear she loved him as he was, whether he chose to revisit his early loss or not.

And there was something else too: patience. Dana did not push. Implicit in the comments of almost every man I interviewed was the desire that his partner not hurry him. Most men hurry themselves, eager for something "productive" to come from the swirl of thought and emotion inside them. From others, and especially their partners, they spoke of a need for "tolerance" of their moods, acceptance of their pace, and permission to be wrong.

In the words of one man, who acknowledged being "a jerk" at times to his girlfriend in the period after his father's death: "The most important thing a partner can do is to send the message: 'Look, I know you're going to be in a weird place for a while. Know that you have a license . . . to deal with it however you choose.' "

H. L. Mencken

—◊◊◊—

Even when a son admires and cares for his father, the death of the father can be liberating. That was the case with Henry Louis Mencken, the cigar-chomping, acid-penned literary and cultural critic widely considered the most influential newspaper writer of the twentieth century. If it hadn't been for the early death of his father—"the luckiest thing that ever happened to me," he would later write—H. L. Mencken might have spent his life making cigars instead of chewing on them.

Mencken's life began in 1880 in the Baltimore bourgeoisie. His father, August, the son of a German immigrant, had early dreams of becoming an engineer, but eventually opened a cigar factory instead. The business was successful, and the boy they called "Harry" got a private, formal elementary education under the tutelage of a German-born schoolmaster.

Though sickly and socially awkward, young Mencken was an academic success, and writing was his forte. He spent much of his free time with the books he pulled from his father's shelves. He later recalled that reading Mark Twain's *Adventures of Huckleberry Finn* was "probably the most stupendous event of my whole life." Decades afterward, Mencken's satirical tone would at times be compared to Twain's.

Mencken always had a fondness and respect for his father. But entering his teens, tension was added to the mix. Biographer Fred Hobson believes Mencken's father probably pushed the boy into going to Baltimore Manual Training School, a technical high school, hoping his son would fulfill the father's lost dream of becoming an engineer.

Mencken, known later for his iconoclasm, did not rebel at first and eventually graduated first in his class at the age of fifteen. Instead of engineering, however, the boy had been attracted to art and literature. During high school, he learned the piano and wrote music. He painted. He read ceaselessly and wrote hundreds of poems. By the time he graduated, he knew he wanted to be a writer.

But his father wouldn't allow it. The elder Mencken was a practical man. If his son did not want to pursue a college degree in engineering—and the younger Mencken made it clear he did not—then it would be the cigar business for him. It was his father's ambition that H. L. would learn the business top to bottom, and then take it over someday.

The ensuing three years were hell for H. L. Mencken. Day after day, the disillusioned youth would drag himself through his working hours; first he learned to roll cigars, then to sell them, then to tend the company's books. Decades later, he would admit that he was so unhappy in those days that he had considered suicide.

A year into his stint at the company, Mencken appealed to his father to let him leave. His father was gentle and understanding, Mencken later recalled, but assured H. L. that he too had once recoiled from the business world, only to adjust over time. The same would happen to the son, the elder Mencken promised.

But it didn't. The young man's passion was writing. He signed up for correspondence courses, focusing his evenings and weekends on developing his skills. His acute observations, clever wordplays, and conversational tone—all precursors of the style that would bring him national renown in later years—were noted even then by his correspondence teachers.

But his misery at the cigar factory continued. Out of fear and respect, he waited two years after that first fruitless conversation with his father to beg again for his freedom. Still, the father said no. For H. L. Mencken, who felt dutifully bound to his family, there seemed no escape.

And then on December 31, 1898, August Mencken, who was then forty-four and apparently in robust health, suddenly began convulsing. His eighteen-year-old son was rousted from bed to fetch help. Later, H. L. Mencken would acknowledge that as he ran to the doctor's home, all he could think of was "that if my father died, I'd be free at last."

Two weeks later, his father died from a kidney infection.

According to Mencken's memoirs, the funeral was held on a Sunday evening. On Monday evening, Mencken walked into the offices of the Baltimore *Morning Herald* and launched his legendary newspaper career.

My father died on Jan. 24 in the early morning. . . . All my dreams
of comradeship with him, of entering Parliament at his side and in his
support, were ended. There remained for me only to pursue his
aims and vindicate his memory.
— SIR WINSTON CHURCHILL

Chapter 9

LIFE CHANGES

IT WAS another spectacular, blue-skied northern California morning as Steve Freedman, twenty-six, cruised the wide, scenic highway between San Francisco and San Jose. Behind the wheel of his black Volvo, Steve's mood matched the wondrous day. A boss with whom Steve had a troubled relationship had just announced that he was leaving, which Steve considered a blessing. And there was more good news: Steve had just had a freelance article accepted by a major magazine, he was making headway with a new woman in his life, and he'd managed to score a couple of tickets to see Bruce Springsteen in an upcoming concert.

On a typical day, a Springsteen tape might have been spinning in Steve's cassette player. But on this morning in 1985, he was tuned to KGO, the AM radio station that carried ABC broadcast news. A week earlier, Steve had learned that his father, an ABC radio correspondent, would be traveling with President Ronald Reagan to Germany. On the phone, the father and son journalists had shared their excitement about the assignment, tossing around storylines the father might pursue. Just before hanging up, the son had borrowed a phrase from broadcast legend Charles Osgood for his parting words to his dad: "See you on the radio."

And he had. His father's first report had come early in the week from Bonn. There had been another broadcast midweek. And now, on Friday, as Steve approached the highway exit near his office, he listened for his father's latest dispatch. It never came. Only when he reached his desk, and answered the phone, did Steve learn why: His father, aged fifty-four, had just died of a heart attack in a hotel room some eight thousand miles away.

The news put him into a temporary state of shock. Steve left the office and the following day caught a plane back to his childhood home in New York City. In the days that followed, he remembered, "a black cloud covered every aspect of my existence." Waking up each morning in his old bedroom, he recalled, "there was fifteen seconds or a minute of relative happiness and calm—and then wham! That thing that's going on lands on my chest, or on my head. . . . There was this blackness in my life."

Along with the pain, however, came something else. Steve didn't see it clearly at first. But as the funeral passed, and the intensity of his grief diminished, he became aware of a nagging sense of dissatisfaction in his everyday life. For a while, he tried to distract himself; he hoped to ride out the malaise. But he couldn't.

And then he faced the problem: He no longer had passion for his work. For five years, he had found a way to make the best of newspaper reporting, competing to break the next story, vying for the next promotion. Now, however, with his father gone, Steve saw that his interest in journalism had been largely an attempt to please his dad. When I talked with him thirteen years later, Steve explained it this way: "I had previously been the seed that fell too close to the tree. Now the tree was chopped down, and suddenly, I was seeing light."

With his father out of the picture, Steve reexamined his options. He could continue to coast in his current job, earning a dependable $50,000 a year. Or he could take a step away from that safety and find a vocation he really cared about. Eighteen months after his father's death, Steve quit the newspaper to take a job managing a homeless shelter. The pay was low, the hours were long, the frustrations were many. But later, he called the choice "the greatest decision of my life." He added, "I wasn't looking to lose my dad. But I don't know how I could have moved on had he not died. I consider [his death] a huge gift, even though it came at a huge cost."

As Steve Freedman's story indicates, a father's death can bring with it not only anguish, but opportunity. According to my survey results, two out of three men said that in the two years following the death, they experienced significant—and mostly positive—changes in their family ties, work lives, or religious convictions. For some men, such as Steve Freedman, the changes were dramatic and consciously chosen: quitting a job, for example. For others, they were subtle, incremental, and barely noticeable until much later, when the son reflected on the different person he had become since the loss.

For sons who had lost fathers in childhood, the changes tended to infiltrate every aspect of life. William Campbell, who was thirteen when his father died, spoke for many who had lost fathers early. He told me that after the death, "It was like living another life. I even changed my name—starting to go by my first name, rather than the middle one. My mom, unable to support herself financially, needed to be close to my grandparents, so we moved. . . . We never spent another night in [our] house. I left all my friends, my school, our church. I quit Boy Scouts and soon quit taking music lessons—both things which my dad had pushed. We moved from a place where our main support group was our network of friends to one where that support group was composed mainly of family. None of which is to say that the biggest difference was not the sheer absence of my dad."

Another son, who was eight when his father died, also moved with his family after the death. His mother began working for the first time. Four decades later, this son told me: "When I reflect on that kid, it seems like I'm thinking about someone else."

Among these younger sons, it was rare to find one who could pinpoint positive changes that might have resulted from the death of their father. It seemed almost a sacrilege to try. On the other hand, among sons I interviewed who'd lost fathers in adulthood, many seemed intent upon finding something hopeful to take away from the experience. It was almost as if they wanted, after their descent, to emerge with a piece of gold.

Frequently, that gold was an improved relationship with their mothers. In my survey, 48 percent of men said the quality of their connection with their mothers changed in the two years following the father's death. And among that population, 90 percent said the changes were for the better.

For Michael Gross, a doctor who lost his father at age thirty-nine after a long illness, his connection with his mother had already been deepening before the death. "Going through this horrible thing together," Michael said, had forced them to collaborate, and to lean on each other. And he was repeatedly impressed by her emotional resilience: "She had a lot of strength, a lot of savvy, real good logic and judgment."

Michael recalled an incident when the father was near death: "It occurred to me that we better ask him where he wanted to be buried. I was sure that I would do it, that [my mother] would step aside. But when I suggested that it needed to be done, she said, 'I'd better ask him that.' She went over to him and in a very clear and steady voice, she asked him exactly what his wishes were. You gotta love him for this. He said, 'We'll talk about it later.' "

Michael's father survived that near-death experience, but died a year later. Mother and son flew together, with the coffin in tow, to the father's birthplace in another country. "In our travel, we had time to talk about the emotional aspects" of the death, "what it all meant," Michael recalled. And mother and son continued to work together through the funeral week. "We functioned really well as a unit. It was almost like two people in there reinforcing a dike as the water leaked in. We were shoulder to shoulder. . . . I had a realization that there was a lot of strength there, a lot of love."

A historian who lost his father suddenly at age thirty-seven was able to lean on his mother for support. In the weeks after the loss, "I told my mom I really felt I could have said things to my father, thanked him. Dad and I, we had a stereotypical male silence. That was the bond we had. It didn't express itself verbally. My mother assured me: 'Your father understood.' She said he was aware of the fact that I appreciated him. Whether she meant it, or was making me feel better, I don't know. But I believed her."

In the process of these conversations with his mother, this son told me, the two became "more at ease, more disclosing." The son also learned from his regrets about not thanking his dad. While talking with his mom, he thanked her for the sacrifices she'd made while raising him.

Another son, a middle-aged business consultant, also found that, with his father gone, he could relate to his mother differently. The father had been a dominant and judgmental force in the son's life. After the death, the son came to realize that he had blamed his mother in part for the father's harshness. In reality, he now saw, she too had suffered under the father's dominance.

"I have a little more respect for my mother" since the death, said the son, who was forty-two years old when his dad died. After the death, the mother, then aged seventy-two, got her driver's license for the first time and forged a full life with many friends and activities. "I can't say we're soul mates," the son told me. "She'll still do the mother-guilt stuff. It angers me, and out of that anger, I'll sometimes stop talking with her. But I believe her dependency on me . . . has lessened with his death."

Not that dependency is inherently bad for a mother-son relationship. One son, who was forty at his father's death, said his relationship with his mother improved because of the increased time and attention she needed after the death. "I started to serve the ballast function, helping anchor her to reality," this son said. "I took over my father's role."

There are, of course, occasions when the mother-son relationship deteriorates after the father's death. One son, who was twenty-five when his father died, told me that his dad had always played "the mediator" in the family, calming disputes, helping his children and his wife find common ground. With him gone, this son recalled, his mother "tried to roll back" the son's privileges and responsibilities. "She became more authoritarian, more directive. Had I been competent then at dealing with emotions, I could probably have gotten around it."

Instead, the son said, even simple disagreements "boiled over into irremediable conflict. . . . Basically, we were two basket cases living under the same roof."

Charles Garten's relationship with his mother became strained in the period leading up to his father's death. A year before he died, the father suffered a major stroke and could not speak, walk, or sit up in his hospital bed. After several months of watching his dad deteriorate in a nonresponsive comatose state, Charles, who was then thirty-three, came to believe his father would want his medical treatment stopped.

Charles recalled: "My mother, during this whole time, was a basket case. She was occasionally suicidal. She was constantly in tears. And she was totally irrational. Her only sanity clung to the hope that he was going to walk out of that hospital, and then come home. And it was just . . . clear that it wasn't going to happen. At one point it became clear to me that my father's suffering was being extended by my mother's selfishness, her blind need to keep her own hope alive. And I finally confronted her on it."

That's when Charles suggested the family begin to pull back on medical interventions. "I'll never forget what it felt like to have my mother say: 'Are you trying to kill your father?' . . . That's pretty much the M-16 of maternal guilt, wouldn't you say?"

Just as a son's relationship with his mother often changes following the father's death, so too do his connections with brothers and sisters. About 36 percent of those in my survey said their relationships with siblings changed after the death, and those changes were nearly four times more likely to be for the better than for the worse.

A mathematician who was thirty-four when his father died told me that after the death, "staying close with my siblings became ever more important." For one thing, his two brothers and sister wanted to coordinate care of their mother, who was still healthy but now living alone in a city where none of her children lived. For another, they wanted to affirm that their important family traditions, including an annual July Fourth football game, would survive even without their father. The son explained: "At first, we wondered: Could we still play the football game, with New York City rules inherited from my father's childhood? The answer is that we could."

In rare cases, sibling relationships got worse after the death of a father. Usually, the mother was already dead, and the siblings' connections were frayed. One son, a gay man who was fifty-four at the death of his father, explained his situation: "As long as Dad was alive, I would not let myself finish the relationship with my siblings. My two brothers hadn't spoken with me for a long time because they didn't approve of my 'lifestyle.' But I couldn't let go. And then, after Dad died, I let go. Basically, I focused on my family [of friends], my real family."

Close friends are often able to provide support equal to that of a sibling. The FatherLoss Survey results indicated that there was no difference between sons with and without siblings regarding the intensity or duration of their grieving after the death of a father.

Many of the men I spoke with said that one of the positive effects of the father's death was deepening bonds with friends, especially male friends. In the period immediately after the death, I found that many sons, gay and straight, seemed interested in connecting with other men. While sons got valuable assistance from wives and female friends, one man told me: "A man's relationship with his father is different from women's relationships with their mothers or fathers. It's unique. There are certain elements that only a man would understand."

While a few of the men I spoke with lamented the lack of male support during their experience with the death, most spoke of positive contact with men in their lives. In the survey, when asked whether male friends or male relatives helped them through the experience, 72 percent of the sons answered in the affirmative. The sons I spoke with said men tended to be less feeling-oriented than women in their support, but just as crucial in helping with their recovery.

Jesse Hefner's father committed suicide when Jesse was thirty-six, shooting himself in a location where he could be sure Jesse would be the first to discover him. On the morning of the death, Jesse's best friend Ken found out about it, showed up at Jesse's house, hugged his friend, then spent the day answering the phone, cleaning up the house, bringing in food, and allowing Jesse to attend to his family.

At the end of the day, Ken sat down with Jesse for what Jesse, a police officer, referred to as "a critical-incident stress debriefing." Jesse explained: "We relived the whole day, everything I had seen. We talked about why it happened. [Ken] was a friend since high school. He had his own history with my dad, and could relate things about Dad that put his suicide into perspective. It helped take what seemed really nonsensical and gave it a framework so it was not so out-of-the-blue."

Ken's most important contribution, Jesse told me, was his rationality. Jesse said: "He's an engineer. He's got an engineer's emotional way. . . . He's not the one who reaches into your heart. He reaches into your head. That first night, he knew that I needed to start to make sense of it. He tried to engage my brain as well as my heart. He saw the patterns that at the time, I didn't see. . . . Not that we don't talk about feelings. We do. But in crisis times, [Ken] moves to his brain. And he helped me kick into my brain too."

Another son, a union official, told me his relationship with his brother-in-law "turned a corner" during his father's illness and death. The union official, who was forty-three at the death, had a brother who was alcoholic; the brother was not around as their father was dying in the hospital. During the final weeks, the family had to make difficult decisions about the father's medical treatment. The brother-in-law stepped up to become a key player in those decisions.

The official described his brother-in-law's influence: "He's an electrician, pretty typical, not talky-feely. But I knew he really loved my dad. . . . When I'd see him, we somehow shared and communicated. A lot of it was unspoken. It was a look, or a story. He'd tell me something my father had said or done, and then give me a smile that said he knew I'd appreciate hearing that. Men need to have that with other men. We know a little more emotionally about where each other is coming from." This man added that during his father's illness, he and his brother-in-law "communicated on a more open level than we had before—even than what we do now. It was a window of opportunity. . . . I jumped at the chance. It's something I was starving for."

A man who was thirty-seven when his dad died told me his male friends "came to my rescue" after the death. "Many of my lake buddies dropped everything, and came and stayed through the Sunday, Monday, and Tuesday of the funeral [week]. There were four friends who had been going on camping trips for many years, and felt that my father was a father to them as well. We split the pallbearers up, and half were my age and the other half were my father's age."

Another man, a lobbyist who lost his father at age thirty-three, told me he needed his friends, both male and female, "just to dump. I needed somebody to talk to, someone from my world. . . . I needed someone to blabber to who wasn't a part of it all, who wouldn't get so emotionally tied up. In the immediate moment, it all seemed so epic, and it was important to have people I could say weird shit to without having to worry about provoking a deep emotional reaction, who would understand my own odd way of seeing it. I don't remember a word of what [my friends] said to me at the time. It didn't matter."

A university professor, whose father died when the son was thirty-four, told me he was specifically interested in talking with friends who had been through the death of a father. He explained: "It's like company. There was no need for counseling. I wouldn't relate to self-help. I was just going through it. . . . If I had a tragic illness, I'd contact people who'd been through it. It's commiseration."

A computer programmer who was sixteen when his dad died, told me his male friends "helped the most just by hanging out, being there, doing what we'd always done. Nothing contrived. . . . What bothered me most was when people tried to console me, to tell me how it was going to be okay."

While these men said their friendships were strengthened by the loss, I heard about a few cases where a friendship died along with the father. The cause was almost always the same: The friend didn't call after the loss or failed to show up for the funeral. One son who was forty-two at the death said he called an old college friend to tell him the news. The friend offered condolences, but moved on quickly to other subjects. Soon, the friend was trying to make jokes about those other topics. The son recalled: "After that, I consciously decided to let go [of the friendship]. He could not be serious. Even in the face of this."

One kind of relationship that almost never gets worse after the death of a father is that between the surviving son and his children. Among the 181 men in our survey who had children at the time their fathers died, none said that their connections with their children worsened in the two years after the death. Meanwhile, more than a quarter of these men—26 percent—said their relationships with their children improved.

Often, the improvements came when the bereaved son reexamined his relationship with his father. After such review, the son would make a conscious decision about how to parent his own children in response to the way he'd been raised by his father.

Brad Richards had never gotten along well with his dad, who

seemed uninterested in him, even in adulthood. When the father died, Brad was fifty-two and was himself the father of a thirteen-year-old girl, who lived with her mother, fifteen hundred miles away. After the death, Brad started to wonder whether his daughter was viewing him in much the way he had always perceived his father. After all, Brad spent time with her only when she traveled to see him over the summer and at Christmas.

After the father's death, Brad decided to change that. He began flying to visit his daughter every couple of months for three- or four-day weekends, staying in a hotel near his ex-wife's home. From his father, Brad said, "I learned how much it hurt to be distant. I had the money [to visit more regularly]. It just never occurred to me to make it a priority."

A real-estate agent who was fifty-three when his father died, said his two sons became a higher priority after the death. In his case, the inspiration was less the failings of his father than a recognition of what's important in life. His father's death, this man told me, "made me appreciate and relish close relationships—family, especially. . . . What is to be valued? Is it things or is it people? Is it relationships? I really find myself making more time when people want to talk with me. When my sons are around, I do more hugging and touch-ing. I love them in a more focused way."

In addition to his relationships with family members, a man's rela-tionship with his work may shift after the loss of a father. Twenty-nine percent of the men I surveyed said that in the two years after the death of their father, their attitude toward work changed. For a few, it became less important. But for most, its importance grew.

At the opening of this chapter, we saw how Steve Freedman felt liberated after his father's death to seek out a new career. For him, his work life became more important after the death. Steve ended up spending a couple of years as manager of that homeless shelter and has since struggled to balance his need for income with a desire to give to his community. When I last talked with him, Steve was forty years old. He was working as a freelance business consultant, charging some clients upwards of $150 an hour, while at the same time offering similar services for free to nonprofit groups he supported.

Another man who had spent twenty years selling financial services said that after his father's death, he quit his job at a small accounting firm to pursue his own business in computer consulting. One reason for the change was personal: "I had a falling out somewhat with my [boss]. He and I were close and built a business together. When my dad died, he didn't even come to the wake." But the son added, "What pushed me over the edge was the finality of my dad's life, knowing I only have so many years left to do what I really want to do."

When I talked with this son, four years after his job change, he was making less money and working more hours than he had in his old career. But he said he got more satisfaction from being an entrepreneur. And his dad's spirit remained close to him. "I often look to my father's memory now. I'm aware of his inner strength. He never complained. He kept plugging along. That's what I'm trying to do."

The death of a father affected men in their work lives in one other way. Several sons who were children when their fathers died told me that the traits they developed in childhood to deal with the death—independence, self-reliance, and emotional distance, among others—helped them in their careers.

An example: A forty-five-year-old special-education teacher said his experience of trauma in childhood helped him empathize with the difficulties many of his students faced. He said he knows, for instance, that special education kids usually need emotional support more than academic insight. He told me that, ironically, he spent more time hugging his students than he did his own kids.

Among his colleagues, meanwhile, he was known as a "bridge-builder," someone who could arbitrate disputes fairly. He explained: "One of my fortes is to see the dynamics of relationships among my peers without getting too involved. My emotional detachment allows me to move in any circle."

Before I leave the realm of changing relationships, there's one more worth noting: the relationship between a man and his god. For many of the sons I spoke with, the death of the father was a test of faith. In the years before the death, a son may have believed in God and afterlife, he may have been an atheist, or he may have adhered to some other theology. With the father's death, whatever beliefs the son had held in the abstract were tested in reality. The result, in about 16 percent of the sons in my survey, was a change in religious convictions.

When religious convictions did change, sons were about six times as likely to report that they'd become more rather than less religious. Those who already attended religious services regularly were most likely to say they became more religious. But even among sons who said they rarely or never attended religious services, 7 percent said they became more religious after the death of a father.

One such son, a high school teacher who was twenty when his father died, began attending a Baptist church after his father's death. Fifteen years later, he told me: "I found that knowing the Lord, Jesus Christ, gave me peace. I could turn to him for guidance. I believe the Lord filled the void left when my father died."

Another son, who as a teenager had rejected his father's fundamentalist Christian tradition, also found himself spiritually affected by his father's death. This man, who was forty-two at the death, said of his father: "I wondered whether I had chosen atheism as the ultimate insult to him. I definitely counted myself as one" before the death. Since the death, the son said, "I'm paying more attention to the transcendent. What is there that bridges this consciousness and any other? I'm more fascinated with what might live on."

Those sons whose fathers had committed suicide seemed most challenged in their religious beliefs. "If there is a God, then how come crap like this would happen?" asked one such son, who was in his thirties when his father shot himself. This son added that even before the death, he was dubious of the Christian teachings he'd been raised with. The loss solidified his skepticism: "I see it more now that we're all on our own, struggling to get by."

Another son, who was sixteen when his dad killed himself, said: "I was so mad at God. I totally blamed him." The boy wondered what would happen to his father in the afterlife. "In the Bible, it goes into detail that you cannot take a life. Dad's dead, so he can't really ask for forgiveness. I'm sure he loved God. So I don't know." Ultimately, this son remained an active Christian. A minister helped him. "He explained that there's God's will and man's free will. You have to separate the two."

Beyond religion, relationships, and work, sons mentioned a few other changes following the father's death. About 13 percent of those in my survey reported changes in their diets, exercise routines, or other health habits following the death. One son, whose father died of a heart attack in his fifties, called the death "a humongous wake-up call" when it came to his own health. The father had been a smoker, and shortly after the death, the son, then in his twenties, actually took up smoking for the first time. But within a year or so, he had stopped and had begun cutting back on meats and other fats in his diet. A few years after that, he joined a gym and started working out regularly. Nonetheless, more than a decade after his father's death, the son told me: "I think about, and am scared of, dropping dead of a heart attack like my father *every day*."

Other men spoke of changes in their hobbies, their dream lives, even their sexual urges. One man said he'd grown up in a Christian denomination that strongly condemned homosexuality. He'd left the church in early adulthood and later got married. After the father's death, when the son was twenty-nine, he experienced a change in sexual feelings: He was increasingly attracted to men and wondered whether he was bisexual. When I talked with this man, it had been three years since his father's death. He was still in his marriage and had not acted on his homosexual urges, he told me, but continued to wrestle with them.

My study is not the only one to find that people who lose parents tend to go through significant changes in the aftermath. In the late 1980s, Dr. Joan Douglas, a psychologist at Skidmore College in up-state New York, was one of just a handful of scientists researching the impact of parent-loss on adult children. In one study, she interviewed forty midlife adults who had experienced the loss of a parent and found that "upheaval and transition" were common themes in the first year to eighteen months after the loss. In an interview, she told me that it was impossible to know for sure whether the changes would have occurred without the death, but that in many cases, her subjects directly linked the two.

A decade after her research had been completed, Douglas and I shared theories as to why change is so common after a parent-loss. First, we agreed, some adult children seem to suppress certain of their thoughts and actions out of respect for (or fear of) their parents. Thus, the man who started having homosexual urges after his father died might have finally felt free to explore an aspect of his personality that didn't seem safe to investigate previously. The same might be true of Steve Freedman, the man who had quit journalism—his father's profession—to run a homeless shelter.

Second, sons may also make changes after a parent-death, as Douglas put it, to "fill in the space" left by the loss. For example, if a son previously depended upon his father for financial advice or emotional support, the son might now turn to his mother, a sibling, a partner, or a friend to fill that need. This may account in part for the frequency with which sons reported changes in their relationships with friends and family members.

Finally, some adult children seem to make changes after a parent-death because they've confronted their mortality; they realize that there's a limit to life, and if they're going to do certain things, they've got to start now. As Douglas put it: "Parent-and-child is a central bond. It's who we start out with and who we frame our whole world around. The loss of this person forces us to reorganize our inner selves. Eventually, this is reflected in our behavior, for better or worse."

Fortunately, based on what sons told me, these changes are usually for the better.

Ernest Hemingway

—⚭—

In his preteen years in Oak Park, Illinois, Ernest Hemingway was close to his father, Dr. Clarence Hemingway. In Ernest's memory, the two spent many weekends hunting, fishing, and exploring the wild. When Ernest reached adolescence, however, father and son began growing apart. Later, the son would blame this estrangement largely on his mother, saying her extravagant spending forced Dr. Hemingway to work long hours away from the family.

By his early twenties, as he began his writing career, Ernest had come to resent both of his parents. And the feeling was mutual. The elder Hemingways, who were religious conservatives, took great offense at their son's first book, *In Our Time*, which they described as "filth." Their letters to him were brimming with disappointment.

It was at about this point, late in 1928, that Dr. Hemingway— deeply in debt, suffering from diabetes, and fearing that he would lose a leg to amputation—withdrew to his bedroom one day with his father's Civil War revolver, and killed himself with a shot to his head.

Ernest Hemingway, then twenty-nine, managed to suppress any initial distress. He was involved in the final rewrite of *A Farewell to Arms* and focused on the literary task at hand. Hemingway did ask his mother to send him the suicide weapon, which he ritually tossed into a lake.

But the ghost of his father endured. As biographer Jeffrey Meyers points out, in the decades after the suicide, the letters and stories that flowed from Hemingway were laden with references to the fact and method of his father's death. Meyers notes that Hemingway discussed suicide in *Death in the Afternoon* (1932), *To Have and Have Not* (1937), and *For Whom the Bell Tolls* (1940). And in an unpublished passage of *Green Hills of Africa* (1935), Hemingway wrote: "My father was a coward. He shot himself without necessity. At least I thought so."

Cowardice, in fact, was a potent issue for Hemingway throughout his middle age, and he regularly strived to prove his courage, most notably through big-game hunting. But by his late forties, Hemingway had become haunted by his own impulse toward self-destruction. Meyers points out that even as Hemingway was winning the Pulitzer and Nobel prizes for *Old Man and the Sea* (1952), he was discussing his own suicide with a friend: "I'm going to try *not* to do it."

By 1961, at age sixty-one, Hemingway suffered from depression, alcoholism, failing eyesight, diabetes, hepatitis, hypertension, and impotence. He could no longer write, nor live up to his standards of manhood. On July 2, almost immediately after returning from a hospital for treatment of his mental illness, he killed himself in exactly the manner his father had thirty-two years before.

After my father's death, I had trouble psychologically. . . . I'll tell you
how it was. I was walking down Dawson Street. And I felt I couldn't
go on. It was a strange experience I can't really describe. I found I
couldn't go on moving. So I went into the nearest pub and
got a drink just to stay still.
—PLAYWRIGHT SAMUEL BECKETT

Chapter 10

———

DOES THERAPY HELP?

———

MEN DON'T readily seek professional help as they come to terms with the deaths of their fathers. The vast majority of those I interviewed said they felt capable of handling the loss on their own, or with help from family members and friends. A few said they thought seeking therapy indicated psychological weakness.

In about 8 percent of the cases, however, faced with intolerable anxiety or depression, sons put aside any doubts about therapy as they struggled to reclaim their equilibrium. And according to my survey, those who sought professional help—in the form of a psychologist, psychiatrist, clergy person, or other counselor—overwhelmingly reported that it served them well.

Most often, these men were motivated into action by a sense of despair. "I thought I was going to explode," one son, a forty-four-year-old sculptor, told me. His intense inner turmoil began about a year after his father's death. That's when he started remembering childhood scenes in which his father hit his mother. As increasing numbers of these memories emerged, his anger escalated. He eventually decided to seek help because "I was afraid of turning my rage on [my family]."

Other sons sought help when the father's death was one of a series of losses, and they felt overwhelmed. Elton Swift, for example, was forty-four when his father died. In the six months before the death, Elton's wife had asked for a divorce, and Elton had been laid off from his job as a coal miner. After his father's death, sitting one day at breakfast in his apartment, he began crying and couldn't stop.

This had never happened before, and Elton didn't know what to do at first. Eventually, although he hadn't been a regular churchgoer since childhood, he drove to a Catholic church, sat in a pew, and prayed. He recalled: "The priest came in, and prayed with me. When I quit crying, he took me to his office and told me where I could get some help." For the next several months, Elton spent one hour a week with a psychologist and two hours a week in group therapy.

Duncan Peters, another man I interviewed, also suffered multiple losses. Nine years before I spoke with him, Duncan's father, grandfather, and a good friend all died within a couple of months of each other. Duncan, a physical therapist, was thirty-two years old at the time. At first, he said, "I thought I'd weathered the storm pretty good. It seemed a little easier than I thought." About four months after his father's death, however, Duncan started feeling alternately depressed and panicky. After a couple of weeks in this emotional state, he said, "I didn't recognize myself. I went to work fine, but I didn't eat. And when I did eat, my stomach hurt."

The more his mood fluctuated, the more focused Duncan became on his mental condition. "Was I psycho?" he wondered. He described one of his symptoms: "It was like someone said 'boo!' to you. No one actually said it, but you still got the thrill." At his worst, Duncan said he wasn't seriously suicidal, but asked himself at times: "What's the use of walking around feeling so dead inside?"

Duncan may never have sought help, he told me, had his brother's wife not been a psychologist. In an unusual arrangement, he chose his sister-in-law as the counselor to help him through his ordeal. (More on Duncan's therapy later in this chapter.)

The men described above all were adults at the time of the father's death. My survey indicates that 6 percent of men who lost fathers in adulthood received professional help to cope with the loss. In comparison, among sons who lost fathers in childhood, the percentage receiving professional help was more than twice as high—13 percent.

This is in keeping with my findings (cited in Chapter 1) that sons who are children when their fathers die are more likely than others to have long-term problems related to the loss. Frequently, these problems don't show up clearly until the son is an adult, as he struggles in his work or intimate relationships. It is common, in fact, for these sons initially to seek counseling for problems that seem unrelated to the father's death.

Jack Matthews was forty-one years old, married, with a teenaged daughter, when he considered therapy for the first time. Jack and his family had moved a year earlier from Oregon to New Hampshire for Jack's work, but the job had fizzled out. Now, his wife and daughter wanted to move back; Jack resisted and kept looking for new employment. He didn't find any at first, and family tensions escalated. That's when the three of them decided to get some family counseling.

The therapy seemed to have nothing to do with Jack's father, who had died thirty-two years earlier. But Jack described what happened one day: "The counselor said: 'Tell me your life story.' The more I talked [about] this alcoholic father, who left his family and then died when I was nine, the more sad I realized the story was. I had never really faced it or discussed it." At the time of the death, Jack recalled, he had not been "terribly sad or morose." In the therapy, however, he realized how the loss "ultimately drives my behavior. . . . I didn't have a good model of how to behave as a man or a father. I thought men were supposed to lay down the law to their family."

One of the results of the counseling was a change in Jack's attitude about moving west. He decided to allow the majority to rule in the family, and they went back to Oregon.

Another son, Gordon Dole, who also lost his father in childhood, told me he went into therapy after an emotional breakdown more than two decades after the death. Gordon's father had died of a staph infection when Gordon was thirteen. It was then the middle of the Depression, and Gordon remembered feeling glad at first about the death because he thought the family now might get extra aid from the government. He also remembered, with far less cheer, how quickly he had to become man of the house and take over his father's farming duties.

Gordon got married in his twenties, had children, and never considered seeing a therapist until one night, at age thirty-seven, while studying to become a minister, he awoke "in a manic state. I wanted to scream. I wanted to yell. I wanted to throw things," he told me three decades later. "It was like I was in the middle of a road, with a Greyhound bus bearing down on me, and I couldn't get out of the way."

Again, the episode seemed unrelated to his father's death—until he began talking with a psychiatrist. Then Gordon realized that he'd been carrying a huge emotional load: his anger at having to take on adult responsibilities at thirteen, his guilt at being initially happy about his father's death, and his sadness over the loss itself. In therapy,

Gordon explained, "I realized how pivotal was the event of my father's death. . . . It created the trajectory, it set me on a course, toward my nervous breakdown."

A number of previous studies have tried to answer the question of to what degree grief therapy helps, and the results have been mixed. About half of the studies I read showed no benefit for bereaved people who got professional help; the other half found that those who got help tended to have shorter and smoother recovery periods.

My own survey showed counseling to be worthwhile for those who chose it. Sixty-eight percent of those who received counseling reported that it was "very helpful" in their coping with the death of their fathers. Another 27 percent said counseling was "somewhat helpful." Only 5 percent of those who tried it said it didn't help at all.

I followed up on some of these failed cases and found that a common problem was a lack of chemistry between the therapist and client. A thirty-five-year-old businessman told me he went into therapy at age twenty-three. He had lost his father at age ten and had struggled through adolescence without professional help. He'd certainly exhibited signs of distress: He had been frequently fearful and angry, he recalled. In high school, he would often eat his lunch alone in the auditorium. "It wasn't like I was depressed. It was a relief [to be alone]. I [didn't] have to be concerned with what people think."

Through his college years, the son continued to spend a lot of time alone, but what concerned him most was his growing sense of apathy. He recalled: "My feeling was not suicidal, but sort of like fatalistic. . . . There was a sense of detachment, not caring."

After graduating from college, the son sought out a male therapist, and they started meeting weekly. But they didn't get anywhere. Looking back more than a decade later, the son said: "I didn't have too good a relationship with my therapist. For three or four months, I felt like: Why am I even going to him? He sat behind a desk; I didn't like that at all. I was angry at him the whole time. I'd walk in many days and not say anything, even though I had a ton of things to say."

After a year or so, the son quit therapy because "it wasn't going anywhere for me." When I spoke with him twelve years later, he hadn't sought counseling again. He continued to struggle with relationships and other issues. He told me he sometimes wondered if he had failed to give himself a chance during the therapy in his early twenties. "My intuition said that this [counselor] was the wrong one. Why didn't I go somewhere else?"

Several other men I interviewed also expressed dissatisfaction with their choice in counselors. One told me he was too smart for his psychiatrist, but continued in part because he could get tranquilizers. "I almost never used them," he said of the pills, "but I kept them in my pocket for years."

Much more common than failed therapies were successful ones, though success was measured differently by each man. At age eighteen, Vince Mays lost his father, suddenly, to a heart attack. Father and son had been close, and Vince told me he felt as if he were "cast adrift." He managed his unhappiness during his college years by drinking to excess several times a week.

By age twenty-four, Vince was a successful computer programmer, but he'd made a daily habit of drinking, and he tended toward sarcasm and anxiety. Vince's mother, noticing that he had no friends outside his drinking pals, gave him the name of a therapist and encouraged him to go.

During the first year of weekly sessions, Vince continued to drink. He avoided direct conversation with his therapist about his dad, focusing instead on struggles in his everyday life. Eventually, the therapist convinced Vince to join Alcoholics Anonymous. The effect was immediate: He started crying in the therapy sessions. Week after week, Vince said, "I talked and sobbed, talked and sobbed." About six months after the crying began, it ended. A couple of months later, Vince and his therapist agreed that he no longer needed weekly sessions; they touched base every few months for another year.

When I talked with Vince twelve years later, he said the physical release helped him most: "I was holding on so tight, clamping down. It's still a tendency of mine."

Another son who'd shut down emotionally after the death of his father benefited from therapy that began more than three decades after the death. The son was seven when his dad died and compared the impact of the death to being "hit by a truck." He said he stopped feeling much of anything after the loss and stayed that way well into adulthood.

When he was in his early forties, he went into counseling when his marriage became rocky and one of his sons began acting out in school. Fifteen years later, he told me: "It took almost a year before [the therapist] could get much out of me. It was very slow." Then one day he unexpectedly shed some tears over the loss. "I wouldn't call it sobbing," but he said he felt good to have finally had "a natural reaction" to his father's death.

More valuable than this physical release, this son said, were the insights he gained in talking with his counselor in the months that followed. When the therapy started, he said, "I had a lot of trouble even naming emotions." After three years, though, he'd gained a good understanding of his inner landscape. He acknowledged that understanding how he felt "didn't correct everything. It didn't alter [you] to . . . be this sensitive person. But it allowed you to see how you're functioning, put it into perspective, and to be aware more of what your limitations are."

The son told me he believed the therapy saved his marriage, and made him a better father. "I see how I run from closeness," he said. "Now, I can catch myself doing it. I can intellectually compensate."

Indeed, among the men I spoke with, success in counseling most often was defined as coming away with *greater insight into behaviors and impulses*. By talking about their fathers, and speaking aloud about their life experiences, these men said they were able to see themselves more clearly and make healthier decisions about how to act in the world.

One insight that was frequently cited by the men with whom I spoke was the realization that their reaction to the death of their father—whether strong or reserved—was "normal." Duncan Peters, for example, the man who entered therapy with his sister-in-law after suffering anxiety and depression, said, "In the first five minutes, she explained what depression was about and that I'd probably get over it in six months anyway." That prognosis, he said, "immediately gave me confidence and hope."

After that, he and his sister-in-law met weekly for an hour or two in his living room, where he was able to talk openly about his ongoing nervousness, lack of appetite, and other symptoms. He recalled: "Just being able to talk would help. It was like taking two aspirin, and the headache would go away." In the early weeks of therapy, the symptoms would return, usually by the next day. But over the course of several months, they began, as predicted by his sister-in-law, to diminish.

When I talked to Duncan, it had been nine years since his father's death. At forty-one years old, he acknowledged that he didn't have "the absolute confidence" in his emotional state that he'd had before the death. "I've never told my wife this, but to this day, if she's gone overnight, I become preoccupied with that. What if I become anxious? What if I start to lose it? I have this thing about being alone."

Despite the lingering insecurity, however, Duncan said he believed his therapy was successful because it helped him through his crisis, and showed him his weaknesses. "In a sense, I was fortunate I reacted as I did," he told me. "A lot of people go to drugs and alcohol."

Duncan said he was still involved in a Bible study group with his sister-in-law, and said of her: "She's my guru in my mind, my life preserver." While professionals generally warn against seeking therapy from a family member, Duncan said he had no regrets about his choice: "I knew her interest was my interest. It wasn't sixty bucks an hour. The idea of going in to a stranger—it was something I wasn't ready for."

Like Duncan, Elton Swift, the coal miner who experienced the uncontrolled crying spell after his father had died, was nurtured through his crisis in one-on-one sessions with his psychologist. But, he told me, the greater benefit came in a different kind of therapeutic environment.

His one-on-one work, Elton said, focused on his belief that he had contributed to his father's death by failing to convince the older man to stop drinking. There was added guilt because of a nasty end to their relationship. Elton recalled the day his father died: "He'd been drinking the night before, and when I saw him, I was disgusted. I told him, 'You could lay in a casket and close your eyes. Nobody would know you ain't dead.' " Then Elton left to visit a friend. While he was gone, his father had the massive heart attack that killed him.

In individual therapy, Elton gradually came to see that his father had died as a result of lifestyle choices that had nothing to do with

Elton. And in part through the insistence of his counselor, Elton said he eventually forgave himself "about 90 percent" for his comments to his dad.

It was in *group* therapy, however, that Elton got the perspective that allowed him to move on with his life. Each week, eight or ten clients met in an office with a therapist and talked about their lives and struggles. Elton recalled: "When I heard other people talking about how bad things were, I'd start crying. It was like watching *Old Yeller*, seeing Old Yeller die every day. You can only take so much."

Elton said that after a few months of hearing other people's sad stories, he thought: "Maybe my problems aren't so bad. Maybe I'm magnifying things. . . . There's people dying on the highways, people getting shot. I just said [to myself], 'This is life. You're not dead. You're not crippled. You got to accept it.' "

Armed with this attitude, Elton quit his individual and group therapies. In the decade since, Elton told me he'd reconnected with his sons and landed another coal-mining job when a new mine opened up. "I'm not perfect," he told me, but he said he'd never felt the need to go back into therapy.

The combination of individual and group therapies also helped Jesse Hefner, who was thirty-six at the time his father shot himself beside a pond near the family home. When the death occurred, Jesse already had been in individual therapy for four months. His wife had insisted upon it, saying she would leave him if he didn't go. "I was becoming like my dad," he recalled. "I was angry a lot of the time. I was seething."

Jesse, a police officer, had chosen a woman to be his therapist. He'd started with the attitude that together, he and she would "fix the problem, and then it'll be done." In the early weeks, he'd focused on the family issues that were bothering his wife. His father had come up in the course of the discussions, but had not been a major focus.

Then came the suicide, and Jesse's therapy took a number of turns. First, his individual work quickly began focusing on his relationship with his dad. He was able to cry in his therapist's presence— and to admit that "some pressure had been lifted off of me" by the death. In Jesse's childhood, his father had been heavy-handed and perpetually angry, he told the therapist; even as an adult, Jesse often feared the older man. The father's absence from his daily life offered some relief.

Over many months, Jesse used his weekly therapy sessions to sort through his complicated relationship with his father. He asked family members for more information about his dad and brought that to his counselor. By the time I talked with him three years after the death, Jesse told me: "I've forgiven my dad for the stuff he didn't do right. Based on where he came from, he didn't do badly. Part of it is understanding that *his* dad was a hugely abusive parent. . . . I recognize [my dad's] weaknesses, but I don't condemn him anymore."

Group therapy helped Jesse in a different way. The day after the suicide, a representative had contacted Jesse from the police department's Employee Assistance Program and invited him to participate in a suicide survivor group. Feeling desperate and confused at the time, Jesse agreed to join.

There, he said, he heard stories similar to his own. He felt less alone. He recalled that in one of the first sessions he attended, "This lady said: 'You will not believe this, but someday you will know that every suicide has a gift.' Well, I didn't believe her. But it's true. My dad's gift to me was: 'This is you in twenty years if you don't try to make your life better. If you don't come to peace with things, you'll be sitting by that pond.' If I hadn't gone into therapy, if I hadn't taken a real hard look at my life, twenty years from now, I'd be in the same spot. I know now that I won't be."

When I spoke with Jesse three years after the death, he was still participating in the suicide group and still seeing his individual counselor.

There's one other kind of help that some men sought, though in a strict sense, it was not therapy. It was the self-led men's group. Several of the men I interviewed had joined groups of men who met regularly to talk about their lives. No money changed hands in these groups, although some of the participants were therapists, and some of the nontherapists were trained in leading men's groups.

One man who attended such a group told me he was most helped by an atmosphere that welcomed the anger he still felt toward his father, fourteen years after the death. "Male rage isn't acceptable everywhere," this man said. He added: "One thing I worried about coming in was that [men in the group] would try to tell me what a man ought to be. It didn't happen. There's a lot of open space. We can explore."

Another son paid $600 to participate in a men's weekend sponsored by a Wisconsin-based group called the Mankind Project. After that experience, the son joined a free, weekly, ongoing group of men who also had been through the weekend.

When I talked with this son, he was forty-seven. It had been twenty years since his father's death. He told me what he'd missed most was the chance to develop a man-to-man relationship with his dad. He had been at the cusp of such a relationship, he said, when his father died suddenly. "I find that [the men's group] fulfills the need of welcoming home the prodigal son. . . . What I lost was being able to come back and be affirmed by my father. Being in the group has allowed other men to affirm me."

The son added: "I don't know why I think of this, because [my father] would never have done this. But the visual image is of him putting his arm around me, sort of grabbing my head, and giving me some 'noogs,' and saying, 'I love you, you knucklehead. . . . You're a knucklehead, we're all knuckleheads. Welcome to the knucklehead club.' "

John Lee, author of *The Flying Boy* and founder of the Austin (Texas) Men's Center, believes men, on the whole, shy away from therapy—to their own detriment. After the loss of a father, he told me, men can usually benefit from talking in-depth about their relationships with their dads. "Most men are recovering from the *life* of the father, not the death," Lee said.

What are the signs that professional help might be needed? Lee said that after the death, if a son notices himself acting like his father in ways the son knows are unhealthy, it's a sign to see a counselor. Another warning sign Lee mentioned was extended inactivity or isolation.

Other counselors said a surviving son might also consider therapy after a father-death if his health has deteriorated, if he's stopped doing things that used to be pleasurable, if he's using drugs or alcohol heavily, or if he has frequent thoughts of suicide.

Choosing the right therapist can be tricky. Thomas Golden, coauthor of *When a Man Faces Grief*, suggests looking for counselors who are experienced in dealing with loss. Many therapists "are petrified of grief," he said. He recommended contacting the Association for Death Education and Counseling (see Appendix II: Resources for Men Facing Loss), which maintains a list of grief counselors around the country.

The most important evaluation, however, must be performed by the client, Golden said. "You've got to feel connected" to the therapist. "You've got to feel the therapist wants to know about you, cares about you, and is trying to give you a safe place to dump your stuff. If a therapist has a big agenda, if he says, 'You need to release,' then run. They need to be there for your agenda, not theirs."

Golden has a suggestion for grief counselors who want to serve men better: Invite them to *do* something, not sit in a circle and talk. For example, Golden said, a Hospice group located near a lake could invite widowers for a day-long fishing excursion in honor of their deceased partners. Golden said: "Men will come to that. They meet all the other men whose wives have died. When that's over, they walk off in pairs and threes." Grief-counseling providers must get creative, Golden said, because "coming in for help is against the masculine code."

Indeed, 92 percent of the men questioned for this book chose not to seek any kind of professional help. Most of those I interviewed said they received adequate support from spouses, partners, friends, and family members. When I asked about whether they'd considered seeing a therapist, a few men became mildly offended. "I'm not *that* bad off, am I?" one said.

Most men seemed to view counseling not as a potential facilitator of normal grief, but as a last resort, appropriate for emergencies. At the same time, virtually all agreed that talking with an interested outsider about the death could be a valuable experience. Toward the end of most of my initial conversations with men, which generally lasted two to three hours, I asked what had helped them the most in coping with their father's death.

More than a few said talking with me.

David Halberstam

It has been fifty years, and David Halberstam, the Pulitzer Prize–winning war correspondent and author, can't remember all the details surrounding his father's death. But even now, at certain times—when he shaves in the morning, or visits a friend in the hospital, or hears the phone ring after 10 P.M.—Halberstam will catch a whiff or a glimpse or a sense of the man who, even in death, continued to help guide his son through an adventurous life and career.

The younger Halberstam had just turned sixteen when his dad, a hardworking, chain-smoking physician, died of a heart attack at age fifty-three. The call from the hospital came late at night. During the year that followed, Halberstam experienced a "sense of coldness, of being more of an island," he told me in an interview. "I was emotionally distraught, frozen."

It's not that Halberstam had spent that much time with his dad. The older man had always worked long hours, and after the bombing of Pearl Harbor (which occurred when David was seven),

Dr. Halberstam joined the Army and spent much of the next five years away from home, attending to the wounded. After the war, the father lived just five more years, and even during that time, he was usually out of the home, working to rebuild his medical practice.

Yet despite their lack of time together, the father had been "the person I was connected to more than anyone," Halberstam said. He remembered from earliest childhood the "sweet-sour smell" of shaving cream and cigarettes in the bathroom each morning. From later years, Halberstam recalled his father's "kindness, his tolerance. When I had a bad report card, Mom would be quite upset. 'Well, do better . . . , let's pick it up.' My mother was always raising the high-jump bar. [My father] had a tolerance with the imperfections of childhood."

After the death, Halberstam did well enough in high school to be admitted to Harvard, where he began his journalism career at the campus newspaper, *The Crimson*. From the start, he said, he could sense that his father would have supported him in his work. "You could feel his confidence," Halberstam said. "You were smart enough to know he was rooting for you."

One of Halberstam's first professional jobs was at *The Tennessean* newspaper in Nashville. It was there that he met Carl Zibart, a middle-aged bookstore owner who ended up serving as a father figure to the young reporter. Halberstam explained: "I think you have proxy fathers, older men you take comfort from, who you can go to for some degree of sustenance, some degree of resonance that you're doing okay. You almost audition older men to play that role. In Carl, I found kindness, intelligence, a sense that I was of value."

During these early years of his career, Halberstam would often dream of his father. In the dreams, the older man came vividly alive. "It was so powerful," Halberstam recalled. "I could really see him. . . . It was painful waking up. That was the hard part. [The dream] was so palpable. The presence was so comforting. The person who appeared was always so kind."

When Halberstam was twenty-six, he left *The Tennessean* to join *The New York Times*. His father's influence followed him. The son accepted overseas war assignments, he told me, in part because his father had done so; at age forty-six, the elder Halberstam had joined the military to combat the Nazis.

David Halberstam eventually would win his Pulitzer for coverage of the Vietnam War. He recounted an incident in Vietnam in which the legacy of his father played a role. It was early fall of 1963, and the war was heating up. At a press briefing one day, Halberstam listened as a U.S. military officer warned him and other journalists to stop being so aggressive in their attempts to report from the front lines of the war. The general specifically named Halberstam and a colleague, Neil Sheehan, in his comments, scolding them for contacting military brass and other higher-ups in their efforts to get to the battlefield.

When the general was done speaking, Halberstam, who was then twenty-nine years old, stood up with barely controlled anger. "We are going to go on calling the generals and the ambassador," he recalled saying. "We're here to report. We are not your privates or your corporals. A lot of Americans went into battle, a lot of American gear was used in combat, and Americans deserve to know what happened. You have every right to write to our editors and tell them we're too aggressive, and you can ask them to send somebody else. But until then, we're going to try and keep going out in the field." Then he sat down.

Halberstam's rebuttal signaled a new attitude among the media, which until this period had been regularly, and often willingly, censored by the military. Thirty-six years later, Halberstam said of his rejoinder to the general: "That was really my father. I always thought that was the kind of thing he taught me. Stand up for who you are. Stand up for what you believe. Don't be pushed around."

A few years later, Halberstam left *The Times* and began a successful career writing books about politics, business, and sports. His books include such bestsellers as *The Best and the Brightest*, *Summer of '49*, *The Reckoning*, and *Playing for Keeps*. Yet even at sixty-four, his age when I interviewed him, Halberstam remained driven. He suggested that his father played a role in this ongoing ambition: "It's rather humbling to know that no matter how accomplished you are, there's this person up there whose approval you still seek."

Halberstam said he sometimes wishes for a conversation with his dad "to go over things, figure out what you did right and what you didn't do well, get something of a report card, share your life, let him look at his granddaughter, who I think he'd like very, very much." For the most part, though, Halberstam said he doesn't dwell on the loss. He said of his dad: "In some odd way, he's a living, organic part of me. . . . There's a great line in *Carousel*, something like, 'You are not dead as long as someone who is alive thinks of you.' In that sense, he's very much a living presence."

Chapter 11

LINGERINGS

THE DEATH had come in the night. Will Kraus, fifty-three years old at the time, had been sleeping at his ailing father's house. He'd set the alarm for 4 A.M., when his dad would need his next round of medications. The alarm had rung, and Will had gathered up the pills and gone to his father's bed. But his father was dead. The mourning was harsh, as Will subsequently watched his mother succumb to cancer. In the months and years that followed, Will would occasionally awaken in the middle of the night, with a strong sense of missing his dad. Then he'd check the clock. More often than not, it read: 4 A.M.

For fifteen-year-old Bill McDowell, his father's death had come without warning; he'd had no time to say or hear last words. Bill had been staggered by the loss, and recovered very gradually. Twelve years later, as the plane ferrying him from Paris to New York settled in above the clouds, the in-flight movie began to play. It was *Shine*, a film about a boy whose relationship with his father shapes the son into a brilliant pianist and troubled man. For much of the next two hours, Bill recalled, "I'm bawling in my seat." He explained: "I still have these moments. [The pain] stays at some level, then comes out, and then goes back in its closet. . . . Sometimes I'll be at the movies. I'll get tears in my eyes in a moment of pathos. And then I'll think of him. When I cry, I think of my father."

The death had come violently, perhaps appropriately for a man who had physically abused his eldest son. That son, Horace Tipton, then twenty-one, had welcomed the loss and savored his anger for more than a decade. But then Horace had forgiven his dad; he'd even named his only son after the older man. Still, forty-two years later, when Horace cut a finger, stubbed a toe, or hurt himself in some other way, he would sense his father's presence. He explained: "That smell of sweat, mixed with his aftershave—it comes to me at the strangest times. . . . I can't put my finger on it, but I look around for him. I can still feel him. In some sense, I guess, he will always be with me."

After the acute pain of the loss, after the period of active mourning, after a son has made whatever changes in his life seem appropriate—even then, the connection between a father and son is rarely over. The majority of men who contributed to this book reported that they continued to experience their father's presence months, years, and even decades after the loss.

Sons cited five particular "triggers" that could bring back memories and emotions about their fathers: anniversaries and holidays; the media; relationships with other men in their lives; their own tendency to act like their fathers; and dreams or visions of their dads. We'll take a look at some examples of these, and then at whether or not they're a sign of trouble.

Typical of the first trigger—anniversaries and other holidays—was a man from Michigan who told me that each spring, as the thaw begins in his home state, he experiences a downswing in his mood. He was eight years old when his father died. Through his teens and early twenties, he didn't know why he became sad each spring. Then he was reminded by a family member that his father's death had occurred in April. I talked with the son fifteen years after this revelation, and he told me that linking his annual depressions with the anniversary of his dad's death had been helpful. He still felt melancholy, but "now I don't plan vacations" for the spring.

While this son had a positive relationship with his dad, a musician who was forty-six when his father died told me he had "an anniversary reaction" although he'd had a troubled relationship with his father during their lives together. The son said that on the date of his father's death each year, "I feel numb and relieved and sometimes a little sad. I remind myself that it is up to me to also remember his good points . . . , his incredible intellect, his magical green thumb, his major contributions to the [immigrant] community. . . . When I think of him now, I also feel empowered. I am the hope of his 'hopeless' life."

For Henry Ravich, who lost his father at age twenty, it's his own birthday that reconnects him each year with his dad. Henry's father died at age forty-seven of a heart attack. I spoke with Henry for the first time when he was exactly that age. He told me: "The past year, I started stressing out over my blood pressure readings, which are borderline high. The doctor said there was nothing to worry about, but I became anxious anyway. I started checking my blood pressure almost once a day. Of course, that only made it higher." Henry said his worry eventually escalated to the point that his doctor prescribed antianxiety medication for him.

When I spoke with Henry a second time, he had passed his forty-eighth birthday, which he called "a milestone." He was continuing to take his medication. "My blood pressure is still up. But I'm not as stressed about it," he said.

A son who was nineteen at the time of his father's death said he too thought of his father on his own birthday. I spoke with the son when he was still a few years short of reaching fifty-two, the age at which his father had died. The son told me he was actually looking forward to catching up with his father: "Every birthday, I realize that I'm that much closer to my father's age. Each year, it's 'I'm seven years younger,' or 'I'm six years younger.' I think it'll help me when I get there. It'll help me put a limit on his life. Still being younger than he was, it's not conclusive yet. It's not over."

Father's Day was the trigger for several other men I interviewed. One middle-aged man said he'd performed a ritual on each of the five Father's Days since his father's death: "Since the graves of my parents are some two thousand miles away, I visit a local graveyard to place flowers, straighten up a bit, and so on. It's a gesture of respect to my parents as well as the parents of others. I hope I have a counterpart back east who does the same." This man acknowledged that he wasn't sure if his action was normal. He added: "You are the only person I've told about this. Even my kids don't know."

Birthdays, anniversaries, Father's Day, and family holidays might be categorized as "predictable trigger events" because they tend to be so closely tied to actual memories of the father. I heard from men about more peripheral triggers: a daughter's graduation, a cousin's wedding, the birth of a grandson. Occasionally, a triggering event at first seemed to have no connection with the father at all.

Brent Williamson was thirty-eight years old, and a longtime Baptist minister, when his boss, the senior minister at his church, suddenly quit. The resignation prompted an extraordinary wave of emotion in Brent, whose father had died sixteen years earlier. I met with him shortly after his boss's resignation. Tears filled his eyes as he explained:

"In the past couple of months, I have missed Dad so much. I can't re-member the last time I've missed him like this."

During this conversation, Brent said he did not know why the resignation of his boss and his renewed mourning had coincided. When we spoke again eighteen months later, however, he saw at least one connection. The resignation had thrown his work life into turmoil, he said, forcing him to reevaluate the whole direction of his career. In this situation, he wanted the advice of his father, who also had been a minister. The son said: "I was aware that no one knew me like he did, and no one knew the ministry like he did. I was confused, and needed insight. He was the man to give it."

Thoughts and feelings related to the father are also frequently trig-gered by events covered by the media.

After U.S. Secretary of Commerce Ron Brown died in a plane crash in 1996, a forty-year-old engineer watched on television as Brown's son delivered a stirring eulogy. The engineer, who'd lost his own father five years earlier, wept at the younger Brown's words. At first, he couldn't understand why he was so emotional. Later, he realized: "Seeing a son speak so highly of his father reminded me of how I felt about Dad."

Movies, especially those with father-son themes, can also reac-tivate a son's emotions about his dad. Several men I spoke with reported strong reactions to *Field of Dreams*, the Kevin Costner film about an Iowa farmer who plows down a cornfield to build a baseball diamond in honor of his dead father. "That picture kicks my ass," said one laborer, who was eight when his dad died.

A thirty-six-year-old photographer, who was a minor-league baseball player in his early twenties, said he watches *Field of Dreams* whenever he gets a chance. This son was eleven when his father died. "I start crying every time I see that movie. It's . . . the [thought] of being able to just for a moment, see your father again. I'm getting choked up talking about it. I can see myself playing catch, having a catch, with my dad." (For a list of other movies mentioned by sons, see Appendix III: *Father Films*.)

Music could also serve as a trigger. Some sons cited particular songs or scores that their dads had loved, while others spoke of songs in which the lyrics made them think of their fathers. Several mentioned "Cat's in the Cradle," the late Harry Chapin's folk-lament about the unfulfilled yearning for connection between a father and son. Another told me that he was moved whenever he heard "The Living Years," the 1988 rock hit by Mike and the Mechanics. The song is about a son whose father has died; the son regrets not having told his father "in the living years" how he felt about him.

Seeing other men that remind a son of his deceased father can provide powerful triggers as well. A forty-seven-year-old insurance salesman who had lost his father twenty-two years earlier, said: "It's strange. When I see a man who is about seventy-five"—the age his father would have been as we spoke—"I wonder about Dad." The wondering doesn't last long, perhaps only a few moments, but it sometimes brings a sting of tears to the son's eyes.

A stay-at-home dad with whom I spoke said that after his father died, he treated older males differently than he had in the past. The son, who was fifteen when his father was killed in a car accident, recalled that he seemed to seek approval from older men. He said: "I became aware of it only when I found myself putting a lot of effort into my thesis [in college], not because I wanted good grades, but to make the head of our institute proud. I had a special relationship with him which I think he also felt."

A fifty-eight-year-old guitar teacher, who was four when his father died, told me he'd been aware of a "mysterious connection" with men for decades. He said: "All my life, I've had men older than me walk up to me and just start a conversation like I was some long-lost friend. And I would never be puzzled by it. I would just take it in stride. I'd have old guys walk up to me on the street . . . and start talking about architecture, or the Depression, or World War II. They'd say: 'You've got a million-dollar smile. You're going to go a long way in this world.' And that would be it. I'd never see them again. But for twenty minutes we were like bosom buddies." This man attributed these incidents to what he called "my Older Man Karma."

One time, when I spoke of my own living father with a man I was interviewing, it triggered his sadness. "I choke up when you mention your dad," this man said. He'd lost his father when he was eighteen; he was sixty-seven when we spoke. "God damn," he said, "I'd like my father to know me now." I felt something akin to survivor's guilt when I heard this comment and was more careful about how and when I brought up my own father in subsequent conversations.

In addition to holidays, the media, and interactions with other men, sons said they were triggered into reconnecting with their fathers when they noticed themselves acting or speaking like their dads. In my survey, 54 percent of men said they had experienced this phenomenon, known to psychologists as "identification."

A middle-aged lobbyist who had lost his father eight years previous to our conversation said of his dad: "Periodically, I become him. Like every time I pack the car to go on a camping trip, I suddenly realize I've become my father. I have these strong memories of my father so methodically packing the car to be sure the space has been efficiently used in the trunk. I'm just as anal about that as my father was—but I have a smaller trunk."

A cattle rancher whose father had been dead six years told me he sometimes heard his father's voice: "I'll say something. And I'll think: 'Son of a bitch. It sounds just like him. Damn, I sound just like Pop.' It says to me: 'Hey, we're all here in the same mold.' "

A church administrator who was thirty-five when his dad died, caught glimpses of his father as he parented his own eight-year-old son. "He's quite a verbal kid. He knows a lot of stuff. He always wants to talk about it. Today, I was taking him to a bus stop. He wanted to talk to me about how people discovered television. . . . He was asking questions, and I was making up answers. This is the same kind of conversations, on different subjects, that I had with my father. It gives me a shock sometimes."

Other men said they were reminded of their fathers in their own choice of words, the tone they used in disciplining their children, or other traits. One forty-five-year-old schoolteacher noticed that he now "putters" around the house in the same way his dad used to, looking for things to fix or paint. A twenty-seven-year-old computer analyst, a decade after losing his father, recalled his dad as distant and introverted. Then he told me he was beginning to see the old man in himself. "A monastic life really appeals to me," the son said.

More than two-thirds of men I surveyed dreamed about their fathers after the death, including 9 percent who said they dreamed about him frequently. For some sons, as we saw in Chapter 7, dreams were integral to their recovery. For others, the dreams provided occasional measures of their current relationship to the memory of the father.

One medical technician, who was thirty-five at the death, said he had very positive dreams in which his father "was in a coffin on top of a train. We were taking him to bury him. We're at the train station. I can't explain why he was in the coffin alive, but all of a sudden he climbs down from the coffin." The son said he had a lot of other dreams in which his father was just "a part of everyday life. . . . I found those to be pleasant, nice to have." He added, "I'm not one to remember dreams, but these were always really vivid."

An educator, who was thirty-six at the death, had always taken pleasure in talking with his father. I interviewed the son when he was sixty-six. He told me of his continuing conversations with his dad in the dream world. "The dreams were never frequent. But three or four times a year, we visit."

A few sons found their dreams less comforting. One man, who lost his father at thirty-three, continued to have regular dreams about his dad for several years: "The dreams all have a similar quality to them. My father is alive again, but after having been dead. They are never about him never having died. Sometimes he's pretty normal, sometimes like a bad horror movie. Sometimes I feel like he goes to all this trouble to come back from being dead, and then I don't really pay him enough attention."

The dreams of a middle-school teacher, twenty-five years after his father's death, were often unsettling. The man was forty-five when I spoke with him: "In some of my dreams, he is young, strong, but I always know that he is not supposed to be alive. In a dream I had recently, my dad was a young man about twenty, twenty-five years old. He was playing football with some friends. I wondered if I should tell him that he was going to be my father someday. Would he think that I was crazy? In other dreams, he appears older, and sad looking. I am not a psychiatrist, and don't know how to interpret these dreams but one common thing stands out: Something always seems to be wrong."

A few men I spoke with told me they had encountered their fathers, not in their dreams but in waking life. Among these men, there was a sense that the father was spiritually present, often looking out for them. One man put it this way: "I've been aware that when I don't know where I'm going [in a car], and I make the right turn, it's my father who was guiding me."

One son who'd lost his father at age eight told me that on one occasion, he had a powerful experience of being guided by his dad. This son was in his early forties when I spoke with him. He said that about two years after the death, he was in the kitchen of his home, preparing toast. The bread got stuck in the toaster, and he picked up a fork to fish out the bread. At that particular moment, this son recalled, "Someone picked me up from behind, lifted me off the floor, swung me away from the toaster, and put me down. . . . I said, 'Dad!' It felt like this presence moved up into the ceiling and was gone."

I asked this man if it were possible that he actually stuck the fork into the toaster and was shocked. He said no. Of his father, he said: "His spirit still is in existence. . . . At critical points in my life, I've felt my father's presence."

Nineteen percent of the sons I surveyed reported that they still were angry with their deceased fathers. But positive connections far outnumbered negative ones among those sons who had ongoing interactions with the father's memory. Dr. Dennis Klass, a leading bereavement theorist and coeditor of the book *Continuing Bonds*, believes that "a certain cleansing" of the father-son relationship often occurs after the father's death. Once the loved one is no longer around in the flesh, the survivor tends to release his resentments—sometimes quickly, sometimes gradually—and focus his memory mostly on the good in the deceased. "The relationship becomes pure in a way that tends to serve the better self," Klass said.

Klass told me that this had happened to him after his own father had died. Klass was in his late thirties at the time and had been emotionally estranged from his dad for almost two decades. After the death, however, Klass felt a softening in his judgments. When I spoke with Klass, it had been twenty years since the death. This was how he described a typical connection with his dad: "My dad was a master with his hands. He could do anything with tools that he set his mind to. I did not inherit this, but any time I'm at the tool bench and I pick up one of his tools, I feel very close. That's the part of him I've kept. Sometimes I'll even say: 'Damn, I wish you were here.' "

Given this tendency for positive feelings to accompany memories of the father, it wasn't surprising that many men I interviewed actively *sought* connection with their dads in the aftermath of his death. Among the sons I surveyed, 72 percent said that after their father died, they spent time with mementos of his, such as photographs or personal items he once owned. In addition, 28 percent said they prayed to, talked to, or otherwise tried to communicate with their fathers. These men seemed to be seeking something from their fathers: comfort, guidance, inspiration, release.

One middle-aged son, who lost his dad in childhood, told me he had a calm feeling when he sat in his own backyard, overseeing a rock garden he'd built. The son said that throughout his life, he'd stopped along roadsides to pick up particularly large or interesting rocks, which he'd place in his yard. Only in his forties did he learn that his father had done the same thing.

A forty-one-year-old lobbyist, whose father had died eight years earlier, told me that "on special days, I'll carry his watch around with me. I use his watch as a sort of catalyst, a device, to create a little ritual of memory of him."

A high school teacher said that after his father died, he had only a handful of photos of his dad. He remembered a poster his father once had on his wall and looked around in stores for a copy of it. He never found the poster, but eventually ran across a beer ad in a magazine that contained a portion of it. The son scanned the ad into his computer, and when we spoke, it served as the wallpaper, or backdrop, for his version of Windows 95. "When this picture comes up on my computer," the son told me, "it puts me in a good mood."

A fifty-year-old bookstore manager, who was thirteen when his dad died, said that a couple of times a year, "I just get the urge to pull out some of his things and look at them and combine them with the memories I have." He continued: "Sometimes, it's precipitated by a particular event, seeing *Saving Private Ryan*, for instance, but more often, it's just when the mood strikes. Fortunately, my dad left good records: scrapbooks and army logs from World War II; a book-let called 'All About Me' [with] all sorts of personal information when he received his diploma from a correspondence school; a lot of pictures . . . , a coffee cup, and drafting instruments. A paper-weight of his is on my desk."

By looking at these artifacts, the son said, he gets a chance to think of the goodness in his dad and to feel some of the emotion he still carries over the death. He said: "As unable to cry as I was then, it is difficult for me to contemplate his death these days *without* crying."

Eighteen years after the death of his father, another son told me he still sought comfort from the older man. The son, a retired la-borer, was seventy-seven when I spoke with him. He was suffering from prostate cancer. "When I'm in the shape I'm in now, when I've gone through some of these crazy tests I've had to go through, and get some of these problems that I'm dealing with, sometimes I wonder: 'Hey, Pop, give me a hand down here.' My mother and dad, to me, they're my saints."

This son said he missed his father desperately. "Here I am, nobody to say Dad to. Who are you going to call 'Dad'? Nobody. And that's important." He added: "I have a pocket knife of his. I used it yesterday. Just a plain old pocket knife, two blades, nothing fancy. I keep it. When I grab that, of course, I know that's my dad's knife. He comes to mind."

Marshall Black, a retired agricultural inspector, was, at ninety-four, the oldest man I interviewed for this book. His father had been dead for fifty-three years. Since then, Marshall had lost his wife, two siblings, and son-in-law, as well as many friends and colleagues. Even at his advanced age, walking with two canes and battling cancer, he was sought after in his community for his wisdom and good humor. He was glad to give advice to others. Yet, he told me, when he faced tough decisions himself, he'd often sit quietly in his easy chair, close his eyes, and conjure up an image of his own father. Then he'd ask the dead man for advice.

He heard no actual voices from beyond, but when he emerged from his meditation, he'd usually have something of an answer. Marshall explained: "The loss of cherished persons is never completely overcome. The relationships continue. They are always with us. . . . I have my father's value system, his frame of reference. I have preserved the father-space inside me."

If, as Marshall Black believes, the loss of loved ones is never complete, what about the mourning? When is it over? The psychologist J. William Worden contends this is a question no more answerable than "How high is up?"

Indeed, among the men I interviewed, each defined "the end of grief" in his own way. Some said it was when they could think of their fathers and smile. Others said it was when they didn't think about their fathers much at all.

When I asked a forty-nine-year-old college teacher, five years after his father's death, whether he had completed his grief, he objected to the question. "I don't know that I need to be healed," he said. "I don't know that I need to be fixed. I'm just sad. Are you going to be cured of sadness? There's no problem to be solved. He's dead, gone, that's it."

A fifty-three-year-old psychologist, who'd lost his dad four years earlier, agreed in principle with this man, but expressed it differently. He said of his father: "I'll always miss him. So the grieving process doesn't end. But a shift has taken place. I finally see my father's story, his life, not as fragmented events but as a whole thing. . . . All the parts fit together. I appreciate the story. And I can see myself in that story. I belong to it."

The son continued: "The remaining sadness is I can't tell him that I accept his story. I don't need a different story to belong to. It's good enough just the way it is. I can't let him know that I see and accept his story. And there's probably nothing my father needed more. That's what I'd like to be able to do. Maybe that's why I'm sitting with you. It's a chance to honor his story."

Several of the men who told me about their dreams, anniversary reactions, and other reconnections with their dead fathers seemed sheepish as they recounted these incidents. A few wondered aloud whether it was normal or healthy for them to have such "flashbacks."

Some grief specialists have wondered the same. For most of the twentieth century, in fact, the conventional wisdom had been that ongoing emotional ties to a dead person was a sign of pathology, of a bereaved person stuck in his or her sorrow. One mid–twentieth-century psychotherapist declared to his colleagues that continuing connection was "a form of regression" that must be "actively opposed." The belief was that until a bereaved person could sever the relationship with the deceased, he or she could not create healthy new relationships.

In the 1970s and 1980s, however, psychologist John Bowlby challenged this notion. He was particularly struck by one study in which more than half of the widows and widowers he observed retained, in his words, "a strong sense of the continuing presence of their partner without the turmoil and disappointment, search and frustration, anger and blame" that had existed previously. He came to believe that people could lose loved ones, and continue to think about, talk about—even talk to—the deceased and still involve themselves satisfyingly in their relationships with the living.

Since the 1980s, more and more grief specialists have moved toward this point of view. They've come to regard mourning as an ongoing "accommodation," in which the bereaved person, throughout his or her subsequent life, may continue to connect with the deceased. These connections may decrease over time or intensify. They may come at specified times of year or without apparent pattern. They may occur only when the bereaved person seeks to establish the connection or, as in dreams, of their own accord.

My own observation, based on the interviews for this book, is that those who continued to have a relationship with their fathers after the father's death were often the most settled with the loss. Through this ongoing connection, these sons seemed to gradually work through any pain, anger, or regret. After that, they were free to focus on the appreciation they felt toward the father, to celebrate his life and their own.

Part 3

———————

THE LESSONS OF
FATHERLOSS

At the very end, I told my father that I would miss him.
I did not say that I had always missed him.
—WRITER ANATOLE BROYARD

Chapter 12

AFFECTIONATE FATHERING

WHAT DOES a son need from his dad?

As the father of a seven-year-old boy, I've long desired an answer to this question. I know how my father raised me, and I've watched a lot of other men commit fatherhood. But the essence of fathering has always eluded me. There's mystery in the relationship between a dad and his child. And you can add to the difficulty the fact that the target keeps moving: Since my own childhood began in the 1950s, fatherhood has changed again and again.

Researching this book, I saw another chance to examine fatherhood. This time, I had access to what I consider to be the real experts: scores of sons, most of whom were also fathers. In the course of probing the deaths of their dads, I asked these men for images and anecdotes from their earliest lives, as well as from their adolescence, young adulthood, and beyond. I wanted their opinions: What makes a good dad? How does a father's role change through the life span?

And what, if anything, can a father do to help prepare his son for the father's death?

Gradually, a consensus formed around these questions. Not an orthodoxy, nor a rule book; fathering is too circumstantial to operate on any rigid scheme. Rather, what emerged were *indications,* hints really, at the essence of fathering.

Distilling these, I found myself remorseful, relieved, and sometimes inspired. I regretted incidents in which I could see in retrospect that I'd hurt my son. I was relieved that he has been so resilient. And ultimately, I was motivated to make adjustments in my approach to fathering, adjustments that may seem small or subtle, but that are making a real difference in my relationship with my son.

What follows, then, is my vision of what a son needs from his dad. Shaped by my conversations with men for this book, it focuses especially on discipline, affection, reconciliation, and farewells.

In the eyes of young sons, fathers often seem gigantic. Again and again, the sons I interviewed expressed wonder at the physical stature and power of the men who guided them in their early lives. Sons spoke of their dads in mythic terms. The older man was "immense," "awesome," "dominating," "imposing."

One son boasted to me about times his father would play softball with other dads at a local playground: "There were short fences, and he had difficulty keeping the ball in the yard." Down at the local bowling alley, meanwhile, this same father regularly "blasted the pins." A son who was eight when his father died told me he remembered the older man as possessing Herculean strength. Thirty-five years after the death, the son recalled: "One year, a tornado blew down a large tree in our yard. Most people would have hooked up a car or something" to lift the tree back upright. Instead, "my dad hooked up a harness to his body, and pulled it up like a plow horse."

The father of another son didn't need to lift a finger, let alone a tree, to impress his child. This son recalled a compelling moment when he was seven: "We lived in a two-story house, and [my father] called me from the top of the stairs. He'd just come out of the shower, and he was asking me to get something for him. And he was naked. He's six-foot-four, weighs two hundred pounds, he's at the top of the stairs. And here I am a little kid. He was a giant."

Given that we fathers tower over our sons, we must be careful to use our power judiciously. Sons told me they wanted their fathers to be strong, but to apply that strength in the service of protecting them. The father was to be a buffer against danger, a shield against the bad guys, the ghosts, and other demons.

Among the sons I spoke with, this desire for fatherly protection was usually fulfilled. One son spoke for many when he told me: "I wanted to be with my dad. I felt safe around him. I knew he would take care of me."

But there were exceptions. A computer programmer who grew up on a midwestern farm in the 1950s, said his earliest memories of his dad were painful ones: "My father and I were never on the same wavelength. I always felt that he resented me. And I was afraid of him. One memory comes back: He was herding pigs, and he had a long two-by-four that he was using to guide them. And one of the pigs got away, and Dad just started beating it with that stick. I started to cry. And that really made my father angry because I was too soft. . . . He started yelling at me: 'I'll use it on you!' "

This son continued: "And that was part of the reason I was afraid of my father—because when he got angry and he would spank us, he would get so carried away. . . . He'd use his hand, unless there was something else available. . . . I don't remember why he did it. All I remember is getting beat."

I heard numerous similar stories of paternal violence. Sons reported that their fathers slapped and punched them or hit them with switches, belts, shoes, razor strops, even chains. The infractions that precipitated the beatings were sometimes large, sometimes small. One son told me that when he was twelve, his father "knocked [him] around" for backing away from a fight. Another said he was hit with a belt from the time he was three for wetting his bed.

Not all spankings were classified by sons as "beatings." About three-fourths of the men I interviewed said they'd been spanked by their fathers, at least occasionally. Among these sons, the majority had either forgiven their dads or felt no need to forgive. "I deserved it" was a common refrain.

Yet even some of these sons acknowledged that discipline other than spanking tended to be more effective. One son, for example, who was in the middle of the pack among eight children, said he got "the belt" perhaps three or four times a year in his childhood. It usually fell on him after he showed disrespect to a teacher or elder in the church.

The son, looking back forty years, did not begrudge his father the whippings. But he said his dad's most effective punishment was "when he let me whoop myself. If I wasn't doing my homework, or I forgot my chores around the house, he'd sit me down and talk to me [about] what it meant to be part of a family, and how important it was to contribute. He'd talk to me for a long time, and then he'd tell me to go sit down and think about it."

A university professor I interviewed also remembered a "calm talking-to" he received from his father when he was about six. The son, who had just started piano lessons at the time, had laughed at his dad and called him "a stupid idiot" for not knowing the notes on the keyboard. The son recalled: "My father said, 'Come into my study. I want to have a little talk with you.' " Then, in a subdued voice, the father told the son: "These are the sorts of things we don't say to other people. It's not the right way to behave. It's not respectful."

The son recalled the rebuke vividly three decades later. Afterward, "I hung my head very low, and slunk out of the room," the son recalled. "I'm sure I didn't do it again. You know, when you speak softly, you carry a big stick."

A father's style of discipline was only one factor mentioned by sons in assessing the quality of the fathering they had received. Another factor was cited even more often: *affection.*

Sons didn't always use that term. Affection has the connotation of holding, cuddling, hugging, kissing, and other forms of physical contact. And indeed, when that occurred between a father and son, it seemed to have an unusually positive effect on the child.

For many of the sons I spoke with, their fondest memories of childhood were wrestling with their dads, being tossed into the air or carried piggyback, or some other form of direct physical play. "When my dad would come home from work, I would jump into his arms," one man told me. "I'd give him a kiss. . . . He welcomed it." Another man reported that "after my father came home from work and cleaned up, he'd set me on his lap and sing to me. I was four or five at the time."

A third son remembers rolling on the bed with his dad. "On Saturday mornings, when he'd been gone all week, I'd climb into my parents' bed. He had horrible breath in the morning. We played a game where he tried to breathe on me, and I hid." This son, who later had three children of his own, quipped that since becoming a father, he had "a dread fear of inflicting morning breath on my kids. As a parent, I breathe a lot through my nose."

Why was wrestling, lap-sitting, hugging, and other physical affection so fondly remembered by sons? For one thing, it seemed to offer the boy a close-up view of the beast he would one day become: a man. The poet Robert Bly, author of *Iron John*, says close contact between a father and son helps the son "tune" himself to the rhythm of masculinity. The boy experiences, in his body and bones, how a man moves, feels, smells. Just as importantly, according to the sons I spoke with, when the father's touch is playful and loving, the son feels accepted and protected.

But physical affection does not come easily to some fathers. Perhaps they were raised without such contact with their own fathers and find it alien, even unmanly. Fortunately, I discovered in my conversations with sons that affection could be administered in a variety of ways. Ultimately, affection was less about physicality than about *loving attention by a father toward his son*.

Some fathers show affection by simply talking with, and listening to, their sons. A middle-aged English teacher told me that in his childhood, he and his father often sat around in the living room on weekends, telling stories to each other. Three years after this son's father had died, the son reflected fondly on those weekends: "I could make him laugh. I'd tell him funny stories, not jokes, but stories. He had a wonderful laugh. He'd really laugh good and loud."

Another form of fatherly affection is intellectual interplay. "My father was always playing games with me," recalled one son. "We played chess and cribbage and bridge. We did the Sunday *New York Times* crossword puzzles together." The son, who later became a mathematician, added: "I do the same thing with my kids."

This same son recalled that he and his dad never said "I love you" to each other and rarely hugged. Yet the son could sense in other ways that his father cared: "I loved to shake his hand. It was fun.

That was an intimate moment for me and my dad. . . . He had an impressive hand. Big, strong. It's not like he squeezed so hard he hurt you. But you could feel some of his power. . . . I think back to the day I drove off to college. There were handshakes then."

I heard about several fathers who showed affection by taking an active interest in a son's school or other endeavors. A businessman who was fifteen when his father died recalled of his father: "He didn't say, 'Hey, let's go out and throw the baseball.' But he did do a lot of activities with me." It meant a lot to this son, for example, when his father took him to auto races and baseball games, and when he volunteered to help at church with preparations for the son's Confirmation. "I don't think he was a touchy-feely person," the son explained, "but he was a real loving father."

Affection even could be conveyed secondhand. A sixty-nine-year-old social worker, who'd been adopted in childhood by a stepfather, recalled the way his stepdad treated the son's mother in the early days. "He was gentle and tender, and listened to her." The son told me his mother had been through two abusive partners before this new man arrived in their lives when the son was about eight. So the son was wary at first of his stepdad-to-be. He later remembered the older man's attitude: "He was patient with me, and I came around."

When a son doesn't get affection, in any form, from his father, the resulting wound can be deep and lasting. Second only to the abuser in generating resentment among the sons I interviewed was the faraway father, the distant dad, the patriarch who was unavailable or uninvolved. Whether the father meant it or not, the message to the son was clear: You don't matter.

"One of the memories I carry from childhood is Dad's bookshelf," a forty-five-year-old man told me. "My dad read a lot. He would come home from work, sit in his chair, and read for most of the evening. Maybe it was his escape. . . . Sometimes, I'd go to that wall of books, and try to figure out what was there that was more fascinating than me."

This son never reconciled with his father, who died when the son was thirty. One of the difficulties in the aftermath of the father's death, the son told me, was that "I'm still mourning what I didn't get from him."

Other men spoke of having fathers who had "checked out" or who were "strong and silent," "a loner," lacking in empathy, "just not involved." Among such fathers, alcohol abuse showed up again and again. The father might stop for a few beers on the way home from work or start drinking when he got home. He'd often become absorbed in a book or TV show, or he'd fall asleep. One son said his daily chores included helping his drunken father stumble from his easy chair into his bed.

Clearly, a father's attention is crucial to his son. But like discipline, it can be overdone. Several men spoke of fathers who were too involved—"controlling," "heavy-handed," "in my face." One man said: "If he'd had his way, I'd have been a marionette." These dads, according to their sons, tended to have an agenda; they wanted their sons to participate in certain activities, even if the sons were not interested.

Sports was a central arena for this struggle. Several men told me they resented being pushed into sports and were hurt when the father's reaction to their lack of athletic interest or aptitude was to grow angry or distant. One fifty-six-year-old recalled: "When I was seven years old, my father told me I threw like a girl. I still feel the wound. After that, I never wanted to play ball again." Another son, a teacher, said: "I couldn't catch a ball. My brother was the athlete in the family. So my father preferred spending time with him."

Beyond sports, when fathers tried to push their children into certain professions or toward the father's vision of success, it also tended to backfire. One forty-two-year-old man recalled "the constant hounding" by his father to go to college and be successful in the business world. At first, the son tried to please his dad, who was a midlevel state employee, but eventually began to resent him. Looking back, the son told me, he quit college in part because he feared he wouldn't measure up to his father's standards.

A few years before his father died, this son told his dad: "No matter what I do, you're not going to like it. If I'm governor of the state, you're going to say I'm not president. If I'm a manager of Kroger, 'You're not chairman of the board.' If I become a priest, 'You're not the pope.' If I'm the pope, 'You're not God.' "

When we spoke, this son was thirty-seven years old and had recently started his own landscaping business. He'd never reconciled with his father, who'd died the year before in a car accident. He still occasionally spoke about his desire to go back and finish his college degree.

If a father is able to provide his son with protection and affection in childhood, he has, perhaps inadvertently, helped prepare the son for the father's death. According to the men who participated in my research, the quality of the father-son relationship in childhood was a key factor in how the son dealt with the death.

In the survey, I asked respondents whether they'd had a generally positive or negative relationship with their fathers in childhood. Those who responded "negative" were more than twice as likely to say they had ongoing problems in their lives stemming from the father's death. Twenty-one percent of sons who'd had negative relationships in childhood said they had ongoing problems, compared to just 8 percent among sons who reported having positive childhood relationships with their dads.

Frequently, sons who'd had positive relationships told me that while their immediate grief over the death was powerful, it generally mellowed over a few weeks or months. Most sons who'd had negative relationships, meanwhile, often reported less intense immediate reactions. But years, or even decades later, their unresolved relationships with their dads still nagged at them.

(One related finding of the survey: Sons who had positive relationships with their fathers in childhood were, after the father's death, more likely to find support with their friends and relatives. Thus, it may be that a positive relationship with a father in childhood contributes to the likelihood that a son will have positive relationships with friends and family members later in life.)

Even when a positive father-son connection fails to occur in the son's *childhood*, there are usually opportunities to compensate later. Another lesson I learned from the sons I interviewed was that fathering does not really end when a son is twenty-one, or forty-one, or even sixty-one. Throughout our lives, right up until the time of our deaths, we fathers have opportunities to deepen our relationships with our sons.

One way a father can help enhance his relationship with his son is by blessing the younger man. One man I interviewed, a business executive, said he had received a traditional Mexican blessing—a *bendición*—from his father when the son left Texas at age nineteen to look for work in California. The blessing, uttered by his father in Spanish, affirmed that the son was ready for the journey ahead and called upon God and humankind to look after him. It also softened the son's feelings toward a father who had often been harsh and uncompromising.

In the introduction to this book, I spoke of the importance of receiving my own father's blessing, the direct expression of his respect for me when I was twenty-seven. He'd said: "I want to tell you now how proud I am of you, of the choices you've made, of the life you've created." At the time, his father had just died, and my father was poignantly aware of having missed his dad's affirmation in his own life.

My father's blessing was especially important to me because I was concerned that I'd disappointed him. He'd put me through college, and now, five years into my career, I'd quit a good job with no plan for what I'd do next. When my father told me he was proud of the choices I'd made, I took it to mean that he supported me in my decision to stop and reevaluate my career direction. I felt the pressure lift and began to trust myself to make the right next steps.

My father's expression of pride was straightforward, but blessings can be subtle too, delivered, like affection, in ways unique to the father and son involved.

One forty-three-year-old son told me he recalled feeling blessed during a chat he had with his dad when the son was about twenty. "We were sitting in a bar at the time, and I remember I wasn't quite old enough to drink. Dad often preferred the atmosphere of a bar, not so much for drinking, but talking. The bar . . . was generally frequented by professors and other educated types like my dad. He was friends with many of them, and liked to engage in philosophical debates with them."

The son said he couldn't remember the topic of conversation on that day, but he recalled demonstrating to his dad that "I could hold my own among the mental giants, and that's what prompted him to say that we were equals . . . , that I was no longer his child, but his peer and friend. In a way, I suppose I had proven my manhood to him, like some sons who bring home their first deer, or pass their Bar Mitzvah."

Another man, an economist, said he felt blessed, in his twenties, when his father started consulting him on business and important family matters. A third man said that when he was invited to accompany his father to American Legion gatherings, "it was almost a rite of passage. . . . The Legion was a place where Dad obviously was accepted by his peers, and his taking me in there and buying me a beer made me feel accepted as an equal. I came into my own in his circle of friends."

All of the blessings just mentioned occurred when the sons were in their early adulthood. But even when a father's blessing comes later, it can carry immense power.

One man I interviewed, who'd been beaten by his doctor-father in childhood for failing in school, steered clear of his dad for nearly twenty years after leaving home. Then, when the son was in his late thirties, he invited his father to visit him at his home, some two thousand miles away. The younger man had become a carpenter, and during his father's visit, led his dad on a tour of one of the million-dollar homes for which he had crafted oak staircases and cabinets.

The son recalled the awestruck look on his father's face and a blunt apology from his dad: "I've underestimated you." In the years following, the son accepted from his father fine tools as gifts and offered the older man advice on how to build things out of wood.

And that was enough for the son. It seemed, in fact, that most sons I interviewed were willing to forgive almost anything if they could hear—in whatever way and at whatever age—the genuine affirmation of their fathers. These declarations of love and pride salved wounds the son had received in childhood. They tended to reduce tensions in the father-son relationship. And they often served as a hand up as well. Sons who received the blessings of their fathers frequently spoke afterward of feeling more mature, more fully adult. It was as if the father was representing not only himself, but the adult male world, and the son had been accepted into it.

———

According to my survey, father-son relationships tend to improve with age. Fifty-one percent of sons reported a "very positive" relationship with their fathers in childhood. That rose to 59 percent during a son's young adulthood, 64 percent in his middle adulthood, and 77 percent among sons lucky enough to still have their fathers in older adulthood.

The son's personal growth and understanding, as he aged, was a key factor in bringing many fathers and sons together. As sons took on more and more responsibilities of adulthood, they tended to see the world from a new perspective—closer to the *father's* perspective. The result was an increase in empathy and compassion for the father, and sometimes, a forgiving of the transgressions of the past.

At least in some cases, however, a father must take deliberate action if he wants to become closer to his son.

In one case, a father who had been absent most of his son's childhood—and harsh when he was around—suddenly lost his wife to cancer when the son was twenty-four. Soon after, the father started visiting his son more often. The frequency of his phone calls picked up. And he invited his son to clear the air. The son recalled: "He would call just to say, 'Hi, how are you doing? If there's something bothering you, tell me. If you want to holler at me, scream at me, go ahead. I understand.' It was like he realized he'd made mistakes himself, but was willing to do whatever he could" to make up for them.

The son accepted his father's peace offering, and their relationship gradually improved through their last twelve years together.

A middle-aged musician, who'd been beaten many times by his dad in childhood, said the greatest thing his father did in adulthood was to acknowledge the abuse. The acknowledgment didn't come easily. At age twenty-one, the son wrote a letter to his father in an initial attempt to reconcile. In it, he suggested to his dad that "we fight because we love each other." At that time, the father refused to take the olive branch. "Love is not an issue here," the father told his son on their next visit together. "You and I were randomly thrown together."

It wasn't until a decade later, when the son was settled in his career, that he broached the subject of reconciliation again. On the first night of a two-week visit with the older man, the son tried a new approach: "Dad, I realize you hate yourself." The son was surprised by his own words and even more by the fact that he'd said them without anger. Most amazingly, his father, who was then approaching seventy, received them without anger and conceded that he'd been abusive in the past.

For the next two weeks, the son told me, he and his father ate together, walked together, took rides in the Southern California mountains together. And they defused most of the tension that had developed between them. "The experience cleared me," the son said. "A great weight was lifted. The truth was out. Despite all the horrible things, he gave me an ultimately priceless gift."

With the reconciliation complete, the son was able to comfort his father with back massages during the old man's final days. When it was over, the son felt settled. "The best thing," he told me, "is that nothing was left unsaid."

In the course of writing this chapter, I asked my son, who was then six years old, what *he* thought made a good father. He told me that a good dad "plays with you," he "takes care of you," he "reads you books." Evan paused for a moment, and then added one more trait: "He waves to you before he goes away."

In concrete terms, Evan was referring to our family's off-to-work ritual. Our driveway runs past the dining room window of our home. As I back my car out in the morning, I usually stop for a moment outside that window and look for Evan, who is often finishing breakfast in a chair by the window. If he's there, I roll down my car window, and we wave good-bye.

For me, this is a satisfying little ritual. But for Evan, who initiated it when he was three, it's evidently more than that. If I forget to stop and wave, he'll remind me about it at the end of the day. Or he'll call me at work for his good-bye. He seems to recognize that my leaving holds in it the potential that we'll never see each other again.

In a way, Evan spoke for all sons, of all ages, when he cited the importance of the good-bye. Our last weeks, days, and even hours as fathers can be important ones.

Clyde Carswell was thirty-four years old when his father informed him just before dinner together one night that he was dying of cancer. The news "knocked me back like a boxer," Clyde recalled. It had been just five years since the two men had begun a reconciliation following a long period of anger and estrangement. Clyde recalled that he'd spent his twenties as a "radical hippie," before starting a successful small business, getting married, and having a son.

In the weeks after his father's diagnosis, Clyde visited the older man regularly, first at his dad's home, later in the hospital. And then the father, a physician, took a sharp turn for the worse.

In the father's hospital room one evening, a memorable incident occurred. Clyde disclosed to me that retelling it was "like walking on sacred ground." In the hospital room, Clyde had been sitting on a couch a few feet from the side of his father's bed. Clyde had been there for most of an hour, as his father alternated between turbulent coughing fits and labored breathing. The older man still maintained his barrel chest, and full gray-black beard. The skin on his face, however, as Clyde could see from the couch, had become pasty and drawn.

During a break from his coughing, the father reached out a hand toward Clyde. Clyde rose from the couch and clasped the hand. He stood beside the bed. For a long moment, the father gazed at his son's face. Clyde noticed his father's eyes; normally brown, they had gone gray.

Then, in his thick German accent, the father forced from his ravaged throat the few words he felt he had to say. Clyde recalled that they went like this: "You've got a beautiful wife, and a gorgeous child. You've got a good life. You're going to be fine." The father then beheld his son's face again, brought it forcefully to his own, and pressed his lips against Clyde's cheek. Then he said: "Good-bye. Now get out of here! Go, go, go!" He then released his son toward the door.

Clyde left the room without looking back. He wept as he drove home. Several hours later, his stepmother called. Clyde's father was dead.

In retrospect, Clyde marveled at "how much selfless effort it must have taken" for his dad, "being pulled in the other direction," to offer such a good-bye. Had the encounter not occurred, Clyde told me, he would "probably have doubted a lot of things. I would have wondered if he was still angry. But I never worried about it. . . . [The good-bye] reduced my mourning to the sadness of losing him."

When I spoke with Clyde, he was forty-five and in fine health. Like most men his age, he rarely thought about his own death. He acknowledged that if he died suddenly, his thirteen-year-old son would receive no letter, no tape, no last words from him. Most fathers I interviewed said that they too had yet to take much action to prepare even their adult children for this almost inevitable loss. A typical explanation came from one forty-two-year-old father: "Since I hope my death is a long way off, all I've done is buy life insurance."

There were a few exceptions. A thirty-six-year-old father said he kept "a loose journal" for his four children, containing notes on "what I was thinking about on the days they were born and other less historic milestones." This man, who'd lost his own father in childhood, also said he made "a very conscious effort of telling my kids 'true stories' before they go to bed at night. They're usually stories about funny things or embarrassing things that I did or that happened to me. . . . I want to give them something to remember about me."

In addition to this man's approach, other fathers I interviewed had ideas for helping prepare young children not only for a father's death, but any kind of loss:

- Speak to children honestly, even when they're young, about the deaths of relatives, friends, and pets, and welcome questions and further discussion.
- Prepare a will.
- Initiate with the children conversation about your religious or philosophical views on dying, death, and afterlife.
- Encourage children to maintain photos and mementos of loved ones who have died and to revisit those keepsakes when they want to remember the deceased.
- Invite them to attend, and participate in, any funeral and memorial rituals.
- Tell children it's okay to cry or not to cry.
- Buy life insurance.
- Give each child some one-on-one time following a death, and invite the child to speak about his or her thoughts and emotions.
- Join children in watching movies in which loss is a theme.

- Maintain a father's "memory box" (one for each child) with photos, cards, and other mementos that represent not only the child's major triumphs, but his or her everyday character as well.
- Compose a brief, personal letter to each child, to be opened in the event of your sudden death.

The fathers of adult sons suggested additional ways of preparing adult children for the father's death:

- Read over your will with them.
- Discuss with them your attitude toward dying and death.
- Invite them to share lingering resentments or anger they might hold against you.
- Make clear to them your wishes for your late-life medical care.
- Keep making contributions to their memory boxes.
- Find a personal item that was previously passed from your father to you, and designate it to go to a male child after your death; attach a written explanation of the origin and meaning of the item. Designate for your daughter something you got from your mother.
- Agree to be interviewed by a family member, on audio- or videotape, about the high points, low moments, and other aspects of your life history.
- Draw up a list of readings, songs, or prayers to be included in your funeral service.
- Write your own obituary.

A LAST WORD

Throughout the writing of this book, I've kept in mind three groups of male readers: those who already have lost a father; those whose fathers are alive, but aged or dying; and those who are themselves fathers of sons.

To summarize the guidance I received regarding each of these groups:

For men whose fathers have died, trust your mourning process. You may want to be alone or to be with others. You may feel deeply or very little. You may cry or not. At least in the beginning, allow your process to take its own course. But monitor yourself too. As the weeks go by, observe your moods, at home and at work. Notice how you think or feel when someone mentions your dad. Take stock of your physical condition. Notice if you've taken up any of your father's bad habits. And if you find yourself struggling, ask for a conversation with a spouse, sibling, friend, or clergy person. If you are fortunate, you will never forget your father, but he will let you rest.

To those who still have a living father: Make a connection with him. Recognize that you still have time to enrich, or reconcile, the relationship. Call him on the phone. Make an extra visit. Ask him what his interests are. If need be, clear the air. Then, thank him for listening and for anything else you feel you want to thank him for.

For those who are raising sons: Give your son your focus. Not to the exclusion of your daughter or spouse. But find a way to meet your son. Read with him, run with him, wrestle with him. Find reasons to admire him. And every so often, no matter what his age, offer him a gift that can come only from you: Tell him how proud you are to be his dad.

Please send your comments to
Neil Chethik
P.O. Box 8071
Lexington, Kentucky 40533
or visit my website at
www.FatherLoss.com

APPENDICES

APPENDIX I:
THE FATHERLOSS SURVEY

RESEARCH for this book involved essentially two parts: in-depth interviews, generally lasting between two and three hours each, with seventy men who had lost their fathers; and a seventy-nine-question telephone survey, conducted on my behalf by a university research center, of 306 additional men whose fathers had died.

Between 1997 and 2000, I conducted all of the in-depth interviews myself, about half in person and half by telephone. All but three of these conversations were audiotaped. In addition to an initial interview, I conducted follow-up conversations, mostly by phone or e-mail, with about half of the men. Each interviewee was offered anonymity.

I took care in this initial stage to seek out a diverse group of interviewees. The respondents were selected with the help of a variety of religious groups, the National Hospice Organization, the American Association of Retired Persons, and other professional and personal contacts.

At the time of the initial interviews, the sons ranged in age from twenty-one to ninety-four. They had lost their fathers between the ages of four and sixty-six. My conversations with these sons occurred anywhere from four months to fifty-three years after the father's death. Of the subjects, 80 percent were of European descent, 11 percent African-American, 6 percent Latino-American, and 3 percent Asian-American. They hailed from twenty-two states, from all regions of the country. About 30 percent attended religious services regularly. All but two men had graduated from high school or completed a GED, 70 percent had attended at least some college, and 20 percent held advanced degrees. Seven of the seventy men identified themselves as gay.

The initial interviews were loosely structured. I usually started by asking about the man's earliest memories of his father, then about their relationship through the son's childhood and beyond, before focusing on the father's death and the son's reactions to it. I also collected information, when available, about the father's life before the son was born.

This approach yielded a wealth of anecdotal information, but few hard numbers. In the summer of 1998, in consultation with Will Schwalbe, my editor at Hyperion, I decided to commission a scientific study that would add hundreds more men to our sample, test some of the findings that had emerged from the in-depth interviews, and produce hard numbers to help create a clearer context for the experiences of the men I'd interviewed.

To create the survey, I sought the assistance of a number of experienced professionals. The initial help came from Dr. James Beninger, a University of Southern California professor. When I contacted him in the summer of 1998, he was president of the American Association for Public Opinion Research (AAPOR), an organization of public and private survey-takers committed to ethical research. Dr. Beninger helped me shape the broad parameters of the survey I intended to do, and then offered to e-mail my intentions to AAPOR members to see who might be interested in conducting the survey. In response to this e-mail, I heard from more than two dozen research organizations, and subsequently contracted with the University of Kentucky Survey Research Center (UKSRC) to conduct the survey. The center's director, Dr. Ronald Langley, had broad experience in collecting social-science data, a stable and well-trained staff, and a strong interest in the survey topic itself. He agreed to directly oversee the project.

At about this time, I also contacted Dr. Robert Kastenbaum, a psychologist and professor at Arizona State University. For more than a quarter-century, he'd been a pioneer in death and dying education, authoring several books and serving as editor of two academic journals on the subject. I shared with Dr. Kastenbaum my vision for the survey, as well as a summary of my research to that point, and asked if he would help me devise the questionnaire and analyze the results. Despite a busy teaching and writing schedule, he said yes.

In the fall and winter of 1998–99, Dr. Kastenbaum, Dr. Langley, and I crafted a questionnaire of seventy-nine questions. We sought basic demographic information, as well as data about the quality of the relationship between each son and his father, the manner of the father's death, and the son's short- and long-term reactions to the loss.

With permission, we patterned several of the questions after those found in previous grief surveys, including "The Parent Death Study" by Sidney and Miriam Moss of the Polisher Research Institute in Philadelphia and "Impact of a Parent's Death" by Dr. Andrew Scharlach of the University of California at Berkeley. We also received generous help from Diane Colasanto of Princeton Survey Research

Associates, who shared data from "Intergenerational Issues in an Aging Society," a survey completed in 1998 for an organization called Americans Discuss Social Security.

On April 20, 1999, about fifteen trained interviewers at the University of Kentucky Survey Research Center began the telephone surveying. Their mission was to complete three hundred interviews with men who had lost their fathers. The potential interviewees were selected using a Waksberg Random Digit Dialing method, which meant that every household in the continental United States with a telephone had an equal probability of being selected.

On May 14, 1999, twenty-four days after it began, the survey-taking ended with 306 interviews of an average of 16.5 minutes each. The margin of error for this sample was plus-or-minus 5.6 percent (at a confidence level of 95 percent). The response rate—the percentage of completed interviews among all eligible respondents—was 45.3 percent.[1]

1. Calculating meaningful response rates is difficult when interviewers are seeking respondents with a particular demographic profile (in our case, adult males who have lost their fathers to death). In our survey, it could not always be determined whether there was an eligible respondent at a home that was contacted. For example, some women who answered the phone declined to put the man of the house on the telephone or, understandably, to say whether there was a man in the house. Also, respondents of both sexes sometimes would not reveal if anyone in the home was eligible for our survey. Thus, the response rate reported above is calculated using an "eligibility estimator," which assumes that the proportion of the eligible respondents among the cases where eligibility could be determined also applied to the cases where it could not be determined. (Further details on this method of calculating response rates are available in *Standard Definitions: Final Dispositions of Case Codes and Outcome Rates for RDD Telephone Surveys and In-Person Household Surveys* [American Association for Public Opinion Research, 1998], and in Judith Lessler and William D. Kalsbeek, *Nonsampling Error in Surveys* [New York: John Wiley & Sons, 1992]).

The demographics of the phone-survey group were similar to those of the group of sons I had previously interviewed in-depth. The age-range of the men in the phone survey was eighteen to eighty-seven. Eighty-two percent identified themselves as white, 11 percent African-American, and 7 percent Latino, Asian, or other ethnic group. Nine percent had not earned a high school diploma or GED; 36 percent had earned at least a bachelor's degree. Thirty-nine percent were regular attendees of religious services, 29 percent attended up to twice a month, and 32 percent rarely or never attended or had no religious preference.

When it came to identifying their "native state," 20 percent of those in the phone survey named states from the Northeast, 30 percent from the Midwest, 16 percent from the West, and 31 percent from the South. Just under 4 percent reported being from outside the United States.

In addition to compiling the direct answers to the survey questions, we explored variations between particular groups of sons. For example, we examined differences in a son's reaction to a father-death based on the son's age at the time of the death, his education level, his race, the age of the father at the time of the death, whether the mother was alive at the death, and the quality of the father-son relationship. Relevant results of these analyses have been included in the text of the book.

I asked Dr. Langley and Dr. Kastenbaum to read the manuscript of this book before publication. Both did so and offered valuable suggestions about blending the stories from the in-depth interviews with the hard numbers from the phone survey.

Clearly, I have had tremendous help in researching this book. Nonetheless, as the designer of the project, selector of the consultants, and writer of the text, I am responsible for any errors in fact, interpretation, or omission.

For more details of The FatherLoss Survey, visit my website at www.FatherLoss.com

APPENDIX II:
RESOURCES FOR MEN FACING LOSS

Organizations serving those dealing with a death.

American Association for Retired Persons
Grief and Loss Program
601 E St. NW
Washington, DC 20049
(202) 434-2260
Jgibala@aarp.org
http://www.aarp.org/griefandloss/

American Institute of Life-Threatening Illness and Loss
630 West 168th St.
New York, NY 10032
(212) 928-2066

American Men's Studies Association
22 East St.

Northampton, MA 01060

(413) 584-8903

Association of Death Education and Counseling

342 North Main St.

West Hartford, CT 06117-2507

(860) 586-7503

info@adec.org

http://www.adec.org

Barr-Harris Children's Grief Center

Institute for Psychoanalysis

122 South Michigan Ave., Suite 1300

Chicago, IL 60603

http://www.barrharris.org

Center for Death Education and Bioethics

c/o Robert Bendiksen

SOC/ARC Dept.

435 North Hall

La Crosse, WI 54601-3742

(608) 785-6781

cdeb@uwlax.edu

Compassion in Dying Federation

c/o Barbara Coombs Lee

6312 SW Capitol Hwy., Suite 415

Portland, OR 97201

(206) 221-9556

info@compassionindying.org

http://www.compassionindying.org

Choice in Dying
1035 30th St., NW
Washington, DC 20007
(800) 989-9455
cid@choices.org
http://www.choices.org

Crisis, Grief, and Healing
http://www.webhealing.com

Death With Dignity National Center
c/o Charlotte Ross, Executive Director
520 South El Camino Real, Suite 710
San Mateo, CA 94402-1720
(415) 344-6489
DDEC@aol.com

Fatherhood Project
c/o Families and Work Institute
330 Seventh Ave., 14th Floor
New York, NY 10001
(212) 268-4846

GriefNet
http://rivendell.org

Growth House Inc.
http://www.growthhouse.org

Grief Recovery Institute
http://www.grief-recovery.com

Hospice Education Institute
190 Westbrook Rd.
Essex, CT 06426
(800) 331-1620
hospiceall@ad.com
http:/www.hospiceworld.org

Hospice Foundation of America
777 17th St., Suite 401
Miami Beach, FL 33139
(800) 854-3402
hfa@hospicefoundation.org
http://www.hospicefoundation.org

International Institute for the Study of Death
P.O. Box 63-0026
Miami, FL 33163-0026
(305) 936-1408

Living/Dying Project
P.O. Box 357
Fairfax, CA 94978
(415) 456-3915

St. Francis Center
4880A MacArthur/Blvd. NW
Washington, DC 20007
(202) 333-4880
sfcgrief@erols.com

National Council of African-American Men
1028 Dole Human Development Center
University of Kansas
Lawrence, KS 66045
(913) 864-3990

National Hospice Organization
1901 North Moore St., Suite 901
Arlington, VA 22209
(800) 658-8898
drsnho@cais.com
http://www.nho.org

National Institute for Jewish Hospice
8723 Alden Dr., Suite 5107
Los Angeles, CA 90048
(800) 446-4448

National Men's Resource Center
P.O. Box 800
San Anselmo, CA 94979-0080
(415) 453-2839
menstuff@menstuff.org
http://www.menstuff.org

Surviving Sorrow
http://www.survivingsorrow.org

Appendix III: Father Films

Forty-four movies in which the relationship between a father and child is a central theme.

A River Runs Through It
Among the Cinders
Boyz 'N the 'Hood
Braveheart
Breaking Away
A Bronx Tale
The Brothers McMullen
Cinema Paradiso
Dad
Death of a Salesman
The Emerald Forest
Field of Dreams
The Full Monty
Get On the Bus
The Godfather

The Great Santini

The Homecoming

I Never Sang for My Father

Indiana Jones and the Last Crusade

Kolya

Kramer vs. Kramer

Legends of the Fall

Life Is Beautiful

The Lion King

Mi Familia

Mrs. Doubtfire

My Life

Nobody's Fool

Nothing in Common

October Sky

Ordinary People

A Perfect World

Pop

Pushing Hands

Rebel Without a Cause

Saving Private Ryan

Searching for Bobby Fischer

Shine

Smoke Signals

Sounder

This Boy's Life

To Kill a Mockingbird

The War

The Wedding Banquet

SOURCES

Listed below are sources directly referred to in the text, as well as readings that generally informed the author.

INTRODUCTION

Allen, Woody. *Without Feathers*. New York: Random House, 1975.

Churchill, Winston. *My Early Life*. New York: Touchstone Simon & Schuster, 1996.

Freud, Sigmund. *Interpretation of Dreams*. Translated by James Strachey. New York: Basic Books, 1955.

Jennings, Waylon. *Waylon Jennings: An Autobiography*. New York: Warner Books, 1998.

Jung, C. G. *Modern Man in Search of a Soul*. New York: Harcourt Brace, 1955.

MacArthur, Douglas. *Reminiscences*. New York: McGraw-Hill. 1964.

Parry, Joan K., and Joan Thornwall. "Death of a Father," *Death Studies*. 16 (1992).

Rollyson, Carl. *The Lives of Norman Mailer*. St. Paul, Minn.: Paragon House, 1991.

Yule, Andrew. *Sean Connery*. Boston: Donald I. Fine, Inc., 1992.

JOHN F. KENNEDY, JR.

Anderson, Christopher. *Jackie After Jack*. New York: William Morrow, 1998.

Heymann, C. David. *A Woman Named Jackie*. Secaucus, N.J.: Carol Communications, 1989.

Klein, Edward. *Just Jackie*. New York: Ballantine, 1998.

Leigh, Wendy. *Prince Charming: The John F. Kennedy, Jr., Story*. New York: Dutton, 1993.

Manchester, William. *The Death of a President*. New York: Harper & Row, 1967.

Reeves, Richard. *President Kennedy: Profile of Power*. New York: Simon & Schuster, 1993.

1. Torn Asunder

Adams, K. S., J. G. Johnrenz, D. Harper, and D. Streiner. "Early Parental Loss and Suicidal Ideation," *Canadian Journal of Psychiatry* (June 1982).

Baker, Russell. *Growing Up*. New York: St. Martin's Press, 1982.

Bendiksen, Robert, and Robert Fulton. "Death and the Child," *Omega* 6 (1975).

Berlinsky, Ellen, and Henry Biller. *Parental Death and Psychological Development*. Lexington, Mass.: Lexington Books, 1982.

Biondi, M., and A. Picardi. "Clinical and Biological Aspects of Bereavement and Loss-Induced Depression," *Psychotherapy and Psychosomatics* 65 (1996).

Corr, Charles A., and Hannelore Wass, eds. *Childhood and Death*. Washington Hemisphere, 1984.

Corr, Charles A., and David E., Balk, eds. *Handbook of Adolescent Death and Bereavement*. New York: Springer, 1996.

Dyregrov, Atle. *Grief in Children: A Handbook for Adults*. London: Jessica Kingsley Publishers, 1990.

Eisenstadt, J. Marvin. "Parental Loss and Genius," *American Psychologist* (March 1978).

Fitzgerald, Helen. *The Grieving Child*. New York: Fireside, 1992.

Furman, Erna. *A Child's Parent Dies: Studies in Childhood Bereavement*. New Haven: Yale University Press, 1974.

Gray, Ross E. "Adolescent Response to the Death of a Parent," *Journal of Youth and Adolescence* 16 (1987).

Harris, Maxine. *The Loss That Is Forever*. New York: Plume/Penguin, 1995.

Hepworth, Jeri, Robert G. Ryder, and Albert S. Dreyer. "The Effects of Parental Loss on the Formation of Intimate Relationships," *Journal of Marital and Family Therapy* 10 (1984).

Jacobson, Gary, and Robert G. Ryder. "Parental Loss and Some Characteristics of the Early Marriage Relationship," *American Journal of Orthopsychiatry* (October 1969).

Kaffman, Mordecai, and Esther Elizur. "Children's Bereavement Reactions Following Death of the Father," *International Journal of Family Therapy* (fall 1979).

Raveis, Victoria H., Karolynn Siegel, and Daniel. Karus. "Children's Psychological Distress Following the Death of a Parent," *Journal of Youth and Adolescence* 28 (1999).

Real, Terrence. *I Don't Want to Talk About It*. New York: Scribner, 1997.

Terr, Lenore C. "Childhood Traumas," *American Journal of Psychiatry* (January 1991).

Van der Kolk, Bessel, ed. *Psychological Trauma*. Washington, D.C.: American Psychiatric Press, 1987.

Viorst, Judith. *Necessary Losses*. New York: Fireside, 1998.

Webb, Nancy Boyd, ed. *Helping Bereaved Children*. New York: Guilford Press, 1993.

Wolfenstein, Martha. "Loss, Rage, and Repetition," *The Psychoanalytic Study of the Child* 24 (1969).

Wolfert, Alan. *Helping Children Cope with Grief*. Muncie, Ind.: Accelerated Development Inc., 1983

Worden, J. William. *Children and Grief: When a Parent Dies*. New York: Guilford Press, 1996.

Michael Jordan

Greene, Bob. *Hang Time: Days and Dreams with Michael Jordan*. New York: St. Martin's Press, 1993.

————. *Rebound: The Odyssey of Michael Jordan*. New York: Signet, 1996.

Mitchell Krugel. *Jordan*. New York: St. Martin's Press, 1994.

2. Too Soon

Erikson, Erik. *Childhood and Society*. New York: Norton, 1950.

Levinson, Daniel J. *The Seasons of a Man's Life*. New York: Ballantine, 1978.

Pollock, George H., and Stanley I. Greenspan, eds. *The Course of Life: Early Adulthood*. Madison, Conn.: International Universities Press, 1993.

Dylan Thomas

Ackerman, John. *Dylan Thomas: His Life and Work*. New York: St. Martin's Press, 1996.

Brinnin, John Malcolm. *Dylan Thomas in America*. New York: Atlantic/Little, Brown, 1955.

Ferris, Paul. *Dylan Thomas: A Biography*. New York: The Dial Press, 1977.

Fitzgibbon, Constantine. *The Life of Dylan Thomas*. New York: Atlantic/Little, Brown, 1965.

Moynihan, William T. *The Craft and Art of Dylan Thomas*. Ithaca: Cornell University Press, 1966.

Sinclair, Andrew. *Dylan Thomas: No Man More Magical*. New York: Holt, Rinehart and Winston, 1975.

Tindall, William York. *A Reader's Guide to Dylan Thomas*. London: Thames and Hudson, 1962.

3. The Body Blow

Anderson, Herbert. "The Death of a Parent," *Pastoral Psychology* 28, 3 (1980).

Guttman, Herta A. "Parental Death as a Precipitant of Marital Conflict in Middle Age," *Journal of Marital and Family Therapy* (January 1991).

Mayer, Nancy. *The Male Mid-Life Crisis*. New York: Signet, 1979.

Neugarten, Bernice, ed. *Middle Age and Aging*. Chicago: University of Chicago Press, 1968.

Powell, Colin, and Joseph E. Persico. *My American Journal*. New York: Random House, 1995.

Sanders, Catherine. *Grief: The Mourning After*. New York: John Wiley and Sons, 1989.

Scharlach, Andrew E. "Factors Associated with Filial Grief Following the Death of an Elderly Parent," *American Journal of Orthopsychiatry* (April 1991).

Scharlach, Andrew E., and Karen I. Fredriksen. "Reactions to the Death of a Parent during Midlife," *Omega* 27 (1993).

Sheehy, Gail. *Passages: Predictable Crises in Adult Life*. New York: Dutton, 1974.

Silberberg, Martin. *On the Death of My Father: A Psychoanalyst's Memoir*. Lewiston, N.Y.: Edwin Mellen Press, 1995.

John Quincy Adams

Adams, Charles Francis, ed. *The Memoirs of John Quincy Adams*. Philadelphia: Lippincott, 1875.

Parsons, Lynn H. *John Quincy Adams*. Wesport, Conn.: Greenwood, 1993.

Nagel, Paul. *John Quincy Adams—A Public Life, a Private Life*. New York: Alfred A. Knopf, 1997.

4. Closing the Circle

Bee, Helen L. *The Journey of Adulthood*. New York: MacMillan, 1992.

Erikson, Erik. *Childhood and Society*. New York: Norton, 1950.

Frankel, Max. *The Times of My Life*. New York: Random House, 1999.

Gilberg, Arnold L., "The Loss of My Dad: An Adult Developmental Issues," *Journal of the American Academy of Psychoanalysis* 22 (1994).

Gross, Francis L., *Introducing Erik Erikson: An Invitation to His Thinking*. Lanham, Md.: University Press of America, 1987.

Gutmann, David. *Reclaimed Powers*. Evanston, Ill.: Northwestern University Press, 1994.

Nemiroff, Robert A., and Calvin A. Colarusso, eds. *New Dimensions in Adult Development*. New York: Basic Books, 1990.

Neugarten, Bernice L., ed. *Middle Age and Aging*. Chicago: University of Chicago Press, 1968.

Neugarten, Gail A., ed. *The Meanings of Age: Selected Papers of Bernice L. Neugarten*. Chicago: University of Chicago Press, 1996.

Rasmussen, Christina A., and Christiane Brems. "The Relationship of Death Anxiety with Age and Psychosocial Maturity," *The Journal of Psychology* 130 (1996).

Sheehy, Gail. *Understanding Men's Passages*. New York: Random House, 1998.

Thompson, Edward H., ed. *Older Men's Lives*. Sage Publications, 1994.

Mahatma Gandhi

Brown, Judith M. *Gandhi: Prisoner of Hope*. New Haven: Yale University Press, 1989.

Fischer, Louis. *The Life of Mahatma Gandhi*. New York: Harper, 1950.

Gandhi, Mohandas K. *An Autobiography: The Story of My Experiments with Truth*. Boston: Beacon Press, 1957.

Green, Martin. *Gandhi: Voice of a New Age Revolution*. New York: Continuum, 1993.

Payne, Robert. *The Life and Death of Mahatma Gandhi*. New York: Dutton, 1969.

Wolfenstein, E. Victor. *The Revolutionary Personality: Lenin, Trotsky, Gandhi*. Princeton: Princeton University Press, 1967.

5. Preparing for FatherLoss

Becker, Marilyn R. *Last Touch: Preparing for a Parent's Death*. Oakland, Calif.: New Harbinger, 1992.

Ilardo, Joseph. *Father-Son Healing: An Adult Son's Guide*. Oakland, Calif.: New Harbinger, 1993.

Meyers, Jeffrey. *Bogart: A Life in Hollywood*. Boston: Houghton Mifflin, 1997.

Rando, Therese. *Loss and Anticipatory Grief*. Lexington, Mass.: Lexington Books, 1986.

Dwight D. Eisenhower

Ambrose, Stephen E. *Eisenhower: Soldier, General of the Army, President-Elect*. New York: Simon and Schuster, 1983.

Ferrell, Robert H., ed. *The Eisenhower Diaries*. New York: Norton, 1981.

6. THE FIRST DAYS AFTER

Haberstein, Robert W., and William M. Lamers. *Funeral Customs the World Over.* Milwaukee: Bulfin Printers, 1960.

Imber-Black, Evan, and Janine Roberts. *Rituals for Our Times.* New York: HarperPerennial, 1993.

Irion, Paul. "Changing Patterns of Ritual Response to Death," *Omega* 22 (1990–91).

Katz, Pearl, and Paul Barton. "Mourning, Ritual and Recovery After an Airline Tragedy," *Omega* 36 (1998).

Levine, Stephen. *Who Dies?* New York: Anchor Books/Doubleday, 1982.

Lister, Larry. "Men and Grief," *Smith College Studies in Social Work* (June 1991).

Lynch, Thomas. *The Undertaking.* New York: Norton, 1997.

McGoldrick, Monica, et al. "Mourning Rituals" *Networker* (November–December 1996).

Romanoff, Bronna, and Marion Terenzio. "Rituals and the Grieving Process," *Death Studies* 22 (1998).

Walsh, Froma, and Monica McGoldrick. *Living Beyond Loss.* New York: Norton, 1991.

Wass, Hannelore, and Robert Neimeyer, eds. *Dying: Facing the Facts.* Bristol, Pa.: Taylor & Francis, 1995.

Wolfelt, Alan D. *Understanding Grief*. Muncie, Ind.: Accelerated Development, 1992.

TED TURNER

Bibb, Porter. *It Ain't as Easy as It Looks*. New York: Crown Virgin Books 1993.

Goldberg, Robert, and Gerald Jay Goldberg. *Citizen Turner: The Wild Rise of an American Tycoon*. New York: Harcourt Brace, 1995.

Heldenfels, R. D., "CNN's Retraction Embarrasses Network's Founder, Ted Turner." *Akron Beacon Journal*. July 12, 1998.

Williams, Christian. *Lead, Follow, or Get Out of the Way*. New York: Times Books, 1981.

7. MEN'S STYLES OF MOURNING

Akner, Lois F., with Catherine Whitney. *How to Survive the Loss of a Parent*. New York: William Morrow, 1993.

Campbell, Scott, and Phyllis Silverman. *Widower: When Men are Left Alone*. Amityville, N.Y.: Baywood, 1996.

Carverville, Philip. "Bereaved Men," *Psychotherapy in Private Practice* 16 (1997).

Doka, Kenneth J., ed. *Living with Grief*. Miami Beach, Fla.: Hospice Foundation of America, 1998.

Doka, Kenneth J., and Terry L. Martin. *Men Don't Cry, Women Do: Transcending Gender Stereotypes of Grief*. Bristol, Pa.: Taylor & Francis, 2000.

Donnelly, Katherine Fair. *Recovering From the Loss of a Parent*. New York: Berkley, 1993.

Golden, Thomas R. "A Tree for My Father," *MEN Magazine*. (March 1996).

Golden, Thomas R. *Swallowed by a Snake*. Kensington, Md.: Golden Healing Publishing, 1996.

Grizzard, Lewis. *Daddy Was a Pistol and I'm a Son of a Gun*. New York: Villard, 1995.

Grollman, Earl. *Living When a Loved One Has Died*. Boston: Beacon, 1977.

Kennedy, Alexandra. *Losing a Parent*. San Francisco: HarperSanFrancisco, 1991.

Rando, Therese A. *Grief, Dying and Death*. Champaign, Ill.: Research Press, 1984.

Rosenblatt, Paul C. *Bitter, Bitter Tears*. Minneapolis: University of Minnesota Press, 1983.

Smyth, Joshua M., et al. "Effects of Writing About Stressful Experiences on Symptom Reduction in Patients with Asthma or Rheumatoid Arthritis," *Journal of the American Medical Association* 281 (1999).

Miller, James E., and Thomas R. Golden. *A Man You Know Is Grieving*. Fort Wayne, Ind. Willowgreen Publishing, 1998.

Smith, Harold Ivan. *On Grieving the Death of a Father*. Minneapolis: Augsburg, 1994.

CHRISTIAAN BARNARD

Barnard, Christiaan, and Curtis Pepper. *One Life*. New York: Macmillan. 1970.

Dougherty, Steven, and Drusilla Menaker. "Lion in Winter," *People Weekly* (April 8, 1996).

8. HOW SPOUSES HELP

Buchalter, Gail. "I Became a Man the Day My Father Died," *Parade Magazine* (March 7, 1999).

Guttman, Herta, A. "Parental Death as a Precipitant of Marital Conflict in Middle Age," *Journal of Marital and Family Therapy* 17 (1991).

Jacobson, Gary, and Robert G. Ryder. "Parental Loss and Some Characteristics of the Early Marriage Relationship," *American Journal of Orthopsychiatry* (October 1969).

Kaltreider, Nancy B., Terry, Becker, and Mardi Horowitz. "Relationship Testing After the Loss of a Parent," *American Journal of Psychiatry* 141 (1984).

Miller, James E., and Thomas Golden. *A Man You Know Is Grieving*. Fort Wayne, Ind.: Willowgreen Publishing, 1998.

Rosenblatt, Paul C., et al. "Difficulties in Supporting the Bereaved," *Omega* 23 (1991).

H. L. MENCKEN

Bode, Carl. *Mencken*. Carbondale: Southern Illinois University Press, 1969.

Fecher, Charles, ed. *The Diary of H. L. Mencken*. New York: Alfred A. Knopf, 1989.

Hobson, Fred C. *Mencken: A Life*. Baltimore: Johns Hopkins University Press, 1995.

Mencken, H. L. *Newspaper Days*, 1899–1906. New York: Alfred A. Knopf, 1941.

9. LIFE CHANGES

Churchill, Winston. *My Early Life*. New York: Touchstone Books, Simon & Schuster, 1996.

Douglas, Joan Delahanty. "Patterns of Change Following Parent Death in Mid-life Adults," *Omega* 22 (1990–91).

Miriam S., and Sidney Z. Moss. "The Impact of Parental Death on Middle-Aged Children" *Omega* 14 (1983–84).

ERNEST HEMINGWAY

Meyers, Jeffrey. *Hemingway: A Biography*. New York: Harper, 1985.

Lynn, Kenneth S. *Hemingway*. New York: Simon & Schuster, 1987.

10. DOES THERAPY HELP?

Black, D. and M. S. Urbanowicz, "Family Intervention with Bereaved Children," *Journal of Child Psychology and Psychiatry* 28 (1987).

Cochran, Sam V., and Fredric E. Rabinowitz. "Men, Loss, and Psychotherapy," *Psychotherapy* 33 (1996).

Davis, D. Russell. "The Death of the Artist's Father: Henrik Ibsen," *British Journal of Medical Psychology* 46 (1973).

Kato, Pamela, and Traci Mann. "A Synthesis of Psychological Interventions for the Bereaved" *Clinical Psychology Review* 19 (1999).

Knowlson, James. *Damned to Fame: The Life of Samuel Beckett.* New York: Simon & Schuster, 1996.

Sanders, Catherine. *Grief: The Mourning After.* New York: John Wiley and Sons, 1989.

Schut, H., M. S. Stroebe, J. van den Bout, and J. de Keijser. "Intervention For the Bereaved," *British Journal of Clinical Psychology* 36 (1997).

DAVID HALBERSTAM

Personal interview with David Halberstam, conducted April 1, 1999.

11. LINGERINGS

Albom, Mitch. *Tuesdays With Morrie.* New York: Doubleday, 1997.

Personal interview with Peter Duchin, conducted April 5, 1999.

Klass, Dennis, Phyllis Silverman, and Steven L. Nickman. *Continuing Bonds.* Bristol, Pa.: Taylor & Francis, 1996.

Lee, John. *At My Father's Wedding.* New York: Bantam, 1991.

12. AFFECTIONATE FATHERING

Bly, Robert. *Iron John*. Reading, Mass.: Addison Wesley, 1990.

Canfield, Jack, Mark Victor Hansen, and Barry Spilchuk, eds. *A Cup of Chicken Soup for the Soul*. Dearfield Beach, Fla.: Health Communications, 1996.

ACKNOWLEDGMENTS

I thank, first and foremost, the 376 men who shared their father-death experiences for this book. I was honored by their openness and have tried to recount their stories in a way that honors them as well.

I am also immensely grateful to Rob Ferguson and John Lynch, editors, writers, and friends, for their unflagging encouragement and faith. I thank also Ann Hagedorn Auerbach, Mark Belletini, Jeff Lamb, Bev Mills, and Tom Owen-Towle for their steady support and advice.

Thanks to Bob Kastenbaum, educator in the field of dying and death, for his generosity and mentoring. Thank you also to Ronald Langley, survey-taker extraordinaire, for his patience and dedication, and to his staff for their sensitivity and professionalism.

My deep thanks to Will Schwalbe, my editor at Hyperion. His passion for this project and wise suggestions kept me on track and motivated. Thank you as well to Mark Chait, Jodi Glaser Taub, and Katie Long at Hyperion. My gratitude also to my agent, Jonathon

Lazear, who saw the promise of this book and found the right publisher for it. And special thanks to another adviser, Todd Musburger, for his confidence and trust.

I am grateful to the members of four groups that helped me develop ideas for this book and offered me a community of support: the nonfiction writing group at the Carnegie Center for Literacy and Learning; the Lexington, Kentucky, chapter of the Mankind Project; the Downtown Lunch Bunch of Toastmasters International; and the Unitarian Universalist Church of Lexington.

I'm also grateful for the indulgences of my officemates, Debra Hensley, Jimmie Roberts, and Sandy Chase, and for Jim Concotelli and Teri Landers, founders of the Lexington Wellness Center. Thanks in addition to William T. Young for his beneficence, and to the staffs of the Lexington Public Library, University of Kentucky libraries, Transylvania University library, Lexington Theological Seminary library, and to Joseph-Beth Booksellers.

Many professionals in death and dying, men's studies, adult development, survey research, and other fields contributed to this book. My sincere appreciation goes out to James Beninger, Bruce Brock, Albert Cain, Diane Colasanto, Phil Converse, Kenneth Doka, Joan Douglas, Thomas Golden, Michael Gurian, Bill Kauth, Peter Kent, Michael Kimmel, Dennis Klass, Thomas Lynch, Terry Martin, Warren Mitofsky, Miriam Moss, Sidney Moss, Ann Olson, Sam Osherson, Brian Rich, Paul Rosenblatt, Andrew Scharlach, John Scheb, David Shenk, Daniel Sizemore, Judith Stillman, Jeremy Taylor, Bill Wilcox, Bill Worden, and Steve Yokich. A special thank you also to the writer David Halberstam and bandleader Peter Duchin.

My father, Morton Chethik, a psychoanalyst and author of *Techniques in Child Therapy: Psychodynamic Strategies*, was tremendously helpful in reviewing the psychological material and in countless other ways. My mother, Beverly Chethik, helped particularly with the structure of the book and was a source of innumerable good ideas throughout. I'm grateful for their love and encouragement, as well as for that of my sister, Jessica, my brothers, Peter and Leigh, and my sister-in-law Harmeen Ahuja and her family. I'd also like to express appreciation to the entire Flood-Dozier clan for their support.

Finally, I thank Evan, for his inspiration and wisdom, and Kelly, for her optimism, patience, and love.

About the Author

Neil Chethik is a writer, professional speaker, and workshop leader specializing in family issues. He has been a staff reporter for the *Tallahassee Democrat* and *San Jose Mercury News,* and author of VoiceMale, a syndicated column on men's issues. His writings have appeared in dozens of newspapers and magazines throughout the United States. He lives in Lexington, Kentucky, with his wife and son. This is his first book.